INFORMATION
SYSTEMS
ARCHITECTURE

INFORMATION SYSTEMS ARCHITECTURE

BÖRJE LANGEFORS
and
BO SUNDGREN

PETROCELLI / CHARTER

NEW YORK 1975

Library of Congress Cataloging in Publication Data

Langefors, Börje.
  Information systems architecture.

  Bibliography: p.
  Includes index.
  1. Information storage and retrieval systems.
2. Electronic data processing. I. Sundgren, Bo,
1946-   joint author. II. Title.
Z699.L357 1975   001.6   75-5521
ISBN 0-88405-300-8

CONTENTS

INTRODUCTION

Information systems and data processing systems have often been failures. This has been documented by several authors, notably McKinsey (1968), who found that about two thirds of the companies studied were disappointed. There are also indications of failures in a majority of applications not subjected to published analyses. In addition, it appears that many systems which may be regarded, for economic reasons, as reasonably successful are disappointing to the human beings who come into contact with them. This may, of course, also be detrimental from an economic point of view on a longer perspective.

1. INFORMATION SYSTEMS ARCHITECTURE

There are many signs and theoretical arguments which indicate that data system failures are common because the designers and programmers tend to emphasize short-sighted and narrow local execution efficiency aspects. The importance of designing systems to suit human needs and also of designing with regard to total system aspects rather than separate, fragmented "computing runs" has been largely ignored in the past and, unfortunately, this still seems to be the rule.

The development of an *information system architecture* should lead to better information systems both from the aspect of developing the right systems (and not only "efficient" ones)—that is, those that the users need or desire—and effective systems—that is, those that show a reasonable balance between the local efficiencies of the distinct processes in the system. To achieve the first-mentioned goal—the adaptation to the users—we develop tools that make it possible to define the needed information as well as the information structure independently of any implementation decisions. We further develop these tools in such a way that, on the one hand, they are nontechnical enough to be understood by nontechnical users and, on the other hand, they are precise enough to permit the use of the documented specification as a basis for systematic analysis—for example, of performance requirements—and also as a basis for the subsequent data design and data processing design (or data system design, for short). This information specification part of the information system architecture is the area of *information analysis* (including information design). Its elements are touched on in this book although a more extensive treatment is left for another volume.

To achieve the second goal, that of obtaining an effective system design from a performance point of view, we develop in this book methods for analyzing and calculating expected performance for different data designs. We also study how distinct alternatives for structuring data and processes to represent any specified information internally in the data system can be devised (Langefors, 1961 and 1963). In this way the data design and architecture can be made in a separate stage, following that of information analysis but preceding that of detailed construction and implementation. In this way the data system designers are also encouraged to study different architectural alternatives and to evaluate them with respect to their suitability as a framework for efficient and reliable detail construction and implementation. This is in contrast to current practice in which it is rare to see different alternatives studied before final design; in fact, it is practically impossible because the design is made on a detailed level from the beginning. The difficulty is aggravated by the fact that on the detail level many dynamic problems are also encountered, which makes it even more difficult to obtain the overview and perspective needed to consider overall and long-range goals.

2. INFORMATION SYSTEMS, DATA SYSTEMS, AND DATA BASES

Data systems or data processing systems are systems that handle data in order to provide information. It is therefore important to consider the information needs that are to be served by the data system and to consider how data can be designed to represent information. This is the basic observation underlying the information systems approach (Langefors, 1961, 1963a, 1963b, 1965, 1966) or the informatological (or *infological*) approach. It would appear that the information systems approach to any data processing design task would be the obvious one. However, it is at variance with the common way in which data processing systems are designed as well as with the development of computer science in general. In these areas of study we usually assume that data and computer programs have to be designed together and that the data are to be designed to suit a certain program. In information systems design a group of data is used to represent each specific information message and can thus be designed independently of the individual programs that will be working with it. All the expected uses are considered in choosing the data representation of any information, not just one single application.

Information systems are systems that handle, or provide, information. In this sense we may regard all information-handling activities in an organization as constituting the information system of the organization. The latter is thus the *object system* of the information system. Usually the information system of an organization consists of several information systems each of which is a subsystem of the information system of the organization. Some of the information (sub)systems are usually implemented, wholly or partly, through data systems. In an information system, data representing some specific information should be available to all those human users or computer programs that can make use of the data and are authorized to do so.

3. THE INFOLOGICAL APPROACH—USER CONCEPTS AND DATA STRUCTURE INDEPENDENT ACCESS

In the infological approach, the human users' need for information is made the basis for data design. This is also true for data that are to be used as input to computing processes because the processes themselves are designed to suit users' needs. One important insight gained from this approach is that it is the conceptions in the minds of the users that determine what information can be extracted from data and what data to use to represent the information they need. Thus different data may have to be used in order to provide "approximately the same information" to distinct users; and some people may not be able to assimilate some specific information at all if they are lacking the necessary concepts.

The infological approach assumes the system to be working in such a way that the users—or the application programs—only need specify the information they want, in terms that they find natural, and the system will then retrieve or compute the data conveying this information, regardless of how these data are stored or structured within the data systems' data base. In contrast, the data processing systems usually require that the location of the desired data in the stored data structure be specified. This is, of course, very awkward and as a rule impossible for a normal user. Thus the infological approach reguires the system to provide "data structure independent access" (Langefors, 1963*b*) to information in the data base. It also provides the means for obtaining such a function. It can be seen that in this way there is an extensive independence between the data and the programs. A further advantage of the infological approach is that the data structure may be changed without changing the programs, and vice versa, as long as the infological structure is retained.

The desirability of data structure independent access has also been pointed out recently by Senko et al. (1973), thus indicating a growing awareness among the computer community of the importance of what we refer to as the infological aspects.

4. INFORMATION KINDS AND MESSAGES, DATA FILES, RECORDS, AND ENTRIES; RELATIONS

To form information about an organization or an operation within it, or about the world in general, people form conceptions about entities or *objects*. Objects then are any real or conceived entities that one informs about or wants information about. A person, for example, is an object and so is a house, a country, a purchase-order transaction, an idea, or a budget. We inform about an object by giving some property of it or some relation between two (or several) objects. We may, of course, also want to say something about a property, in which case that property appears as the object. To organize our conceptions we conceive of classes of objects (object classes or entity classes) that are similar in some sense, usually by having identical kinds of properties. "Persons" or "purchase orders" are examples of object classes. A certain kind of property, such as the attribute "age in years" or the relation "owning a car" together with a certain object class (or group of object classes) form a certain information kind (for example, the owning of cars by persons) or "information concept" (or i concept). It follows that the messages or information entities form classes of messages of similar kinds. These classes are exactly the information kinds (or i concepts).

A certain message or information entity can be represented by a certain group of data terms (or data items), which group we refer to as a *data entry*. Thus a certain information kind will correspond to a set (or some sets) of similar data entries. Such sets are referred to as *files* (or data sets).

Any data entry, representing a message for a certain user or group of users, can be represented by an endless number of alternative data entries embedded in more or less complex data structures. The *data designer* may choose any of these alternative forms to suit the needs for storage or processing efficiency. Thus the infological approach encourages the data designer to evaluate several alternative data structures before choosing one to represent the information structure specified by the users or by the information analysts. An information kind (or i concept as we have defined it) is a combination of an object class and a property class. This may be treated formally as a relation between the object class and other object classes. In "relational approaches" to data base design this view is taken. We then associate one "domain" (value set) with the object class and other domains with the associated object classes and property–value classes. Each "relation" is then a relation name together with a list of the domains involved (Bachman, 1968; Codd, 1970). A message corresponds to one instance of relation.

It appears that the "relational approach" is a special case of the infological approach, and a more formalistic one. In any case, both are closely related, although developed in distinct places. One difference is that the infological approach emphasizes the fact that the same i concept can be represented by distinct alternative logical data files.

A collection of messages constitutes a set of information relations and thereby forms an information structure. Thus if two messages inform about the same object, they are thereby related to each other.

Likewise if one message states a relation between two objects *A* and *B*, it thereby also establishes a relation between any message stating a property of *A* and any message stating a property of *B*. It is obviously required that if the messages are represented correctly and completely by data entries, the corresponding relations will hold in the data. In addition, however, the data designer may introduce structural data, such as pointers and delimiters, to improve the processing or storage performance in the system. Likewise additional structure is given to data by storing them in common physical areas.

5. INFORMATION PRECEDENCE RELATIONS, ALGORITHMS, AND PROGRAMS

Although messages state properties of objects, including relations between an object and other objects, there are also relations between messages in the sense that the property value of one message has a certain relation to the values of some other messages. The latter ones may then be said to be *information precedents* to the former one. Information precedence relations are defined when the users or the analysts specify what other information kinds are to be considered when producing information of a certain specified kind. When these precedence relations have been defined, the input and output for the associated computing program have been defined. It then remains to define how the output is produced from the input; that is, after the existence of a precedence relation has been established, the analyst will, in a succeeding step, work out the functional properties of the precedence relation. This can be done, for instance, by writing a mathematical formula or an algorithm. Any of these may then be represented by a computer program. It is the precedence relations that tie together the parts of an information system by binding together different messages or different information kinds so that they form a system. The precedence relations also provide a means for systematic information analysis, because once an information kind has been found to be required, then a step of precedence analysis systematically defines additional candidate information kinds.

6. DATA TRANSPORT AND ACCESS

In the system architecture stage we are interested in comparing alternative system structure layouts for performance. The difficulty here is that many details that will affect the data processing workload are only determined later in the detail construction stage. Our problem is the way in which the main system architecture affects performance and other design aspects such as reliability and flexibility. The key observation here is that when we handle the large data sets or files of information systems, we have to use mass storage equipment of distinct kinds, and they are all slow in comparison to the central processing unit (CPU) of the computer. Therefore the data transport between file storage and CPU will be a dominating factor in determining processing time and response time. Different overall architecture of the data file system will lead to vastly different data transport workloads. By data transport we mean here all that is involved in making the data in the file system (data base) available to the users or to the application programs. Thus "file directory decoding," access to the file records, and transfer to main memory are all included.

When a certain message is to be produced by a process in the system, all its precedents are to be made available to the process. This will normally imply data transport involving the file storage. Thus the information precedence relations determine the potential need for data transport. By putting all the precedents of one message in the same access block in the file storage we would obviously reduce the data transport for that process. We will, however, usually increase transport for other processes. This, on the other hand, may then be reduced by grouping the processes together. It can be seen already that by studying the information precedence relations over the entire system, or a major part of it, we may be able to find the efficient ways of organizing the file system in the architectural stage. We will study this important aspect fairly extensively in Chapter 3 and related questions will be covered in subsequent chapters.

7. OVERVIEW OF THE BOOK

The task of systems architecture is the development of a framework within which the needs of users and the object system will be implemented and the information technology will be efficiently exploited. In the first chapter of this book, we study how information can be defined and specified and how this information can be represented by data and data structures. Also the sizes and the transport requirements of individual files or data sets are briefly studied. The distinct data sets or files in an information system have relations to each other and this is what makes them form a system. Such relations are *associative relations* obtained by some messages referring to other messages as well as *precedence relations*, which imply that some messages can be produced from other messages—their information precedents. Obviously the relations that join the information and data sets to make them form a system are of the utmost importance for the design of the system. In Chapter 2 we learn how the precedence relations can be described such that system analyses can be made, based on these descriptions. Different system matrices, precedence matrices between information kinds, incidence matrices between information or data and processes, and so-called coincidence matrices are defined and studied. Also how each information precedence relation is represented by a data process is discussed.

As the precedence relations will be implemented by data processes, it follows that in the system the transport of data needed to provide processes with their input and to take care of their output can be determined from the precedence and incidence matrices. Organization of the data into files and records in distinct ways can influence the data storage and transport. As data are used in several processes, the data organization will have to consider the different uses in order for an organization to be found that will be efficient with respect to all usages. Obviously this means that we need to have overall system descriptions available, such as the system matrices. In Chapter 3 we see how data can be organized into files through different degrees to file consolidation and how the data transport generated in the system, using different consolidations, can be computed using the system matrices and associated information. Similarly, the data processes can be grouped together to save data transport, and how this can be computed using the system matrices is studied.

In systems built by means of modern file storages the data can be organized in many distinct ways. Usually all data associated with a certain object are formed into an "entry" consisting of several segments of groups of contiguously stored data. These segments result from consolidation of smaller records, so how to structure file entries requires consideration of the consolidation problem as well as several other problems. In Chapter 4 we study many distinct forms of file organization and many distinct "file-structuring operators."

Having seen what different file-structuring possibilities are available, we encounter the problem of how to choose the file structures. This raises the question of how the distinct organizations perform in distinct applications. Hence we are led to consider how distinct applications can be defined and characterized. Thus in Chapter 5 we are presented with distinct kinds of interactions between the system and its environment and in Chapter 6 we learn how a file organization can be designed to suit a certain object system, depending on the precedence relation and on the mix of interactions expected for the system.

It should be pointed out that there are many important problems of data system design that are not treated here. This is especially true with respect to the dynamic properties. We are concentrating here on the structure. This is not quite the same as being restricted to static phenomena. Our view is that to design large information systems we need to specify the desirable information content first, and this can be done without regard to details of the dynamical events during its production. Then, to handle a large system we need to design the main structure which will define the framework under which the dynamical stream of events can occur and obtain resources. To do this the structural resources must be evaluated as to their capacity for supporting the streams of events as well as the control of this dynamic. This can be accomplished by considering the average effect of the dynamic streams such as data transport and access operations and its variations. It is thus not necessary to become involved in the detailed design of the control of individual events. That is a class of problems that can be brought up at later stages during the design project. Of course, this may call for iterations of earlier stages, as is always the case in large system design. These stages are not treated here. Much of the current research in computer science is done in that area, however, so supplements to what is treated here are widely available. On the other hand, to develop computer-aided system design the formalism treated here can be developed so as to be formally connected to the subsequent design stages. In the meantime this interface will have to be handled in a less formalized way.

We end this introduction by giving in the next section an orientation of a basic general model for designing large systems, which constitutes an important background for the whole presentation made in this book.

8. A GENERAL MODEL FOR THE PROCESS OF DESIGNING IMPERCEIVABLE SYSTEMS

To design large (imperceivable) systems so that they satisfy established specifications is extremely difficult because the design involves a buildup from a large set of parts. Even if the kinds of parts are given, the extremely limited capacity for overview that characterizes human beings makes it impossible to start at the bottom, combining parts. It is impossible to know in such an approach whether the combination with which one starts contributes to the system specification or not. What happens is usually that systems are built up from bottom to form small systems with limited scope. Then a few of these are combined to solve some larger system problem, and so on. A usual result of this "bottom-up" approach is that designs are developed for which one then searches to see if there are any problems around that could use the design as a solution. It is thus that we obtain all the known "solutions hunting for problems." To be able, instead, to design so as to fulfill a given specification is, of course, highly important. This is one of the tasks to which systems theory, or even systems thinking, addresses itself. What is needed are enough structured methods to make sure that design is approached as a sequence of decisions, each of which closes down the total remaining degree of freedom in such a way that a good solution is always known to exist in this remaining degree of freedom, if a solution exists at all. To solve this problem we may start with an approach that is well established in algebra. When we have to solve an equation we start by imagining that we have a solution and by giving a name, for example, x, to the variable that is the solution. We then work on formulas containing x until, if successful, we get x expressed in the variables given.

The system design problem can be thought of as indicated by the formula

$$s = f(p_1, p_2, \ldots, p_n) \qquad (1)$$

where $f(p_1, p_2, \ldots, p_n)$ is the *part structure* or detail structure of the system; s is the given specification of the required external properties of the system S to be designed; $p_i (i = 1, 2, \ldots, n)$ are the parts (or part types) from which the system S is to be constructed; and f is the "structural design" function of S determining how the parts p_i are connected to form S.

The problem is that we have no chance of conceiving of f if the system is large, that is, if n is large. The solution approach is to assume that we have a set of large system components or subsystems $x_i (i = 1, 2, \ldots, k)$ such that

$$s = F(x_1, x_2, \ldots, x_k) \qquad (2)$$

with $(F(x_1, x_2, \ldots, x_k)$ being the *subsystem structure* of S and k being small, such that already a few x_i will suffice for a solution of the *whole* problem. Then *if* the x_i have enough simple external properties, it may be possible for the designer (or, sometimes, even a computer program) to draft one or a few candidate structure functions F because the problem is now a much smaller one. The crucial point here is that although the design problem $s = F(x_1, x_2, \ldots, x_k)$ could be in terms of very few subsystems only because the latter are very large, it is only a few external properties, x_i, of each large subsystem, i, that are considered. Hence the problem (2) could be made as small as needed to obtain enough overview to permit a reasonable chance of finding a possible solution, or a set of solutions. Equally important, we may now be able to deduce, or at least intuitively construct, the total system properties that result from each such drafted candidate subsystem structure. This makes it possible to test each design layout against the system specification and to modify the design when it does not fit the specification well enough. After a number of such iterations, we may find a satisfactory solution alternative. Then we may continue by repeating the procedure for each of the subsystems.

In this way we replace the problem (1), which may be an impossible one to solve, by the problem (2) plus a sequence of problems of a kind similar to (2) but concerned successively with x_1, x_2, ... , and, then, a subsystem of x_1, x_2, ...

A different and more extensive treatment of the general method for system design was presented in *Theoretical Analysis of Information Systems* (Langefors, 1966), where it was also given an axiomatic development. Recent work in "software engineering" (Dijkstra, 1968; Zurcher and Randell, 1968) presents applications of methods of this kind to software system design. We have, ourselves, found that it provides an important guidance in all problems of design and of management of large systems. Consequently much of the treatment of information system and data base problems in this book will follow, more or less closely, the principle of this method of system design.

Fundamental to the theory of system design is the concept of external property. A designer of one level only needs to specify the external properties of the subsystems he wants to use as building blocks. He can then estimate the resulting properties of the system based on the external properties of the subsystems. To communicate between persons concerned with a system it is only necessary to communicate about external properties. Likewise, for one subsystem to communicate with the rest of the system only some external, structural properties need to be satisfied. In information system design the information to be represented in the system specifies the external properties the data will have in the system. Data designers may choose among an endless number of alternative data structures as long as they have the external property for conveying the right information. Also the information entities specified by an information precedence relation constitute a specification of some basic external properties of the data process that will be designed to realize the precedence relation. Similarly, at a later stage the logical data descriptions specify external properties for succeeding physical data construction.

CHAPTER 1

INFORMATION AND DATA

To design information systems—also to use them properly or specify their functions—we must be able to talk about their information content. We therefore discuss information elements, or messages, as well as kinds of information. We also study how data can be designed to represent information whereby a group of data elements, or data terms, will represent one information element or elementary message. Thus we find how information system design specifies wanted information first and then designs the data to provide it. We study how one piece of reality can be informed about in different ways by distinct "elementary messages." When one of these alternative message forms has been chosen, according to which ones best suit the information users, we have an endless number of alternative data structures that can be used to represent the messages. When choosing which data structure to use in the system, consideration is given to the effect it will have on the data transport work and data processing work in the system. When a data structure has been chosen, the details of it must be designed so as to suit the structure of the data handling and processing hardware.

The data files, or "data sets," that result from the information and data design will lead to certain demands for file storage volume and data transport. To determine these demands in detail will, of course, require that we study a sequence of design problems, which become successively more and more dynamic and transient. In later chapters we will proceed along this sequence but in this book we do not go as far as to the detailed, concurrent event control considerations or algorithmic considerations. We study instead that which can and should be handled before those problems.

1.1 INFORMATION ELEMENTS AND DATA ELEMENTS

We use the view that *data* are symbols used to represent and communicate knowledge and that the term *information* refers to this knowledge. Thus we see that in dealing with information we may sometimes restrict ourselves to the data aspect, concerning ourselves with the design of data structures and data processes. We then are concerned with *datalogical* questions. Contrary to this it will at other times be in portant to consider the *informatological*, or *infological* (*conceptual*) aspects, dealing with the knowledge to be treated, that is, information.

Conceptual Terms and Data Terms

In natural language we communicate information by combining words to make sentences. A single word does not, in general, convey information, only certain groups of words do that by forming sentences. For this to happen the words in the sentences must have *meaning* to the receiver. The meaning of a word is a concept or an idea to which the word refers or associates. Thus we have a conceptual or infological aspect of a word. Often this concept or idea is a certain class of objects, real or abstract, or an individual member of such a class.

> EXAMPLE 1: The word "dog" and the German word "Hund" are distinct symbols but refer to the same concept: that associated with the class of all dogs. If we express just the word "dog," we do not convey any information about the real world in spite of the fact that the listener may understand what the word means, that is, refers to. (However, the sequence of words "my dog is black" does convey information about the real world.)

On the other hand the formal aspect or the datalogical aspect of a word is concerned with the set of spoken sounds (phonemes), which are the data (or symbols) constituting the spoken word, or the set of characters that constitute the written word or computer-stored word. Similarly, from a datalogical point of view a written sentence is the set of written words and their interrelations, whereas the infological view of the sentence is the information or knowledge that can be obtained through the set of concepts referred to by the words of the sentence plus the relations between these concepts as indicated by the structure of the sentence.

EXAMPLE 2: The sentence "I saw a black dog" conveys some information about myself. Thus I can be regarded as the object informed about and this follows from the grammatical form of the sentence. In other words there is an accepted rule that makes it possible for the receiver of this message to know that in the string of words making up the sentence, that substring which follows "I" in the string is related to the word "I" in a certain way. This rule belongs to the language. It makes use of the meaning of the individual words (and may therefore be regarded as not purely formal).

In natural language the content of a sentence—its message—may be ambiguous because a word may have more than one meaning or because a word in the sentence may have a certain relation to one part of the sentence or to another part, depending on the context. In using data processing to handle information we try to avoid this ambiguity and simplify processing by using words, or terms, with uniquely defined meaning (within each system) and using defined relations between the terms as well as using simple and defined structuring of the data.

EXAMPLE 3: The sentence "my dog is black" may be represented more formally, for instance, as

Object		Property	Time
Dog	Jossy	Being black	Presently
Dog	Jossy	Belonging me	Presently

Elementary Situations, Messages, Entries, Records

We cannot determine the information represented by a written text by just listing the words in it. We have already mentioned that the meanings of individual words do not, by themselves, convey information; this is obtained by suitable combinations of and relations between the individual word meanings. Thus a single word is not an information element in the sense of a unit of information. Instead the information element must consist of a number of words or terms combined in certain specific ways.

We may refer to the information content of a combination of word meanings, or "conceptual terms" (we also will use the term *reference*) as a *message*. We might account for the information content of a text by describing which messages it contains. These messages may themselves be so complicated as to require their own content to be described. Thus we may need to break down messages into smaller messages until we come down to such simple messages that they are directly understood. This raises the question as to what are the smallest messages possible. It is not important for us to be using the smallest possible messages, although that would entail some advantages. What is important is that we define messages which are small enough to be understood by themselves. We find it natural to look for the smallest messages possible as a methodological device. We note first that "smallest message" can be given different meanings. Therefore we can make a choice of "smallest possible" in some natural and simple sense.

It is easy to see that there is one view of what constitutes a minimum message (or minimum piece of information) which is natural both from a general-intuitive perspective and from a system theory point of view. To constitute information a message must at least make known (a) what object (or unit, or entity, or concept) it informs about, (b) a property (or behavior or situation) of that object, and (c) the period of time for which the property holds true or has been been observed. That this is natural from a general point of view follows from the fact that it is inherent in any concept of knowledge or information known (to this author).

That the message described above is natural from a system theory point of view is easy to see. A system is a set of objects of any kind with different relations between the objects. To observe or study a system we thus observe or study the properties or the behavior of the objects or the relations. Thus elementary facts about systems will have to be facts about the property or status or behavior of an object or about a relation between an object and the rest of the system. In the latter case the relation is the object we inform about; for instance, we shall later talk about precedence relations such as "A precedes B". If we define what we mean by "precedes," then we inform about the relation "precedes." In that sense the precedence relation becomes the object of the object of the discourse. If we cancel a part of a message so that it no longer makes known what object it informs about or what property it states, or at what time it holds, the rest of the message does not even convey information about an elementary situation in the system.

As we have seen any message must encompass (a) an object part, (b) a property part, and (c) a time part. However, the property part may be a compound property such that it may be decomposed into two or more *elementary* properties. The message can then be split into several smaller, elementary, messages.

DEFINITION 1: Elementary Message (*e*-Message). A message the property part of which states an elementary property (or an elementary behavior) is an *e* message.

We define an *e* message as the smallest piece of information in the sense that if any part of what it makes known is ignored, then the rest does not carry information. "Elementary property" here means one that could not reasonably be regarded as consisting of two or more factors each of which is itself capable of being regarded as a property.

EXAMPLE 4:
(a) "Weight 100 pounds" is an elementary property.
(b) "Buy five apples" may be, by some, regarded as two properties combined:

BUY APPLES   AND   QUANTITY, FIVE

It is important to note that the definition of an *e* message will apply to distinct types, depending on what we will accept as an elementary property. From experience we find that the most simple form (similar to a binary relation) will always do. (This would, for example, imply regarding "buy apples" as an elementary behavior but regarding "buy five apples" as not elementary.) It also appears that the only alternative necessary to consider is to extend the class of elementary properties (or behavior) so as to include also ternary relations, that is, a binary relation with a quantity relation.

EXAMPLE 5: The message "Tom buys five apples" will correspond to one or two *e* messages depending on whether to "buy five apples" is regarded as an elementary property (behavior) or instead to "buy apples" is regarded as an elementary property.
In the latter case we have two *e*-messages:
    *e*1: Tom buys apples
    *e*2: quantity in *e*1 is five.

It is important to note that we have defined the *e* message (and a message in general as well) in terms of *what is made known*—that is, which *reference concepts* are involved—without specifying anything about *how* it is made known. Thus, for instance, we have said nothing about how the *e* message is to be represented in writing, that is, how the message might be represented by data. In other words, we are defining *e* messages as pieces of knowledge or information and not as data. In this way we have, of course, avoided making the definition strictly operational in a sense that would leave only one way for implementation. This has the advantage of leaving open how we would design *e* messages in different practical situations, which is necessary because we do not know which implementations would be best in any future application. Although we purposely avoid being too specific in our *definition*, we may, of course, present detailed *examples* of how we *might* implement the definition in many cases.

It would have been possible for us to choose the more general and less specific definition of an *e* message as any kind of minimum information message that one would *like* to choose in each specific case. Such a general definition would still be very useful. This was our earliest definition (Langefors, 1966) because at that time it was too difficult to know what disadvantages would be involved in making a more specific and, hence, more restrictive definition. Now, after almost a decade, we have found that the more specific definition used above has always worked.

DEFINITION 2: Elementary Situation (Elementary State or Elementary Event). If one single, elementary property or behavior exists at a specific interval or moment of time *t* at a specific object *o*, this characterizes an *elementary situation or* e *situation.*

THEOREM: An *e* message informs about an *e* situation. The proof is immediate in view of Definitions 1 and 2.

It would be in accordance with ordinary language and the above definitions to say that an *e* message is the information about the *fact* that an *e* situation is prevailing. We could therefore say that *an* e *message that is true expresses an* e *fact.*

DEFINITION 3: *e* Entry and *e* Record. To record an *e* message or to communicate it we usually use symbols, that is, *data*. Those data that together represent an *e* message will be referred to as the *e entry* (elementary entry) associated with that *e* message. If the *e* entry is stored in one contiguous area of storage (or printing), it will often be referred to as an *e record* (elementary record).

Typical Information Structure of an *e* Message
Definition 1 of an *e* message that we presented above was purposely chosen to be not wholly operational. The definition was based on the external property: what is *made known*. It left open the question of how the *e* message is built up. Of course, the definition itself has some structure in that it specified three reference concepts or *conceptual terms* to be made known by the *e* message: which object, which property, and

which time are referred to. Many different designs of *e* messages are possible in accordance with the definition. We can be somewhat more specific about the design of *e* messages in general and we prefer to do this by way of illustration of a *typical design*, rather than to let the *definition* be that narrow. Thus we keep the definition general and conceptual and use illustrations in order to be concrete.

We turn to the question of *how* the *e* message makes things known. *To make known what object the e message is about* we could use an identifier or a name, for instance, a number. This would require one single standard procedure for constructing identifiers for the "whole system" that would be accepted by everyone concerned. This is too complicated to work in large systems (such as companies or organizations) and the natural system–theoretical solution is the common one: The system we wish to inform about, the *object system*, is partitioned into classes of objects that are similar in some definable or generally understood way. Such object classes may be persons, articles, sales orders, or machines.

If the object or property classes are suitably chosen and appropriately managed within the object system (for example, a company), it may be possible to establish for each class a set of names or identifying numbers such that there is a one-to-one relation between the names and the objects in the set. This is the case, for instance, with the class of persons for which it has been possible to design and use unique identification numbers over whole countries (for example, in Sweden). It is interesting that this was possible even without a formal definition of class membership, being based instead on a *general understanding* of the reference concept "person." Thus general, unanimous understanding may be as useful (and more) as a strictly formal definition. In such well-behaved cases the object reference of the *e* message is solved by using two conceptual terms:

identification of object: $<$object class name, identifier$>$

Note that the conceptual terms *object class name* and *identifier* are of the same character as in Definition 1 in that they are supposed to *make known* (by whatever means) what the message refers to. Thus to make known which object, we make known which object class and which individual member of the class. The advantage is that by partitioning the reference concept *object* into the two reference concepts *object class* and *identifier within the class* we make it easier to define data terms that can be understood by many people and, hence, be used as reference data or *devices for making known what is referred to.*

EXAMPLE 6:
(a) Identification of a person:
  <person, identifier of the person>
One way to represent this by data may be as follows
(b) Data to identify a person:
  <'person','150321–1912'> (in Sweden)
(c) Another way of identifying a person might be
  <'department','department#','person','employee#.

Primes are used here to signify *data* representing a reference. Thus in (a) *person* is supposed to indicate the concept *person*, whereas in (b) 'person' is used to indicate the written word (or magnetically recorded word). It will make known to those who "understand" it that *person* is what is talked about. It has been assumed in this example that it is known from the context that we are only concerned with people in Sweden at the moment. Otherwise more data would be needed in order to make known that which is indicated in (a).
(b1) Data to identify a person:
  <'person,Sweden,"150321–1912'>
We might have chosen other data, for instance.
(b2) Data to identify a person:
  <'human being,Sweden,"150321–1912'>

Often the object classes are more complex, or less well-known, so that it may be necessary to refer to an element of a subclass of a subclass of an object class, in many levels and, maybe, in an undetermined number of levels.

EXAMPLE 7:
(a) Identification of a company C which is a subsidiary of B which, in turn, is a subsidiary of A:
  <company A, subsidiary B, subsidiary C>
(b) Data to identify the company:
  'company, A;' 'subsidiary, B;' 'subsidiary, C'

Of course, the distinction between the knowledge aspect (conceptual aspect) (a) and the data aspect may appear subtle to an inexperienced reader. This is partly so because we are making this discussion in writing. Thus, in fact, we are using data (written text) also to describe the conceptual level. However, (a) describes what concepts or ideas must be available to those who are to be able to interpret the data representation (b).

One very concrete and formal distinction between the info-logical aspect (or knowledge aspect) and the data aspect is that an indefinite number of data representations is possible for making known the same object or concept. Hence the choice is an important design decision. Among the objects that cause some problem with their identification are events or transactions because of their transient nature.

EXAMPLE 8: In Example 5 the message
    Tom buys five apples
was split into the two *e* messages
    *e*1: Tom, buys, apples
    *e*2: *e*1, quantity, five

In *e*2 the identifier *e*1 has the position of object identifier and identifies the event in question as the object informed about. Thus *e*1 might be the order number that has been given to the sales transaction talked about. Now a user may not know the number *e*1 but may know the complete *e* message *e*1. He would then be served by being allowed to write *e*2 in the form
    *e*2′: (Tom,buys,apples),quantity,five
We observe that if the user knows everything about *e*2′ except the value five then he may specify
    Tom,buys,apples,quantity,?
in his query. We may consider this as formulating the query as an incomplete *e* message *e*2′, having the first three terms as its object identifying part. Alternatively, it is possible to regard the message
    Tom buys five apples
as an *e* message rather than as a composite message composed from *e*1 and *e*2 and write something like
    Tom buys ? apples
We see that essentially the same query results so the choice of point of views is not very critical.

EXERCISE 1: We have pointed out that information is always tied to some conceived object. It is therefore dependent on common conceptions among people in the object system about classes of objects. Many such classes are well established and problem free, for instance, classes of objects that are regarded as real objects such as persons or machines. Other classes are more artificial but can nevertheless be fairly easily recognized and identified because their definition is kept invariant for a fairly long time. This is the case with departments and product groups and also with properties such as age or inventory on hand. These are not too difficult, but they call for more careful definition in system design than is usually done. There are also other objects which may be fairly concrete but nevertheless cause trouble with their individual identification because of their transient behavior. These are what we used to refer to as events or transactions. As we have discussed earlier, events are difficult to identify when needed. Of course, an event such as a customer ordering an article is usually given an identity number, but this number will often be difficult to know or remember because of the transient nature of the event. We found that as a consequence it is often convenient to identify an event by means of a complete *e* message describing the event. Such a complete *e* message would thus take the place of object identifier in any other *e* message about the event. This may be a feasible, though somewhat complex, solution in individual retrieval situations but it is not always suited for more systematic use, for example, in accounting. Discuss the means for systematized identification of events (transactions) normally used in accounting or budgeting systems with respect to the discussion just given and with respect to the concepts of *e* messages and *e* concepts.

We may conclude that to make known which object it informs about, the typical *e* message will contain one conceptual term that refers to (makes known) (a) an object class by a name or a group of names and (b) a member of that class by an identifier.

To make known what property the e *message states* (of the object it informs about) we use a device similar to that used for objects in that we assume that properties can be assigned to classes. Thus an "attribute" or a "relation" is a *kind* of property and is naming a property class. Typically a property is determined by an attribute–value pair or a relation–object pair. Thus, for instance, a person *Pete* may have the property

   age is 32 years

where "age is" is the attribute and "32 years" is the value (of the property). Likewise

   Pete, has as father, Tom

defines a property of Pete and this property is

   has as father, Tom

where "has as father" is the relation and "Tom" is the second object (*counter object*). Here the value in the property of the object *Pete* is another object *Tom*. Such attributes are often called *relations* or object relations. We see that typically we have

PROPERTY = ATTRIBUTE–VALUE   OR   RELATION–second OBJECT

where "second object" refers to the fact that this is another object than the main object, that is, than that which the *e* message informs *about*. Of course the second object is identified in the same manner as the main object, that is, by means of object class and identifier within the class. The class of main objects is often called the *domain* of the relation. The second object or *counter object* then belongs to the *counter domain*. Note that in another situation the "second object" may instead come to be regarded as the "main object."

To make known which interval or moment of time the e message is about we only have to observe that time is one kind of attribute, although a special kind, and thus is treated in a similar way as the property part of the message.

The *typical* e *message*, we may conclude, consists of (a) name of object class, identifier within the class. (This is repeated a number of times if subclasses of object classes are used); (b) name of property class (attribute, relation or event), value of attribute; and (c) name of time attribute, value of or identification of time.

> EXAMPLE 9: The message is
> person, Pete
> weight, 150 pounds
> time, 720802
>
> *Recall* again that what we talk about here are the concepts referred to by the terms written (that is, the reference concepts) and not the data or written words. We have thus described the *information structure* of a typical *e* message by describing how it is constructed from conceptual terms.

As we have seen the value of a relation is an object. However, the relation itself may also be associated with an object or an object class. For instance, in the *e* message

Stockholm is the capital of Sweden

"Stockholm" is the object informed about and the property stated is "is the capital" to which is associated the value "Sweden." Time is simultaneously specified in the property by the verb form "is". Thus this *e* message mentions three object classes or objects. On the other hand that object class which is involved in the name of the relation "is the capital" is combined with the verb "is" and many people would prefer to regard "is" as the relation and "the capital of Sweden" or "the capital of the country of Sweden" as a combined object. This kind of choice is a matter of "information design" to be handled by the users and the information analysts, in cooperation. Note also that we will often want to form a message to say something about a property or a property class, in which case the latter takes the position of the object informed about by the message. As the time interval involved in a message may also be formally regarded as an object, it may be possible, formally, to define an *e* message as a group of five objects or object classes, which, however, play distinct roles in the message.

EXAMPLE 10: "Course of <student> is A4 in the fall term 1973" or
(<student>, fall term 1973, course = A4)
or (in "prefix form")
course (<student>, fall term 1973) = A4

Data Structure of a Typical *e* Entry

The information structure of an *e* message—that is, how it is built up from three groups of conceptual terms, one for each of the main conceptual terms, which identify the object, the property and the time—forms a natural basis for definition of the data structure of the associated data, the *e* entry. This is obtained by observing that each conceptual term will be represented by one data term or a group of data terms (see Formal Definition of the file concept in Section 4.1) in such a way that each data term (or group of data terms) refers either to a conceptual term and thus to the corresponding reference concept (as, for example, "person" refers to the concept *person*) or to other data in the system, which data refer, in their turn, to the intended reference concept (as when the data term "person" refers to a set of "person data" which may actually be regarded as a *partial*, physical representation of the reference concept *person*).

Note that in addition to the data terms representing the terms of the message, an *e* entry must contain data (or data structure) that binds the terms together to form the entry. Thus every *e* entry must have a data structure that makes known which terms belong to the same entry. We may call this the *entry-forming-structure data*.

Not all conceptual terms in the *e* message need to be explicitly recorded as data terms because the data terms to use are those needed to make known what the *e* message makes known. Thus if something is known already from the design of the system, the corresponding data terms may be omitted. For instance, if the system is known to contain only *e* messages about system states existing *at present*, then the time reference data can be omitted from the *e* entries. Likewise if a certain instrument in a display room is known to be connected, on line, to a specific object *A* in the system and is known to be a thermometer, then the current reading *T* of that instrument is the only data term explicitly indicated in the *e* entry (its property value term) that represents the *e* message.

  object, *A*; temperature, *T*; time, present

Note carefully that when in these illustrations some data terms of the *e* entry could be omitted the underlying conceptual terms are still there, given by the context or by the physical structure.

Attributes and Relations

  We have made a distinction between attributes and relations. The reason for this is conceptual rather than formal. Some properties of an object are naturally conceived by most people as relations whereas others are not. Thus "Tom is son of Bill" would be regarded by most people as expressing a relation between Tom and Bill. Instead, for instance, "age of Bill is 37 years" would be regarded by many as a property of Bill, which assigns the value 37 to the attribute "age (in years)."

  Formally it is possible to regard the attribute as a relation. We would then, in this case, regard the attribute "age (in years)" as defining a relation between Bill and 37. For this reason it is quite common among people with a formalistic orientation, such as mathematicians or computer programmers (and computer scientists in general), to disregard the usefulness of the concept of attributes as distinguished from relations. We see two drawbacks (at least) of this attitude. Information is not a matter of formalities only. The understanding of people is fundamental in information systems, and so what is natural to people is often more important than what is formally simple. In fact, many failures of data system design have been caused by too little regard for what is natural to the people involved. There is, however, also a formal reason for not disregarding the distinction between attributes and relations. Thus although attributes *can* be formally regarded as relations, this does not mean that there would be no formal differences between the concepts. There are differences, and those differences mean that what make relations interesting in information systems are characteristics that are missing in attributes.

  Relations form the information structure, and relations between objects form the systems that we usually represent in our information systems. Attribute–value pairs instead are associated with individual objects. Thus whereas chains of relations go from object to object and thus join corresponding object records in a data base, attributes do not form a chain but only single links ("atoms").

EXAMPLE 11: The messages
    son of Tom is Bill
and
    Bill purchased a car from a dealer in A-town
set up a chain of relations that bind together the objects so that Tom is chained to A-town.

$$\text{Tom} \xrightarrow{\text{son}} \text{Bill} \xrightarrow{\text{purchased}} \text{car C} \xrightarrow{\text{sold by}} \text{dealer} \xrightarrow{\text{in}} \text{A-town}$$

Instead "age of Tom is 53" and "price of car C is P" set up a link from Tom to 53 where it ends and a link from car C to P where it ends.

$$\text{Tom} \xrightarrow{\text{son}} \text{Bill} \xrightarrow{\text{purchased}} \text{car C} \xrightarrow{\text{sold by}} \text{dealer} \xrightarrow{\text{in}} \text{A-town}$$

Tom → age → 53   car C → price → P

Thus in the information structure the attributes "age" and "price" have an appearance that is different from that of the relations "son," "purchased," "in." Although there may be retrieval processes in the information system that will have to follow the chains of relation, there will be no chains of attributes.

1.2   *e* CONCEPTS AND *e* FILES, PROCONCEPTS, *c* CONCEPTS, AND RELATIONS

e Concepts

It is common in data systems to organize records (or data entries) of "the same kind" into a common file, or a small set of files, the underlying reason being the assumption that the records in a file carry information *of the same kind* (but for distinct objects and distinct time periods). Thus the idea behind files is that a file is associated with a certain *kind of information*. As our approach is to take the information itself as the basis (the infological approach), we turn the idea around and study first information kinds and from there on we study how files in a data system may be designed to correspond to kinds of information. When we say that file records "carry information," we are, more precisely, referring to the fact that a data record or a data entry is a group of data chosen to represent a message. Then to define the information *contained* in the file we define the *e* messages it contains.

An important type of similarity of *e* messages is when they all contain the same kind of property, that is, the same attribute (or the same relation). All *e* messages with the same attribute may be distinct with respect to all the other terms: object class, object identifier, value of attribute, time value. However, many of them will also have the same object class, so it will be very natural to regard classes of *e* messages that have the same attribute and the same object class or, in other words, have the same kind of property and the same kind of object. In conclusion we say that *e* messages of the same attribute and object classes are of the *same elementary kind of information*. This specific sort of "sameness" of elementary kind of information we will refer to by the term *e* concept. Thus an *e* concept is characterized by being associated with a specific pair ($<$object class$>$,$<$elementary property class$>$). For instance (person, age) is an *e* concept and so is (articles, inventory on hand). Sometimes the way used for the specification of time may be of interest, so this will also be included in the *e* concept specification ($<$object class$>$, $<$property class$>$, $<$time attribute$>$).

One would then have, for example, the *e* concept

(person,age,years)

or, in "property prefix form"

age(person,years)

EXAMPLE 1: The *e* concept

inventory on hand(articles)

might be given the more precise specification

inventory on hand(articles,number of pieces)

but then

inventory on hand(articles,pounds)

would be regarded as a distinct *e* concept, which may or may not be desirable.

EXAMPLE 2: In practice we may often prefer to regard inventory on hand as the same kind of property regardless of whether it is measured in pieces or in pounds, for instance. Then the unit of measure would be a variable: "quantity" which in each individual record will be specified by a term that may take on such values as "pieces" or "pounds." In this case the detailed specification of the *e* concept might be inventory on hand(articles,quantity type)

EXAMPLE 3: It is likely that we may want to regard
     inventory on hand(articles,quantity type)
and
     inventory on hand(articles,money value)
as distinct *e* concepts.

    Although we may or may not want to present the unit of measure (such as "quantity" or "money value") for the value associated with an attribute, we probably will always want to have the second-object class associated with the relation represented when the property is of a relation kind. This is so because all object classes are potential entities for retrieval.

EXAMPLE 4: The *e* concept may be
     (article,ordered by,customer)
or, less conveniently this time,
     ordered by(article,customer)
However, when both domains of the relation are always identical it may be unnecessary to mention the second-object class.

EXAMPLE 5: The *e* concept
     (person,is father of,person)
or
     is father of(person,person)
may equivalently be described by
     (person,is father of)
or, less appealing,
     is father of(person)

EXAMPLE 6: The *e* concept *el*
     el = (*e* concept, is precedent of,*e* concept)
may be described by *el'*
     el' = (*e* concept,is precedent of)
but
     (*e* concept,is precedent of,process)
can, of course, not be represented without mentioning the second-object class "process."

As we have seen it is sometimes preferable to use the property prefix form of an *e*-concept description similarly to the case with *e* messages whereas in other cases the other form (infix form) is more convenient. It is, of course, likely that in system documentation we will choose one of these forms and use it consistently.

Some Examples of *e* Concepts Taken from Real-Life Cases

EXAMPLE 7: From the information system of a university department we present some *e* concepts from the *e*-concept catalog. They are presented here in prefix form.

3A1   First term registered (student,course)
3A2   Latest term registered (student,course)
2A   Result of examination (student,course,examination,date)
514A Score in course (course)
511A Number of new registered (course,current term)

We may illustrate the use made of the *e*-concept catalog by looking at the description of the *functional relation* which defines how an *e* message of the *e* concept 511A is produced from information from 3A1 and 3A2.

Functional relation 511

1   For one specified course
2   For each student
3   If First term registered,3A1 = Latest term registered,3A2
4   Then add 1 to number of registered,511A

Note that in each of the *e* concepts shown, the property (shown as a prefix in front of the parenthesis) happened to be an object, thus illustrating the fact that both the property part and the object part of a message may be objects.

Note that 1, 2, and 3 in the functional relation together specify the value of the property of two *e* messages. Thus 1 and 2 identify a course and a student for each application of the relation, and this pair makes the object informed about by the *e* messages and 3 states the property parts of these *e* messages.

EXAMPLE 8: From the information analysis for the design of an on-line order-processing system in a Swedish company. In this system some 800 *e* concepts were identified and documented in a catalog to form an important basis for the system design, implementation, maintenance, and development. (This example is based on a system documentation worked out by Torsten Lundquist.)

Figure 1.1 is an extract from the *e*-file catalog (closely related to an *e*-concept list).

An example of a functional relation is given below.

11131 Deduction of requested quantity
        Transaction ‡ (1033) = 7

if

Quantity on hand(1212) $\geq$ Quantity request (1176)

then

Quantity on hand (1212) = Quantity on hand (1212) −
Quantity request (1176)
Quantity ordered (1180) = Quantity request (1176)

if

Quantity on hand (1212) $\leq$ Quantity request (1176)

then

Quantity difference (1302)= Quantity request (1176) −
Quantity on hand (1212)

Number	Attribute	Type	Size	Object	Type	Size
. . .						
1176	Quantity request (order line)	N	6	Order # Article #	N N	6 6
. . .						
1180	Quantity ordered (order line)	N	6	Order # Article #	N N	6 6
. . .						
1212	Quantity on hand (division, stock, location, article)	N	6	Division # Stock location # Article #	N N N	1 2 6
1302	Quantity differ- ence (order line)	N	6	Order # Article #	N N	6 6

Fig. 1.1

A Group of *e* Concepts as an *n* Relation

In an information system we will often have groups of *e* concepts. There may be different reasons for this. For example, we may have a *natural group* where it is more natural for the users of the system to regard a group of *e* concepts as the smallest conceptual unit rather than as individual *e* concepts. In such cases it is appropriate to regard the natural group of *e* concepts as a natural *n* relation. (The trouble with this view is that what is natural for one group of users may not be natural for others.) We may instead have groups that occur because retrieval or processing considerations lead to the consolidation of *e* files even when this was not motivated for conceptual reasons. In such cases it does not seem appropriate to talk of *n* relations.

EXAMPLE 9: The message,
> Customer C
> ordered
> 5 pieces
> of article A
> at time T

may be regarded by many people, as an instance of a time-varying natural ternary relation (over the three domains, customers, articles, number of pieces), rather than as a group of the two concepts,
> (customers,ordered,articles)
> ((customers,ordered,articles)quantity,number of pieces)

where in the latter *e* concept the object domain is that of events of the kind (customers, ordered, articles).

EXAMPLE 10: The message,
> Person Tom
> is a student, at present
> was born in 1948

would be accepted by most people (who know the idea of *e* concepts) as a group of two distinct *e* messages related by both being about Tom. In this case it seems totally artificial to talk of a three relation (although this is formally correct).

EXERCISE 1: We might think that the use of a three relation would avoid the complication of having a whole *e* message or *e* action (such as customers, ordered, articles) as the object of the *e* message about "quantity." However, the reader may find that this is not the case by determining which parts of the message expressing the three relation must be stated in a query that would retrieve the value of "quantity." He will find that exactly the same terms have to be present as were used in Example 9.

e Files and c Files

Each *e* concept that will be used in an information system will give rise to one or several sets of *e* messages and these will be represented by data entries. In this way collections of *e* entries, which we call *e* files, will be used in the system to represent information belonging to the *e* concepts. We shall look further into the structures of *e* files in subsequent chapters.

Usually several distinct *e* files are wanted for a class of objects. These may often have to be taken together because the users may want them in the same reports or because data storage and transfer then becomes more economical or efficient. We then say that the *e* files are consolidated into one (or more) consolidated files or *c* files. This part of data system design will be discussed in later chapters. We shall sometimes say that a *c* file represents a *c* concept.

1.3   INFORMATION STRUCTURE AND DATA STRUCTURE

Data Entries to Represent a Message

There are still people who find it difficult to grasp the concept of information as something different from that of recorded symbols (data) and perhaps unnecessary. Thus we are facing the question of whether it might not be sufficient to consider only the object system (the reality) and the data used to describe it (another reality). There are, however, both fundamental and methodological reasons why the reality and the recorded symbols are not enough for us to consider. The fundamental reason is that the data cannot refer directly to reality; data cannot point to the real objects and still less to their properties. Thus we are bound to use human conceptions about the real world as the bridging concept between data and reality. The importance of the conceptions of human beings, the knowledge or information, cannot be wiped away. Indeed, not only are the conceptions of people necessarily involved, the *motivation* of people is critical for communication and, thus, for use of data, as has been shown clearly by psychological research.

The methodological reason for needing to study information and data as distinct, related concepts is that to design an information system we must tackle both of the problems: (a) to find out *what* information the users want and to describe this in a way that the users can understand

and verify, and (b) to give the data system designers freedom to design the data structures and processes most suitable for meeting the needs or desires of the users by specifying to the designers *what* data are required but *not how* one should produce them.

We shall try now to reduce the amount of talking in terms of information by casting the problem in a form that focuses on sets of equivalent data entries as a basis for information system design. We assume that we have on the one hand the object system (OS) (including the users and their conceptions) and on the other hand we have sets of data to serve the object system. Among the sets of data we have "written messages" chosen to describe the messages the users want. We have other sets of data that are entries used to represent the messages in a way that is suited for storage and processing in the data system (DS). We illustrate this idea by an example.

EXAMPLE 1: In Fig. 1.2 (a) we have illustrated a piece of reality (an *e* situation) and in (b) we show a written *e* message about (a) as it might be written by an observer, Pete. Then in Fig. 1.2 (c) through (i) are shown distinct *e* entries, having distinct data structure while being equivalent to the written message (b). Thus (b) through (i) belong to the set of equivalent *e* entries that corresponds to the *e* message describing the *e* situation.

We would make the claim of equivalence between the *e* entries, (b)-(i) formal by demonstrating that for each *e* entry there can be designed an *interpreting algorithm* that transforms the *e* entry to the written *e* message (or to any other *e* entry in the equivalence set).

Interpretation of an *e* entry would be to let "term pair" refer to $<$term$>$ ($<$term$>$) in an *e* entry.

Algorithm Ac

   1 Form the string "object informed about is $<$first term pair in *e* entry$>$"
   2 Append the string "it has the property: $<$second term pair in *e* entry$>$"
   3 Append the string "at $<$third term pair in *e* entry$>$"
   4 Stop

If we apply algorithm Ac to *e* entry (c) we obtain

   1 Object informed about is person (Tom), it has the property: profession (teacher) at time (presently)

(a)

Tom

(b) Information content of the *e* message about the *e* situation as described by the written message,

"Tom is a teacher, presently"

e entry recording the *e* message

(c) Complete *e* record

Person (Tom)
Profession (teacher)
Time (presently)

(d) Graphical *e* entry

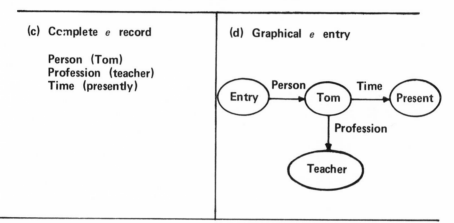

(e) Formatted *e* record (with record format description)

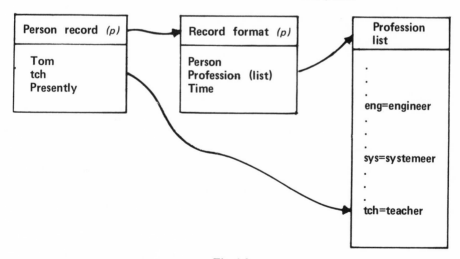

Fig. 1.2

(f) *e* entry embedded in formatted *c* record

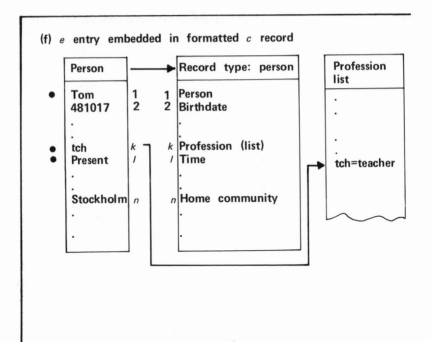

(g) *e* entry in list format

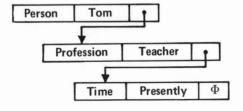

Fig. 1.2   (Continued)

24

(h) *e* entry embedded in an expanded list structure

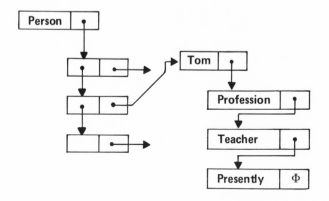

(i) Profession matrix *P*

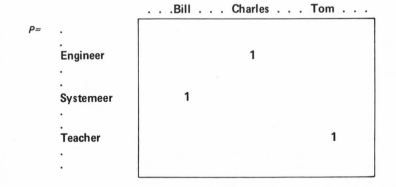

Fig. 1.2   (Continued)

Algorithm Af

1 Form the string "object informed about is <first term in c record type: person>(<first term in c record>)"

2 Append the string "it has the property: <kth term in c record type: person>(<kth term in c record>)"

3 Replace the previous term by its equivalent term according to "profession list"

4 Append the string "at <lth term in c record type>(<lth term in c record>)"

5 Stop

We may thus state, symbolically,

$$Ac \ (e \text{ entry } c) = Af \ (e \text{ entry } f) = (e \text{ entry } b)$$

Thus if

$$(e \text{ entry } f) = Afc \ (e \text{ entry } c)$$
we would require

$$Af \ (Afc \ (e \text{ entry } c)) = Ac \ (e \text{ entry } c)$$

∴ formally

$$Af \ (Afc) = Ac$$

Data Entry and Interpretation Algorithm

It is seen that we can obtain the same written message (or "preferred data entry") from many rather different logical data structures but *only when* we know (or the system knows) which interpretation algorithm to use in each case. The same data entry may give rise to many distinct written messages, depending on the algorithm used for the interpretation. Thus to obtain a specific written message from stored data it is not sufficient just to identify the data entry (or the part of the data structure) to use, but also the interpretation algorithm to use must be identified. Note that it follows that the data system designer is free to choose whatever data structure he finds efficient, but only to the extent that he provides the needed interpretation algorithms *as well as* means for identifying the right algorithm. We may thus be allowed to specify the information we want from the system and obtain the desired written message, regardless of which data structure is used inside the system, and without having to know the data structure.

Whenever a user, or an information designer, has chosen a certain written message to represent the information content of a message that he has in mind, he may delegate to a data system designer the choice of any pair of data entry interpretation algorithms he (the latter) wants to represent the written message in the system.

We may thus say that *the message* is *represented* by the *written message* chosen by the users as well as by the *data entry* (entries) designed by the data system designer. "The message" is used here to denote "the information content in the written message."

Although many distinct data entries may be interpreted into the same written message (which is, of course, itself a data entry), it would be misleading to say that they *contain* this written message. It is, however, reasonable to say that they all *contain the same message* (information), because they are equivalent to the written message in the sense that they may be (formally) interpreted into it. The message (info) is (in a narrow, formal sense) equivalent to all its possible data entries together with their respective interpretation algorithms. (Note the analogy with the theory of invariants in theoretical physics.)

Deducted Information. Associative Relations

So far we have considered the most simple and, perhaps, most natural requirement on data to provide information: to be able to produce (and print out) a written message in a form that conveys the intended information (message) to a user. Another important requirement on data to represent information is that if a certain message can be inferred from a set of other messages, then the corresponding deduction should be possible to obtain on the data representations. Thus a data entry suitable for the representation of the inferred message should be possible to generate using a suitable algorithm that works on the data entries which represent the set of other messages.

We may describe the two required properties of data to provide information as (a) the data must be able to *convey* specified information (messages); and (b) the data must be able to support the deductions that are possible on the corresponding information. The deducted information obviously has to do with information involved in certain relations between the individual messages. We refer to such relations as *associative relations*. The deduction potentialities are, of course, an important aspect of the information structure of a collection of messages which, clearly, has to be realized also by the structure of the corresponding data entries. Associative relations between messages are, typically, manifested by the related messages referring to each other or to common objects or concepts.

EXAMPLE 2: The two *e* entries (1) and (2) are associatively related by having the term pair "class (2B)" in common and this makes some deduction possible.

1. [person(Tom),teaches,class(2B)]
2. [person(Jim),student in,class(2B)]
      the inference rule
   (
   (person x,z,class y (that is, x and z are persons and y is a class)
3. (
   (if [x,teaches,y] and [z,student in,y]
   (then x is teacher of z
      together with the data entries (1) and (2) gives
4. (1)(2)(3) ⇒ Tom,is teacher of,Jim ⇒ Jim,(is teacher of), $^{-1}$ Tom
5. (is teacher of) $^{-1}$ ≡ is student of (( ) $^{-1}$ denotes reverse relation)
   (4)(5) ⇒ Jim, is student of, Tom

Note that it was not necessary to introduce separate structure data such as address pointers between (1) and (2). Their inherent associative connection is quite sufficient to make the inference possible as, indeed, all information processing systems should be able to explore any information structure. However, it may happen during the data system design that structure data may be introduced, but this would then be merely for data processing efficiency reasons.

EXERCISE 1: Outline an algorithm that would produce the answer to the question, Which persons are students of Tom? Assume a data base containing entries of the form (1) and (2) of Example 2, above.

EXERCISE 2: Draw an outline of an entry "person," of the form *f* but extended to contain also the information contained in (1) and (2) of Example 1. Outline an algorithm for this data base, to answer the same question as in Exercise 1.

EXERCISE 3: Outline an algorithm that would retrieve records of the form (1) and (2) of Example 1 from the data base of Exercise 2 and discuss the possibility of solving Exercise 2 using the algorithm of Exercise 1 in combination with this algorithm.

Computed Information. Precedence Relations

It may be possible to compute new messages from existing ones when there are no explicit associative relations between them or when existing associative relations are not complete. In fact, this is presently the common way in which data systems work, whereas deductions are still in the forefront of research. When a message A may be computed from B and C the latter are said to be precedents of the former. Of course, to compute A it is not sufficient to know that B and C have *precedence relations* to A. We must also know the *functional properties* of the precedence relation.

EXAMPLE 3: The messages represented by (1) and (2) in Example 2 have a mutual associative relation but this is not complete enough to enable one to deduce the message M "Jim, is student of, Tom." However, (1) and (2) are precedents of M and a program can be written that would compute M from (1) and (2). This requires the work of programming but does not require the system to have deductive capabilities.

Precedence relations are studied extensively in the next chapter.

The Added Amount of Information from an *e* Message. Virtual Data

We have seen that when an *e* message is added to a system that already contains some *e* messages to which it has associative relations —as when (2) was added to (1), in Example 2—then the amount of information added to the system amounts to more than one *e* message. This is so because the *e* messages that can then be deduced are also added. Because the deduced *e* messages are not explicitly represented in the system by *e* entries, they are sometimes referred to as *virtual* data or implicit data.

We have seen that once we have learnt how to specify any desired information message, then we can leave it to the data designer to invent an endless number of distinct possible data entries, embedded in various sorts of data structures, to represent it in a data system and to choose a suitable one for implementation. Now that we have also seen that data entries may be deducted from other, stored data entries—whenever the corresponding message can be deduced from messages contained in the stored entries—we see that the data designer may even, for some messages, have the choice of not storing at all a data entry representing a certain message but rather of generating the written message, when needed, from other stored entries.

EXAMPLE 4: If we want to be able to obtain from the system such messages as "Tom is a teacher" as well as "Tom teaches class 2B," then we may, for instance, make the decision during data design not to store any entry of the form "Tom is a teacher" but to design an algorithm, instead, which generates that fact from the message "Tom teaches class 2B" (or, of course, from any message "Tom teaches ... ").

Data Structure Data and Data Structure. Information Structure

As we have seen there are some information relations that must necessarily be represented by special structure data which have to be added to the data terms in an entry representing the conceptual terms of the message. This was the case with the *entry-forming structure data* that represent the *message forming relations* (or the concept relations). For any given data term they are needed to tell which other terms it combines with in order to provide information. In Example 1 we gave illustrations of several distinct entry-forming structure data. For instance in (c), (e), (f), and (i) of Fig. 1.2 they were manifested by contiguous arrangements of the terms of the *e* entry, together with entry begin and entry end marks (brackets in this case). In (g) and (h) they were given by pointers and end marks (for example, ϕ). Also in (e) and (f) some use of pointers was made.

We have also seen that there are other information relations, such as *associative relations* and *precedence relations* in which structure data are not necessary but still may be used as a data system design device. Again these structure data are typically of the kind of pointers or contiguous arrangement in the storage. (Note that the pointers themselves need some device to tie them to other terms. This is usually done by contiguous arrangement.)

It is common even in recent literature of computer science or data processing to see that the term "data structure" is only used in connection with structure established by structuring data*; in fact, often only structuring by pointers is recognized as data structuring. As we have seen, associative relations between messages are represented by equal value of data terms in the corresponding entries (*infological pointers*). It is not easy to find a good definition of data structure that would exclude such structure from the class of data structures.

CONCLUSION We conclude from the study of this section that any information structure, inherent in *e* messages and their interrelations, which reflects a certain structure of the object system, as conceived by some users, can be represented in several distinct ways by data structures. Such data structures are often referred to as "logical data structures" as soon as they have some degree of "device independence" or are described in a way that ignores hardware details. The use of the attribute "logical" in such contexts* seems to indicate that one believes the structure of the problem itself (the object system structure) would be reflected by such data structures. Our results demonstrate that this may easily be very misleading. It is the information structure or infological structure that reflects the problem, not always the data structure.

Some Further Remarks on Data Structure

The representation of systems structure and infological pointers in data systems was probably first implemented through the use of structure matrices, borrowing from such fields of mathematics as algebraic topology and graph theory. (For instance, one of the present authors has used computer models of this kind since 1951 for the treatment of aircraft engineering problems [Langefors, 1963 b 16].)

Somewhat later the use of computers to handle problems regarding the theory of computations and artificial intelligence led to the introduction of so-called list processing structures in which the structure representation was through the use of address pointers as in Fig. 1.2 (g). Figure 1.2(c) instead is a kind often used in the implementation of the system matrix models.

It was not necessarily just a coincidence that scientists in the distinct areas mentioned above chose different ways of representing structure. The artificial intelligence and computation theory field usually experimented with models such that the structures could be mainly kept in main memory while the processing was performed. They could be chosen small enough for this as the experimenter had the choice himself. In this kind of processing the address link (address pointer) is much more efficient than a name link which has to involve a retrieval-by-name mechanism. Thus the pointer was the obvious choice in the field of "list processing" (in "small data bases").

In working out methods for representing structures in large data

---

* For instance, the technical report *A Survey of Generalized Data Base Management Systems,* May 1969, by CODASYL Systems Committee states: "The conventional procedure of using a normal item value from one file to locate a second item value in another file is not considered to be a data structure feature." (It is not known why the committee said "another file" instead of just file or, rather, why they did not use "record" or "entry" instead of file in the sentence quoted.)

bases it has been natural to learn from list processing which has been much used in computer science. It is then easy to forget the reason for making address pointers the obvious structuring device. Thereby alternatives that may become feasible when switching to large structures (large data bases), for which the structure processing has to involve traversing over records stored in backing stores, tend to be ignored. Instead the workers on engineering structures could not make their own choice but had to accept the given size of the practical models and thus usually had to have their structural data in backing storage. In such cases the use of a link in the model, which connects two components—such as proceeding from "Tom" to "profession" in Fig. 1.2(g)—may induce the same amount of data transport for name links and address links (or the difference may be minor). And this, of course, is the typical situation in information systems. Then address links are no longer the only alternative for representing structure. Name links, for instance, may be good alternatives in such environments.

1.4   FILE SIZE AND VOLUME , NOMINAL AND ACTUAL SPEED, TRANSPORT SIZE AND VOLUME

File Size, and Speed of File Transport Unit

To the system designer it is, of course, important to have a measure of how large the different files are. This determines how much storage space will be needed and how much time to transport them in total (as in sequential processing of the files) will be required. It thus determines cost and choice of type of file storage. Unfortunately there is not a single measure of how large a file is or how fast a file storage and transport unit is. Nevertheless the designer needs to have simple measures for these factors to base his early decisions on. For instance, before the choice can be made as to what file storage equipment to use for the files and how to organize the files on the equipment, such estimates must be made. The estimates that can be made before the final design is detailed are, of course, bound to be crude, sometimes very crude. So what we are looking for is not precise computations before the design, but estimates from which the worst errors can be eliminated. To see that even fairly crude estimates may be important we may agree that if a user estimates that one of his files will contain 20 million characters and if he finds in the brochure of a computer manufacturer that a certain magnetic tape unit stores 20 million characters on a tape reel, he might conclude that his file will go on one tape reel. In fact, many offers by computer salesmen and, unfortunately, quite a few preestimates by system analysts, for example, during the so-called feasibility study, have fallen into this trap. In reality (which comes much later) these people will find that they will need two reels at least and, in many cases, their early designs would turn out to require three to five reels.

Similarly, the user or the analyst may find in the brochure of a manufacturer that the tape speed is claimed to be 100,000 characters per second. If he then estimates that 200 seconds will be required to transport (scan) his file, he will be drastically in error. Not only will he have to transport at least twice this amount of file storage, as we noted above, but, in addition, the actual speed (as seen by the user) may be far below the nominal, brochure figure. This is because after a tape has been read or recorded upon, time will also have to be spent on tape rewind and on set up and dismount of tape reels. There may also be other lost time involved. The effect of this time will be that the actual tape speed as seen by the user may be only half the nominal, brochure figure.

Of course, in this typical situation an estimate procedure that is in error by about 50 percent only is a big advantage; and so is an understanding of where the main fallacies are. It is this problem of early stage, simplified estimates that we take up in this chapter. More precise, detailed computations, after design specifications, are much less problematic, although time consuming.

The number of storage positions (bits or bytes, for instance) that is required for the storage of the same file entries may vary by several hundred percent depending on system design structure; and for a given design structure the time to transport the file, or given parts of it, will depend greatly on the speed factors of the file storage used. Thus the apparent volume of a file, as seen by the time it takes to transport it, will vary with the speed and "operation times" of equipment. To compare distinct files for transport-time considerations, the designer may thus want to have a measure that takes the transport time into consideration.

To bring some order into the confusing picture of how large a file is, we start by observing that we could use one measure based on *how many symbols* correspond to the amount of information contained in the file. This we will call the *file size*. We could then use another measure based on the *number of storage positions* used by the file when it has been given its structure by the designer. This we call the *file volume*.

The designer has available to him some means that would make the volume smaller than the size, but he will also be subject to restrictions that would make the volume larger than the size. The combined effect may result in a file volume that is larger or smaller than the file size. He will be interested in obtaining a small volume but only because this has desirable effects on storage cost and transport time. These are, of course, also influenced by other factors so that the relation

$$\frac{\text{file volume}}{\text{file size}} = \textit{file volume factor}$$

will be one among several indices that are of interest.

To estimate response speed or processing economy in the system the designer wants to estimate file transport time. Again this is more complicated than is apparent on the face of it. Thus "transport" may mean different things, and it involves different operations which may bring different influences on the time. Before final design, all of these different factors must be considered and their effects computed. However, at an early stage of the analysis and design this will be impossible. It will also be meaningless, because at this stage many alternatives have to be analyzed and many changes will be made. Therefore crude estimates of average values are more interesting. Thus at early analysis stages the time to transport a file will be estimated on the basis of estimates for the volume of the file and estimates for the "actual speed" of the file unit. [If n_v is the volume factor and n_s is the speed factor (see below), then the estimated time for file transport will be $n_v \cdot 1/n_s \cdot$ file size/nominal transport speed.]

At an early stage, before design decisions have been made, estimates on file size, processing periods, and nominal transport speeds are possible because they are not dependent on the design decisions. It is therefore practical to make these estimates, and document them, as a basis for predesign time and space estimates and for design decisions. Thus alternative design calculations can be based on the same file size, processing timing, and nominal speed figures.

File Size and Entry Size

As the file is mainly a set of entries, it seems natural to determine the file size as

file size = (number of entries)·(average size of one entry)

Thus we are left with the problem of determining the size of one file entry. As a file entry contains one or more e entries, we are led to the problem of determining the size of an e entry. When several e entries are taken together to form a file entry, some data may be deleted. For instance, we may decide to store the object identifier only once. There are so many different ways to obtain such data reductions, however, that it seems wise to regard them as design decisions that influence the final file volume but had better be disregarded at this stage. Our suggestion (subject to future reconsideration) is therefore to *define* the entry size as the sum of the sizes of all the *e* entries contained in it.

entry size = sum of the sizes of the *e* entries contained in the file entry

This choice of definition also has the advantage that it allows the following statement as a theorem:

file size = sum of sizes of the *e* files contained in the file

To determine the size of an *e* entry we determine first the *conceptual terms* of the corresponding *e* message. We know that often they will be

(object class name
(
(object identifier

(time kind
(
(time value

(attribute name
(
("attribute value"

To each conceptual term in the *e* message there will be one data term or one group of data terms. We notice that already the conceptual term may be defined as a group of conceptual terms. For instance, the object identifier may consist of the group,

(company name)   may be unnecessary
division name
department name
number within department

The important thing here is that this structuring of "object identifier" is not made for data system reasons but for conceptual reasons. It is thus not determined in the data system design but by the object system design or object system analysis. Consequently, it seems best to consider this structure when determining the file size figures. As a result a change in structure in the object system will lead to a change in file size, whereas a change in the design of data structure or the storage structure will change the file volume but not the file size (that is, it will change the volume factor n_v).

The size of an *e* entry is, of course, equal to the sum of the sizes of all its terms.* Each term—whether it represents a name of an object, or an attribute (or whatever), or an attribute value—is, in principle, a value that identifies one element in the set associated with the term. Thus, for example, the object class name identifies, by its value, one element in the set of object classes and a department name identifies one department out of the set of all departments. The smallest data term that can identify all elements in a set of *n* elements (that is, of *cardinality n*) is a binary word which has a size of 2 log *n* bits. Thus we obtain a unique measure of the size of a term if we define it to be 2 log (cardinality of the set for which the term is an identifier).

Often we do not know the magnitude (cardinality) of the sets involved but are able to make quick estimates as to the *range* of values, that is, the maximum and the minimum value that a term can take on. For instance, the age of a person might be estimated to stay between 0 and 150 years. The cardinality of the value set will then be determined by the range, together with the resolution required.

EXAMPLE 1: If age of a person is to be represented in years, the resolution is one year and the cardinality of the value set would be determined by the range (= 0 through 150 = 151) and the resolution equals one. The size of the term will thus be 2 log (151).

EXAMPLE 2: If *a*, *b*, and *c* are the terms of an *e* entry (strictly speaking they ought to be six, at least) and if *A*, *B*, and *C* are the cardinalities of the corresponding sets, then the *e* entry size will be

size (*e* entry) = 2 log *A* + 2 log *B* + 2 log *C* = 2 log(*A·B·C*),

which is equal to the logarithm of the cardinality of the "product set" $A \times B \times C$.

Note that each term in an entry acts as a *pointer* that points to either an element in the set associated with a reference concept or to a location in a storage.

Note also that the same *e* entry (or, perhaps, the same *kind* of *e* entry) will have a larger size if it is defined within a larger system that contains more entities in the different sets referred to by the terms (for example, if the system consists of more objects in a certain object class). Thus if we regard the information content of an *e* message as equal to

---

* Excluding any structure data terms introduced in the data design stage. These are to be included in the entry volume overhead.

one, there will be more bits required for a unit of information if it occurs in a larger system. In this sense, a bit would not correspond to a standard quantity of information but would merely appear as a data unit.

File Volume and Volume Factor

We have studied how file size can be defined as a measure of how large a file is. How large a file is determines how much space is needed to store the file and what is required to transport the file (for example, between file storage and main memory). However, the number of storage positions in bits that are occupied by the file may be different from the measure (in bits) of the file size. There are several reasons for this, all of which depend on decisions and choices made during the file design stage. Although the file size is determined by the needs of the object system, the file volume factor n_v is determined by the properties of the storage system used and by the way the designer chooses to structure the file.

Nominal and Actual Transport Speed; Effective Speed

In making estimates about how to design the system for handling data files, we not only need to consider file sizes and file volumes. In some cases it will be the time it takes to transport a file or a pair of files that is of prime importance. In such cases a file A which is 10 times smaller than a file B but is to be handled by a file medium that is 20 times slower, will appear as the larger file from a transport-time point of view; the incautious analyst might disregard this in his estimates because of the minor size of the file. Thus we see that it may be important to

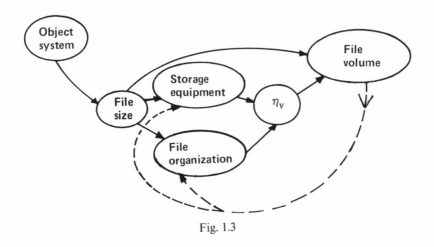

Fig. 1.3

include the awareness of the time for transporting a file in considerations of file sizes and volumes.

The file transport speed is, of course, dependent on the file handling unit used with the file. At the early stage of analysis it is not known exactly what equipment will be used for the individual files. What can be done, however, is to make assumptions about which *class of equipment* to consider for each file, sometimes considering more than one possible alternative. Thus it may not be too difficult to estimate for a certain file that a slow and inexpensive magnetic tape handler may be an economic choice, whereas other files are to be used in such ways that fast tape handlers and a direct-access store of a certain performance class seem more appropriate. Similarly, an input data file may be known to have to be handled as a punched tape or punched card file and thus is bound to be transported with very slow speed (as compared with magnetic file media).

As we have seen we obtain estimates for the transport speed for a file by making an assumption as to what *kind* of file storage unit it will be put on. Using commercial data we may establish typical *nominal transport speeds* for each kind of file handler. We now have to make an important observation: The time it takes to handle a file (reading or recording) may be significantly longer than that involved in the simple file transfer. Thus we have to allow time for mounting and dismounting the tape reel or disk pack, and a tape file will also need time for rewinding. A disk file may need time for check reading after writing. Also, with disk or drum storage an additional rotation may be called for between each pair of blocks. Movement of read/write heads also needs time on some storage types. The speed that is apparent to the user will thus be determined by the file volume divided by the total time, involving all the handling operations of the file. Thus the *actual transport* speed will be significantly lower (typically around 50 percent) than the nominal speed, enough to be considered even in early (predesign) estimates.

Classes of File Storage Equipment

The reason we study file data transport as a separate problem for information system architecture is that we talk of data files when we have to do with sets of data that are too large to be stored in the main memory of the computer. Then, for economic reasons, we use storage equipment that is "slower" than main memory and has different characteristics from it. In the main memory we have, typically, "full speed" and "random access." "Full speed" means that any data word can be brought into a working register of the computer at about the regular instruction time or less. "Random access" means that the time for fetching a new word is independent of the word last fetched. File storage equipment is characterized by having a speed that is much slower than the main memory and, usually, is of nonrandom-access type (even though it is often called "random-access storage") in that the time to fetch the next word is strongly dependent on the last word fetched. As a consequence we experience a time and resource consuming data *transport* operation to move data from file storage to main memory. Most file storage devices (disks, drums, tape units) are of a *pseudo-direct-access type* (Langefors, 1961) which is characterized by the fact that to access a certain data term we first have a direct-access operation with the access time a_1, to a certain main part (which we may call "band") of the file storage, then a second direct-access operation, access time a_2, to a part (called "part") within that band (followed perhaps by one or a sequence of further direct-access operations to successively smaller parts), and thereafter have to perform a sequential scan (scan time equal to a_s) of the smallest part accessed in the access sequence to reach the desired *access block*; this access block is then transferred to main memory (transfer time equal to a_t) whereupon, finally, the data term desired is fetched by the computer. Thus a file storage unit may be described by

$$(a_1, a_2, \ldots, a_n | a_s | a_t)$$

for its data transport characteristics.

For example, a typical magnetic tape file storage may have the vector

$$(60 \text{ sec} | 300 \text{ sec(average)} | 0,01 \text{ sec})$$

which corresponds to a one-minute time interval to mount the tape reel carrying the desired file data, followed by a tape scan of five minutes and, finally, a transfer of one file block in 10 milliseconds. The 60 seconds to mount the tape reel may be realistic if an empty tape unit is available. Otherwise we may need several minutes in order to rewind a tape on a tape unit before we can replace the tape reel. The 300 seconds may be less than the time needed to scan a full reel, as we only expect to have to scan part of the tape to reach the desired access block. This time depends heavily on the processing situation. In a typical system the computer CPU (central processing unit) and the data channel will have to spend some time during the 300 seconds of scanning as well as during the 0.01 second for transfer. However, there do exist (or have existed) tape file devices that could scan the tape to locate an addressed access block without any supervision by the CPU.

A magnetic disk storage unit might have the vector

(60 sec,0.05 sec(average),0.02 sec(average)|0.02 sec average)|0.01 sec)

corresponding to mounting a disk pack (60 seconds), moving the read/write heads to the right disk (0.05 second, average time), moving the head to the right disk track (0.02 second, average time), waiting for the disk to rotate to reach the desired block (0.02 second, average time), and transferring the block to main memory (0.01 second). In this case the CPU and the data channel need be engaged only during the 0.01 second for transfer (and, possibly during the rotation wait time).

The distinct access times and scanning times of a pseudo-direct-access device depend significantly on the *distance* to traverse in the file storage, to access a certain block after another block was accessed. This means that the data transport (access movements, scans, and transfers) may be strongly affected by the way the file data are placed in the file storage devices as well as on the way the locating of the desired block is organized, that is, the *access method* or directory operation being used. Thus the organization of the directory/file pair becomes an important element of information systems architecture whenever pseudo-direct-access devices (tapes or disks) are used.

In tape file devices the scanning operation dominates heavily, which results in such devices usually being thought of as *serial-access storage devices*. This fact makes it necessary, in general, to restrict the use of such devices to files that can always be processed in the "batch processing" mode in which the scanning distance between two successive desired blocks has been made small by processing a large enough batch of transactions against the file in one and the same processing run. In the sequel when we talk of *pseudo-direct-access* devices, we shall be referring to devices *not of the serial-access types*.

Most of the times needed for access and transfer are functions of relevant distances between stored data. For instance a_2 may be a function of the number of disks to traverse, a_3 may be a function of the number of tracks to pass, and in a tape device a_2 may be a function of the length of tape to be scanned. Thus the examples of times that we used in the vectors above will vary depending on the circumstances, but it is usually possible to estimate them fairly well, given the positions of the access blocks involved and the (class of) file storage device to be used.

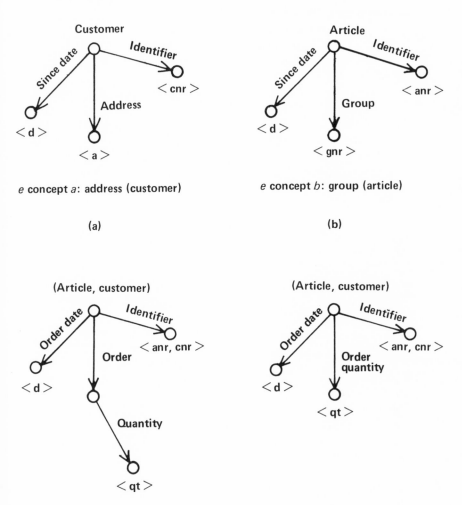

e concept a: address (customer)

(a)

e concept b: group (article)

(b)

(c)

(d)

Fig. 1.4

EXERCISE 1: Discuss the equivalence of the diagrams in Fig. 1.4 and the *e* concepts and *e* messages

e concept (a):address (customer)

e concept (b):group (article)

e concept (c):order (article, customer) and quantity (article, cost, order)

e concept (d):order quantity (article, customer)

For instance, in (a) "address" appears as an attribute whereas in (c) "order" appears as a ternary relation over the three domains (article, customer, time).

e message (a): customer$<$cnr$>$,address $<$a$>$,since date$<$d$>$

e message (b): article $<$anr$>$,group$<$gnr$>$,since date$<$d$>$

e message (c): article $<$anr$>$,customer$<$cnr$>$,order, order date$<$d$>$; *and* article$<$anr$>$,customer$<$cnr$>$, order,quantity$<$qt$>$

e message (d):article$<$anr$>$,customer$<$cnr$>$,order quantity$<$qt$>$,order date $<$d$>$

EXERCISE 2: If we introduce the further *e* concept order transaction (article, customer, "order") and the corresponding *e* message,

e message (e): article$<$anr$>$,customer$<$cnr$>$,order,order transaction$<$onr,line$>$order date$<$d$>$

then we can write

e message (f): order trans$<$onr,line$>$,quantity$<$qt$>$

so that, from then on, order transaction appears as a new object class.

The object class order transaction has the form of a relation involving the objects article and customer. In this sense, the transaction type is equivalent to the relation "order" of the *e* concept (c). Draw the corresponding diagram for (e).

EXERCISE 3: Discuss the equivalence of the diagrams (a) and (b) in Fig. 1.5

CONCLUSIONS

We have found that it is possible to specify exactly *what* information to have without having to use data design or programming terminology. Thus it is shown that it is possible to specify information needs in a way that can be understood by the users. This specification is nevertheless precise enough for the design of the corresponding data structures. But it still leaves full freedom to the data designer to choose an efficient structure—indeed it encourages the designers to look at several alternatives.

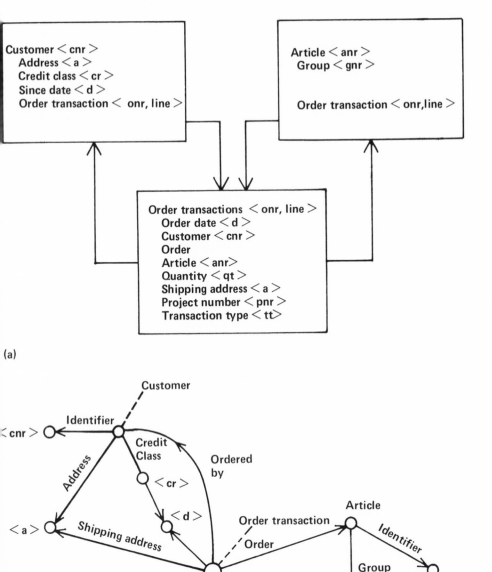

Customer < cnr >
 Address < a >
 Credit class < cr >
 Since date < d >
 Order transaction < onr, line >

Article < anr >
 Group < gnr >

 Order transaction < onr,line >

Order transactions < onr, line >
 Order date < d >
 Customer < cnr >
 Order
 Article < anr>
 Quantity < qt >
 Shipping address < a >
 Project number < pnr >
 Transaction type < tt>

(a)

Customer

Identifier

< cnr >

Credit
Class
< cr >

Ordered
by

< d >

Address

Shipping address

Order transaction

Order

Article

Identifier

< a >

< anr >

Identifier

Group

Quantity

< gnr >

Project

Transaction type

< onr, line >

< pr >

< tt >

< qt >

(b)

Fig. 1.5   Sets of *e* messages associated with three distinct classes, two
            alternative representations.

43

Information elements were found, the so-called *e* messages, and "kinds of information" were defined as kinds of *e* messages of similar types. This made it possible to obtain a well-structured information system.

It was shown how data structures that represent the desired information can be systematically developed. Information units are related to each other corresponding to relations between units in the object system. Thus an information structure is defined. Data representing the information must, of course, contain representations of the information relations. In addition the data designers may introduce "data structure data" to add structure that may make the processing more efficient.

We also saw how sets of needed *e* messages define the sizes of the data files and that the file volumes then depend on these sizes but also on data design decisions.

An important observation is that the necessary connection between a piece of reality and the data, which are other pieces of reality, that we want to use to represent it or refer to it can only be obtained through the means of conceptions in the minds of human beings. Thus what data to use depends both on what is to be informed about and who is to be informed.

REVIEW QUESTIONS

1. A single word does not convey information but must have a meaning to a person in order to take part in an information communication. How can it do this?

2. An elementary message, or *e* message, may inform about a "piece of reality." What name did we give to such a piece of reality?

3. What is the relation between an *e* message and an *e* entry?

4. An *e* message conveys information by "making known" three distinct things. What are they?

5. An *e* message expresses a "property" of an object. The property may be expressed by an attribute–value-pair or by a relation–second object pair. Give an example for each of these two and discuss the differences and similarities between them.

6. Write down an *e* message (that is, its "written message form" as natural to yourself). Show four distinct data structures that may represent this *e* message. In what sense are they equivalent to "the written message" or to either one of them?

7. Explain how two *e* messages may be regarded as containing together more than two *e* messages.

8. What did we mean by "data structure data"?

9. What is the "size of a file" and what is the "volume of a file"? Why do we need both of these concepts?

CHAPTER 2

INFORMATION SYSTEMS STRUCTURES

The information that is specified to be provided by the system has to be collected from the object system—the application or the environment—or it will have to be produced from other information, its "information precedents." In this way an information precedence structure exists in the system and it is this which ties the information units together. The information precedence relations also are important in that they can be exploited to enable a systematic information analysis. When the information units are represented in the system by data structures, the precedence relations will be represented by data processes. The efficient design of the data system, the files and data sets, depends mainly on the information precedence structure in the system in its totality. It is therefore important that the system, as it results from the information analysis and design and as then modified during data design, can be documented in a way that displays the total system structure or makes it available to formal design. System matrices, or equivalent data structures, meet this need. As such matrices can easily be obtained through the analysis of the information precedence relations, they are important system documentation tools.

2.1 INFORMATION PRECEDENCE RELATIONS

We have seen how e messages can be defined as elements of information systems. For these elements to make up a system, mutual relations must exist between them. An e message itself is based on relations in that it is built up as a small aggregate of reference concepts—object reference, property reference, time reference—all of which have relations to each other, as stated by the e message. In addition the "property" in an e message is often a kind of relation between the object and a class of objects or values. The relations between the reference concepts within an e message are seen to be *intramessage relations* forming the e messages which are the information elements of the system. *Intermessage relations* (between e messages), however, act to build up the information system by defining the relations that build up the object system from its elements. The way this occurs is, typically, that a certain e message (that is, its information content) is obtained from (or defined in terms of and thus has relations to) other information contained in other e messages. As an illustration we may consider the e message that informs about the area $F(r,t)$ enclosed by a rectangle r at the time t of length $l(r,t)$ and height $h(r,t)$. We know that $F(r,t)$ is determined from $l(r,t)$ and $h(r,t)$. This knowledge we may express by saying that if we obtain, first, information about $l(r,t)$ and $h(r,t)$, then it is possible to produce the information about $F(r,t)$. In somewhat more technical terms we express this by saying that $l(r,t)$ and $h(r,t)$ are *information precedents* of $F(r,t)$. Further, $F(r,t)$ is said to be a *succedent* of l and h. As we shall have to deal a lot with information precedence relations, let us now introduce a formalism for this sort of statement as follows:

$$\mathscr{P}(F) = l, h \qquad \text{and} \qquad S(l) \supset F(r,t)$$

or, equivalently,

$$l \ll F \qquad h \ll F$$

This precedence relation holds for any rectangle r and any time t; hence the indices were left out. Thus the precedence relation holds for the e concepts of which $F(r,t)$, $l(r,t)$, and $h(r,t)$ are individual e-message instances. In classical mathematical notation we would write this as

$$F = F(l,h)$$

and the e concepts F, l, and h are usually called *variables*. Notice that both of these formulations display the fact that we only wanted to state the dependence of F on l and h without having as yet determined precisely the properties of this dependence or how this dependence could be calculated. The information kind and its precedents form a *precedence bundle*. Thus F, l, and h form the precedence bundle associated with $\mathscr{P}(F) = l, h$. The precedents l and h form the *domain* of the precedence bundle and its associated relation. The current information kind, F, forms the *counterdomain* or the *range* of the relation. From here on we have to move in three distinct directions (Fig. 2.1).

1. What then, in the next step, are the e concepts that are the information precedents of l and h and what information is there in the system that will have F as one precedent? In other words, what information precedents x_i, of higher than the first order, with respect to F, $(x_i < F)$ and what succedents y_i of F are there ($y_i \in S(F)$)?

2. How can data files (or data sets) be constructed to represent the information kinds?

3. How can the relation $F = F(l,h)$ be defined and implemented in a mathematical model or in a computing system? In other words, if $F = f(l,h)$, what are the properties of the function f?

The first of these questions, the *information precedence analysis*, is mainly a *system theoretical* question. It raises the questions of what the *system* has to do to support the determination of F. Actually the question is a deeper one: What are the *relations to other parts of the object system*? It also raises a question of *succedence analysis*: What are all the distinct uses of F, in the whole system, that is, of what other information is $F(r,t)$ a precedent? Thus the first question is a global system question and so is the second question. It has to do with what we refer to as *information analysis*. The third question is a local question about a single, delimited part of the system.

Many applied mathematicians or computer programmers tend to ignore the questions (1) and (2) and address themselves directly to question (3). This is, in fact, so deeply rooted in their way of thinking that they usually believe that they can only identify the information precedents (or the independent variables) through working out the mathematical formula implementing the precedence relation. In information systems analysis this mistake turns out to be an unfortunate one, leading, for instance, to an unsatisfactory handling of (or even ignoring) the important system-theoretical first question. We therefore find it important to look somewhat deeper into this problem.

Information Analysis

In information systems design, questions (1) and (2) discussed above have to do with how to imbed the small subsystem $\mathscr{P}(F) = l,h$ in the

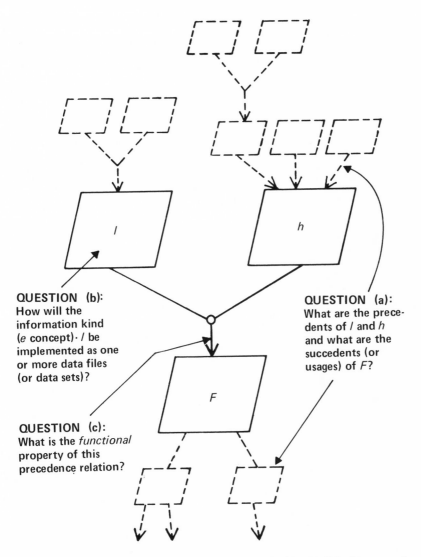

QUESTION (b):
How will the
information kind
(e concept)· l be
implemented as one
or more data files
(or data sets)?

QUESTION (a):
What are the prece-
dents of l and h
and what are the
succedents (or
usages) of F?

QUESTION (c):
What is the *functional*
property of this
precedence relation?

Fig. 2.1   The precedence bundle of the information F. F is the area of a
rectangle, l is the length of the rectangle, and h is the height of the
rectangle.

larger information system. This is a question of *system integration*. The third question, instead, is the local, separable problem of how to design a computation module that will compute F from l and h. To a programmer this is the main question and, indeed, being less trivial than the present example, it will also be a major question in real-life systems. However, it is a mistake to believe that questions (1) and (2) are therefore of minor importance. The experienced systems analyst knows that they are of at least equal importance and difficulty. For instance, is the subsystem $\mathscr{P}(F) = l,h$ the one that should be in the system? Before putting a lot of advanced work into modeling and implementing a computing module, it is important to make sure the one chosen is the right one and also that its external properties have been carefully specified and the right people are involved with it. This may sound obvious and trivial and, indeed, the only reason we stress it is that it is too often ignored in practice. It is in this way that "clever solutions to the wrong problems" often occur. The first step to take to insure the right subsystem being specified is to do enough information analysis to make sure the subsystem has a satisfactory environment. Thus the interface requirements to the rest of the total system are obtained and the actual and potential users are identified; a survey of what possible alternative information precedents there might be in the system is also made. When this preliminary analysis has been done, the construction and implementation of the computing (or processing) module, which will transform the precedents to the desired data, can be assigned as a separate task guided by the proper specification. This is one of the really fundamental system theory-based methods for system construction. It is also important to make further use of the separability of the module construction from the rest of the system design, once the module has been properly specified, by designing the module to take care of variables in general and not just the actual e concepts. Thus if the module to take care of is $\mathscr{P}(F) = l,h$, it will be designed as a module $\mathscr{P}(y) = x,z$, where a binding can be established at the time of initiation of the module process such that y is bound to F and x and z to l and h, respectively. (This systems logic is automatically taken care of if Algol is the programming language used for the system implementation through the mechanism of transformation from *actual parameters* (F,l,h) to *formal parameters* (y,x,z) but other devices may often be used for reasons (of efficiency).)

Because the information analysis problem is so important to information systems design and is also a necessary aid for improvement in systems, design, even while at the same time it is neglected, we find it mandatory to treat it at some depth in our discussion of information systems theory. The local problem of designing and implementing computing subsystems is, however, so extensively treated by computer scientists and practitioners that we do not find it necessary to devote much space to it in an information systems theory text. How to specify the external properties of computing subsystems to form a basis for construction and programming as well as program testing is, nonetheless, highly pertinent to information systems theory and we shall take it up later.

Definition of a Precedence Bundle

The definition of a precedence bundle is not dependent on the definition of the computation, but the converse is true. It should be clear from what we have found above that a *precedence bundle* (that is, an *e* concept together with its precedents) is not necessarily associated with an information process. We stress this because experience shows that this fact is seldom grasped by students and practitioners. Note that a precedence bundle is a *model* of *some* property of the object system. It reflects our knowledge, or assumptions, about properties of the object system. We may *decide* to represent it in the information system, in which case it is true that we need to design an appropriate information process. We may, however, alternatively decide *not* to represent it in the system, in which case it will *not* have an information process associated with it. The precedence bundle is still defined, of course.

Alternate Precedence Sets

There may be distinct, alternative precedence sets for an information kind. We mentioned above that one and the same *e* concept may have distinct alternative, precedence sets. This, of course, is fundamental to information systems theory, so it may be useful to illustrate this fact a little more concretely. This is the more so as one precedence set may be much better than another and one of them may be much more easily available than another. We shall try to give the reader a feeling for the meaning and general importance of this aspect by presenting a few simple illustrations. Figure 2.2 shows distinct ways of representing a precedence bundle. In (a) the three *e* concepts are each represented by a pair of circles, one of which is common to all three. For instance, one such pair is (rectangle *r*, time *t*) and (*h*) joined by the arrow marked height. The precedence arrows, $\mathscr{P}$, are to be thought of as joining the *e* concept and not just the entities *h*, *l*, and *F*, respectively. In (b) the *e* concepts are shown as three typical *e* messages and in (c) they are shown as one single "consolidated" message containing all three.

As a further illustration we study in Fig. 2.3 the problem of representing an arrow or *vector* **L** by means of its *components* along a set

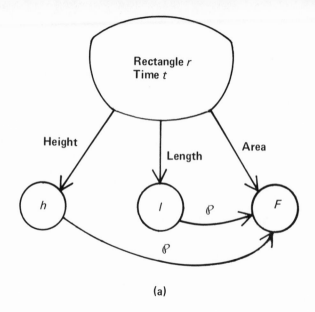

(a)

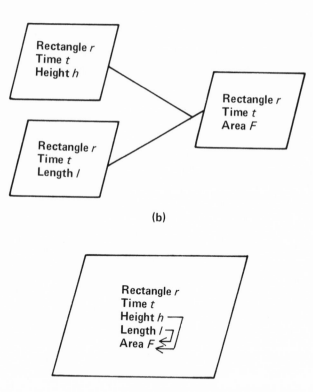

(b)

Rectangle r
Time t
Height h ⌐
Length l ⌐
Area F ⤶

(c)

Fig. 2.2   Three distinct ways of representing (and implementing) the precedence bundle $\mathscr{P}(F) = l,h$.

54

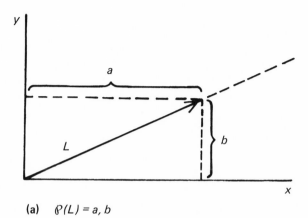

(a) $\wp(L) = a, b$

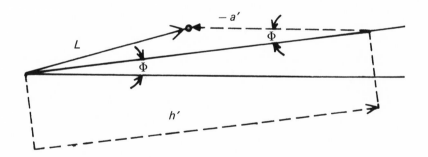

(b)

Fig. 2.3 $\mathscr{P}(L) = a,b.$

of coordinate axes. In particular we study what information precedents can be used to compute the length L of the vector **L**. In Fig. 2.3(a) the components a and b along two orthogonal coordinate axes x and y are used as information precedents for L. In (a) the functional relation is

$$l(x,y) = \sqrt{x^2 + y^2}$$

Thus the precedence relation $\mathscr{P}(L) = a,b$ is implemented by $L = l(a,b)$, that is, by substituting a and b for x and y in the function $l(x,y)$. In the case of Fig. 2.3(b) with the *coordinate axis p* replacing y, it is obvious from the diagram that also the angle ϕ between the x direction and the p direction influences the length L. Thus we find

$$\mathscr{P}(L) = a', b', \phi$$

Note that this observation can be made without taking the time to establish the details of the mathematical formula for computing L.

For instance, it is seen that if we turn the line p while retaining the lengths a' and b', then L will increase as ϕ is increased. If we keep L fixed, a' and b' will decrease with increasing ϕ. Conversely, when ϕ is decreased, the values a' and b', which correspond to a fixed value L, will increase. Thus in Fig. 2.3(a) the angle ϕ is equal to 90 degrees, whereas in Fig. 2.3(b) it is much smaller, and this is seen to result in $a' > a$ and $b' > b$. Indeed, although $L > a$ and $L > b$, we have $a' > L$ and $b' > L$. This implies that the coordinate system (x,p) is inferior to the coordinate system (x,y). To make this obvious we note that if we would have chosen p and x such that a' and b' become about 100 times longer than L (by making ϕ small enough) and if we measure a' and b' within 1 percent error, then the magnitude of this error would be of the same order as L; so we would have to expect L as computed from a' and b' to be in error by about 100 percent (disregarding errors from the numerical computation process). Instead, in Fig. 2.3(a), using orthogonal components, the components a and b turn out to be of the same magnitude as L so the percentage of error in L would only be about the same as that of a and b.

We may conclude from this illustration that to use the e messages a and b as precedents for L—that is, by using the e concepts x and y as precedents—we obtain a better representation than by using the e concepts x and p. There are two reasons: x and p are not a complete set of precedents—we had to add ϕ—and further we expect from what we have seen above that $\mathscr{P}(L) = a, b$ will be less sensitive to errors of data collection (measuring) and of computation than $\mathscr{P}(L) = a', b', \phi$. Note that we were able to reach this conclusion without going into details of the computing process design.

Independent Precedents. Orthogonal Precedents

It is of interest to note that our simple example illustrates not only what we set out to demonstrate: that distinct alternative precedence sets are possible, some of which are better than others. We illustrated more: that the coordinate variables (x,y) which are orthogonal to each other are better than (x,p) which are not orthogonal. This, of course, was a very specific and very simple case but the concept of orthogonality (and nonorthogonality) is a very general one. It plays a fundamental role in modern, abstract algebra and in statistics. Without going deeper into these subjects we can illustrate the generality and importance to information analysis of the concept of orthogonality (and hence of this simple illustration) by noting that the reason ϕ was necessary in the representation of Fig. 2.3(b) was that p and x are not independent and the dependence stems from the degree to which ϕ is different from 90 degrees (degree of nonorthogonality).

The simple illustration used above and its association with orthogonality and independence of different information (different e concepts) can be developed to illustrate one more aspect of importance to information analysis. It has to do with the fact that in real life we seldom have exact representations of reality but only approximations which may (sometimes) be improved by using more information. This amounts to observing that when asking for the precedents of an e concept, we will often not define a *complete* set of precedents but only a *satisfactory* set. This introduces the fundamental question of how we can estimate whether a given set of precedents is sufficient or not. This problem can be illustrated by the above example.

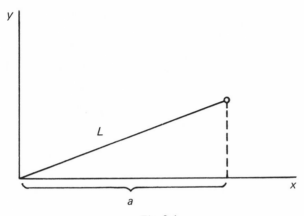

Fig. 2.4

If the information I that we want to determine was dependent on an endless number of variables, we would have, for example, $\mathscr{P}(I) = x_1, x_2, x_3, x_4, \ldots$ and we could decide to use only a limited number of the precedents. Similarly, $\mathscr{P}(L) = a,b$ had an exact number (two in this case) of precedents, but we may still want to use only a smaller number. Thus we might try to see if $\mathscr{P}(L) = x$ would be a satisfactory representation. In this case we might use the *orthogonal projection a* of L upon the x axis as an approximation to L (Fig 2.4). We see that if we could choose the coordinate direction x so that it would be fairly parallel with L, then this might be a satisfactory approximation. In other words if we could choose an e concept x that is *strongly correlated* to L, then x might suffice as a single precedent. We would thus use

$$L \approx a \qquad (\approx \text{ denoting "approximately equal to")}$$

If we found instead that $L \approx a$ would not be satisfactory, we would need to add one or more further precedents. If we chose b as the next precedent (that is, the e concept y), we would obtain $L^2 = a^2 + b^2$. The important thing for us to note here is that in adding the new precedent y we only had to add b to the earlier result. We did not have to redo the earlier estimation. Similarly, if L existed in a three-dimensional space, rather than in the two-dimensional space of the paper, a further increase in precision would be obtained by adding c^2 (see Fig. 2.5) (assuming c to

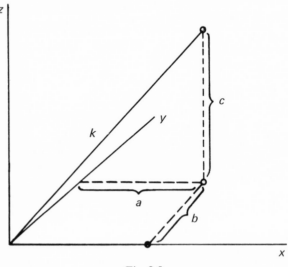

Fig. 2.5

be the orthogonal projection of L in the third dimension z). Thus we would then obtain

$$L^2 = a^2 + b^2 + c^2$$

and we see again that, thanks to the mutual orthogonality of the precedents (x,y,z), we could simply add c^2; so we have an *incremental* computation of successive, improved representations for L. Instead, if we did a similar analysis of the model in Fig. 2.6, we would obtain

$$L \approx a$$

if we used $\mathscr{P}(L) = x$, but

$$L \approx \quad f(-a',b,\phi)$$

where f is a function of a,b, and ϕ; so without going into the details of the function, we may observe that $-a'$ would replace a when we take also b' into consideration. Thus in this case the whole calculation must be redone, a consequence of the nonorthogonality of x and p (Fig. 2.7 and 2.3b) when we introduce the additional precedents b' and ϕ.

The incrementality of the orthogonal set of precedents, making it possible to introduce improvements by simply adding new precedents (new e concepts), is important for system design in general. It is not only that we save computational work but also that it allows successive, incremental improvements in the design of a system. Thus if we implement a system and test it in practice and find that we need to improve it, this can then be done—if we used an *orthogonal* design—by adding more components without having to change the existing design.

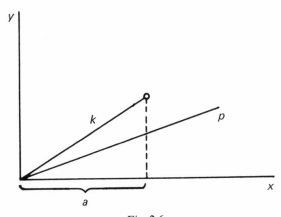

Fig. 2.6

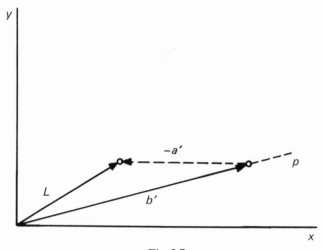

Fig. 2.7

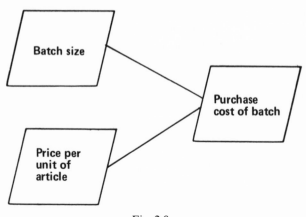

Fig. 2.8

EXAMPLE 1: As another very simple example of information precedence analysis, let us assume that the information we want is the "purchase cost" of a batch of articles.

Obviously we expect the cost of the batch to depend on batch size and on price per piece (Fig. 2.8) and, again, we see that we can make this observation without stopping to develop the formula guiding the computation (even though in this simple case this formula is trivial). However, we may expect the price per piece to vary as a function of the batch size. This leads to the precedence graph of Fig.

2.9. In Fig 2.9 we indicate that under this assumption we could state the need of the additional information "price modification by size of batch" without having, as yet, decided *how* the computation process is to be designed. Instead, now that we know that these are the three precedents we want to have considered, we can start the study of *how* they are to enter into the computation. This can be done in a large number of distinct ways and is a matter for economic estimates and policy decision before it can reasonably be specified for computer programming.

EXAMPLE 2: One real-life case that many people may be familiar with in which the kind of problem we have illustrated does occur is the measurement of the length of a certain route using a map. If the road is not too curved, we may perhaps find that just measuring the straight line between the end points of the route will be a useful first approximation. Thus we would use the distance between the two points as the only precedent of estimating the length. If higher precision is needed, we can use more precedents by measuring

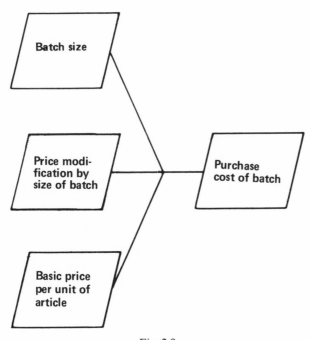

Fig. 2.9

distances between a set of points along the road. If the road passes hills and dales, we may also want to take into account the vertical components (the heights) of the points along the route, thus bringing new information precedents into the estimation procedure.

It is of interest to note that it is possible to assess the importance (or value) of bringing in additional precedents in the route estimation. This can be done in several ways but a simple way, which is often enough, is to observe the amount of change in the result that any new precedent will introduce. If this change is small, the precedent may be dropped. Note, again, that this whole analysis was possible without having worked out the computing procedure for computing the route. The cost of computation is, of course, one estimate to consider when deciding which precedents to use.

Degree of Significance of an Information Precedent

When an i concept x (an information kind or information class) is suggested as a precedent of another i concept y, it is because it is estimated that the value of x, in any given situation, has a significant influence on the value of y. Thus to decide whether to use x as a precedent for y we have to estimate how significant x is for y. This is one of the central problems within statistics.

EXAMPLE 3: A Heuristic Program for Selecting Precedents. Research in "artificial intelligence" is relevant to information analysis in several ways. One result produced by Floyd A. Miller (1967)* can be looked on as a program finding information precedents. A set of possible precedents or factors $(x_1, x_2,...x_n)$ is presented to the program in terms of a set of n-tuples of numerical values of these factors, each together with a corresponding value of the e concept (of factor) y whose precedents are wanted. The program generates a model of the form

$$y = a_0 + a_1 x_{il} + a_2 x_{i2} + \cdots + a_k x_{ik}$$

containing k (a factor chosen by the experimenter) of the precedents, $k \leq 5$ and $k \leq n - 2$. The a_j are the *multiple* regression coefficients. The program finds and outputs the three sets of k out of the n precedents that are best as predictors of y. Standard linear least-squares regression analysis is used to determine the quality of the prediction of y values in each case.

---

* Improving Heuristic Regression Analysis. Sixth Annual Southeastern Regional Meeting of the ACM. June 15–17, 1967 (see Slagle, 1971).

Modification of Precedence Analysis Because of Existing Information

When a step of precedence analysis has been made, we have defined a set of information kinds (*e* concepts) that are needed to produce a certain *e* concept. We then have to check whether the precedents so specified already exist in the system specification. If they do not, we will also have to check whether *e* concepts that do exist in the system specification might replace the *e* concepts now specified. If that appears to be the case, we will repeat the step of analysis to see if the replacement can be accepted. This may be especially important when the *e* concepts found by the last precedence analysis step are initial *e* concepts, that is, *e* concepts that have no information precedents but are to be collected from the object system.

Conditional Precedence Relations

An *i* concept *B* is an information precedent of an *i* concept *A* even if it is only potentially a precedent. It is necessary to have wide interpretation of the meaning of the information precedence relation because the strength of the influence of the value of a precedent on the information produced varies, in general, and thus may be nil in some computation instances.

EXAMPLE 4: A relation of the kind

$$\text{if} \quad f(B) < k \quad \text{then} \quad a: = b \quad \text{else} \quad a: = c$$

where *a*, *b*, and *c*, respectively, are values associated with the *i* concepts *A*, *B*, and *C*, making *B* and *C* information precedents of *A* (Fig. 2.10).
In the data processing design this fact will mean that data files or records representing *B* and *C* will both have to be accessible to the process producing *A*, as it is not known in advance of an execution whether *C* will be necessary or not.

Message Precedence Relations

We have, so far, discussed information precedence relations merely on the *i*-concept level; so when we say, for example, that *B* is a precedent of *A*, we state that to produce information of the kind *A* we need to have access to information of the kind *B*. Of course, when we come to more detailed design decisions or to performance calculations, we need to be more specific. The next step of increased specification will usually be to specify on the message level rather than on the *i*-concept level. Then, for instance, we will specify not only that some information of the kind *B* is needed to produce *A* but also how many, and which ones, of the messages of kind *B* are needed to produce a certain message of the kind *A*.

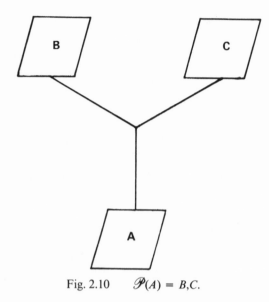

Fig. 2.10 $\mathscr{P}(A) = B,C.$

EXAMPLE 5: In a very simple forecasting model (Fig. 2.11) we may compute expected demand d_{at} of a certain article a in a certain time period t as the mean value of the four preceding periods ($t - 1$, $t - 2$, $t - 3$, $t - 4$). Then we have the precedence relation on the message level.

The corresponding precedence relation on the concept level is, of course, as shown in Fig 2.12.

2.2   INFORMATION SYSTEMS STRUCTURES AND MATRICES

Information Graph, Precedence Matrix, and Incidence Matrix

As we have seen that (a) it is possible to do information precedence analysis without having to dig into details of process or program construction at the same time and this makes it possible to achieve an overview of a wide part of the information system desired (or required) fairly quickly and without necessarily involving computer programmers; (b) there may be distinct, alternative, feasible sets of information precedents; and (c) the choice among the alternative, feasible sets may have to be based on considerations involving different, related parts of the information system.

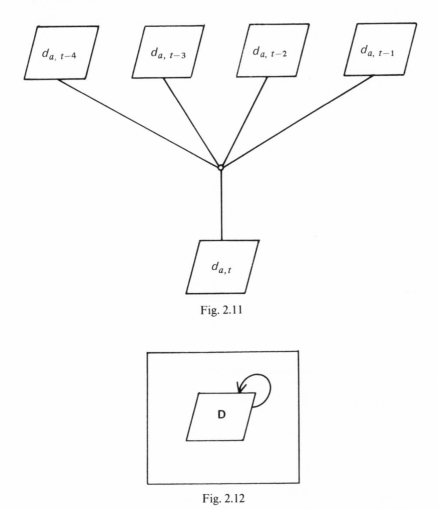

Fig. 2.11

Fig. 2.12

We may thus conclude that if we stop to construct the program that would produce a certain information kind, as soon as that information kind and one set of feasible precedents are defined, we may find it necessary to construct another program, which would utilize another feasible set of precedents. We avoid this by doing enough information analysis of a sufficiently large part of the system before starting program construction.

When we do information analysis over a system, we have the problem of how to document the result of the analysis. In other words, we must select a way of describing the system analyzed. The system designer wants a description that gives him enough overview of the system desired for him to find designs suitable to meet the desired specification. In addition the designer needs a description that can be analyzed with precision so he can verify the correctness of his design drafts. There are two well-known methods for describing a system in a way that gives some overview and, simultaneously, makes analysis possible: system graphs and system matrices.

A description of an information system, whether in graph form or in matrix form, will have to represent the major system components and the relations among them. For an information system this means that the information kinds (or the corresponding data sets) and the information processes together with their interrelations should be represented. As we have seen, however, it may be unnecessary in early analysis–design stages to represent the information processes. Their places in the structure will be obvious. We may take advantage of this fact by leaving out symbols for processes. The advantage will be that the descriptions will contain fewer elements (symbols) and this will make it possible to obtain a better overview. As a consequence larger parts of the system can be covered in each picture.

To get a feeling for the properties of distinct system description methods we look at a small system which we describe in four distinct forms (Fig 2.13) two of which are graphs and two are matrices. In one matrix and one graph form, processes are left out and in another pair of descriptions they are represented.

The incidence matrix E_{10} contains references to all the processes defined and all the information kinds (i concepts) or their data files, in addition to defining the relations between these sets of entities. As a consequence it is possible to document a separate (set of) description for each process and for each i concept. There will automatically be connections between each individual process or i concept (or file) and the matrix. We might say that there is an *infological* pointer from the matrix to each process or file description and from these to the matrix. For instance, a description of the process Al will contain Al as a name and this will be an infological reference to the row Al in the matrix E^{10} and conversely. In an implemented documentation system there may be added data pointers to support the infological references. Thus, for instance, the stored data representing the row Al of the matrix E^{10} may contain a data term that represents the address in file storage of the description for Al (and vice versa).

It should be noted that the system descriptions presented above are structural descriptions only. They do not convey enough information about the system to allow the computation of the performance of the

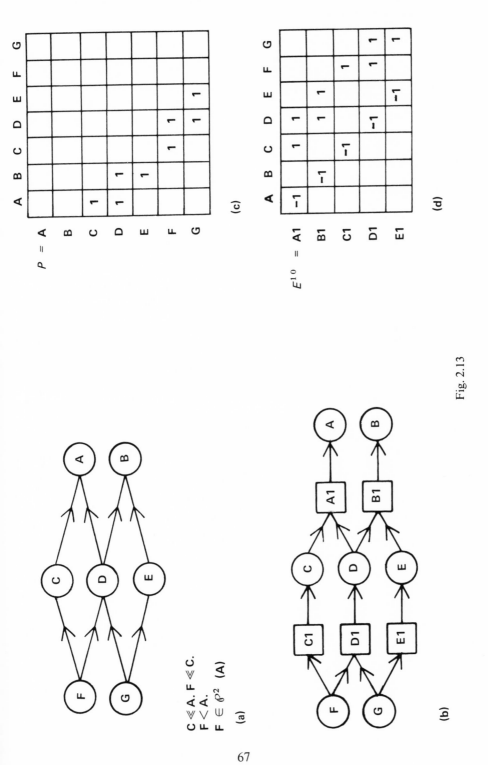

Fig. 2.13

67

system or for the monitoring of the system. Thus to handle those questions that are, of course, necessary for the design work we shall have to amend the descriptions by adding further information to them. We shall look at these problems later.

Precedence Lists and the Precedence Matrix

The matrix $\mathscr{P}$ is equivalent to the set of lists

$$\begin{aligned}
\mathscr{P}(A) &= C,D \\
\mathscr{P}(B) &= D,E \\
\mathscr{P}(C) &= F \\
\mathscr{P}(D) &= F,G \\
\mathscr{P}(E) &= G
\end{aligned}$$

In practical information analysis the precedence list for any specific information kind (that is, i concept) will, typically, be a document form (Fig 2.14). The precedents lists shown in Fig. 2.14 define the precedence matrix *incrementally*, in Fig 2.15.

The Coincidence Matrix and the Processes

The incidence matrix E^{10} defines the incidence of each process with the files in the system. The *coincidence* matrix (Langefors, 1966) is closely related and specifies for each *terminal point* of a process the i concepts or the files it coincides with. Thus to define the coincidence matrix we have to add a definition of the terminal points for each process, as we have done in Fig 2.16, which corresponds to our earlier system in Fig 2.13.

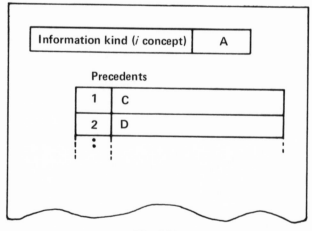

Fig. 2.14

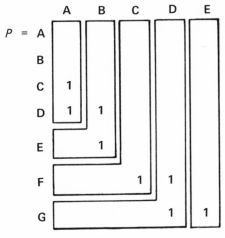

Fig. 2.15

The coincidence matrix M for this system is given below. The three rows in M, which correspond to process B1, are equivalent to the statements

Process B1
in point   1   coincides with D
in point   3   coincides with E
out point 2   coincides with B

and similar statements correspond to the other groups of rows of M. The set of all such statements is thus logically equivalent to the matrix M.

	A	B	C	D	E	F	G
A1 in 1			1				
in 3				1			
out 2	1						
B1 in 1				1			
in 3					1		
out 2		1					
C1 in 1						1	
out 2			1				
D1 in 1						1	
in 3							1
out 2					1		
E1 in 1							1
out 2					1		

$M =$

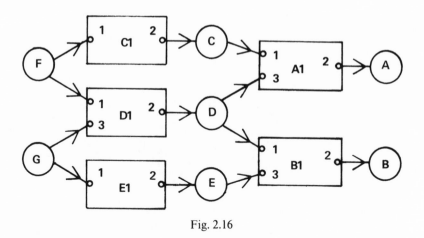

Fig. 2.16

It is, of course, more likely that the program corresponding to process B1 refers to the terminal points 1, 2, and 3 by local names of the kinds of information regarded as associated with these terminal points, for instance, using the names x, y, and z. Thus the coincidence statements associated with process B1 might be written as

x · B1   coincides with D
y · B1   coincides with E
z · B1   coincides with B
(x · B1   reads "x of B1")

or, for example,

B1	x	D
	y	E
	z	B

In this way the whole matrix M might get the form (directory form of M).

$M =$

A1	x	C
	y	D
	z	A
B1	x	D
	y	E
	z	B
C1	x	F
	z	C
D1	x	F
	y	G
	z	D
E1	x	G
	z	E

We see that the coincidence matrix (in either of its forms) can serve as a *linking dictionary* which translates between local process information names and system information names (external names). This linkage between external information names and local data names is often referred to as "binding." (It is usually the task of the "loader" or "linker" of the system software to implement the binding.) We know (Langefors, 1966) that the coincidence matrix can also be used for matrix algebra calculations about the system it describes.

Distinct processes may well have the same program. They are then distinguished by being incident with distinct files. For instance, suppose processes A1 and B1 have the same program P.* The linker dictionary form of the coincidence matrix may be used to make this quite clear.

	Process	Program	Local variables	System i concepts
$M =$	A1	P	x	C
			y	D
			z	A
	B1	P	x	D
			y	E
			z	B
	C1	Q	x	F
			z	C

Thus, for example, P realizes A1 when its variables x, y, z are made to coincide with the i concepts C, D, A, respectively.

The coincidence matrix also applies to the function of a file directory in a generalized data base management system. Thus the coincidence matrix concept serves to illustrate how such computer concepts as program linking and file directories appear, in principle, as fairly straightforward applications of system algebra concepts.

---

* Note that as can be seen in M, files C and D must both have a data format that is compatible with x of program P.

An *i* Concept as a Precedent of Itself

An *i* concept as a precedent of itself can be the typical case of "updating," where a message of the *i* concept A is produced from an earlier message of A plus a transaction message B_1.

$$P = \begin{array}{c|c|c|c|} & \text{A} & \text{B} & \text{C} \\ \hline \text{A} & 1 & & \\ \hline \text{B} & 1 & & \\ \hline \text{C} & & 1 & \\ \hline \end{array}$$

$$E^{10} = \begin{array}{c|c|c|c|} & \text{A} & \text{B} & \text{C} \\ \hline 1 & -1.1 & 1 & \\ \hline 2 & & -1 & 1 \\ \hline \end{array}$$

In Figure 2.17 the *i* concept A as a precedent of itself is neatly represented in the precedent matrix $\mathscr{P}$ by a 1 in the main diagonal (in position A,A). This fact (A $\ll$ A), however, introduced some complication into the incidence matrix E^{10} in which we would have to have both -1 and 1 in the position (1,A)*. We escape this complication in cases in which we consider a data system where the *i* concept A is implemented by two distinct files A' and A" (A" is an updated version of A'), process 1 being the updating process.

$$E^{10} = \begin{array}{c|c|c|c|c|} & \text{A'} & \text{A''} & \text{B} & \text{C} \\ \hline 1 & 1 & -1 & 1 & \\ \hline 2 & & & -1 & 1 \\ \hline \end{array}$$

e Processes and *e* Computations

An information process usually outputs a compound message, consisting of several *e* messages, for each of its executions. A process which, on the completion of one successful execution, outputs one *e*

---

* Of course, we may use one symbol, *x*, for example, to represent the pair -1 and 1.

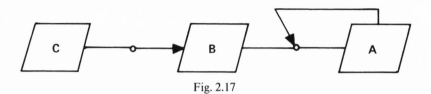

Fig. 2.17

message that is always of the same kind—that is, is an instance of one specific *e* concept—will be said to be *out elementary* (*an* oe *process*). Notice the specification "successful execution." Many processes must have the capability of producing an error message when an unsuccessful execution is encountered and this error message must be allowed to initiate another process than the one (or those) receiving the normal output from the process. This is necessary if a workable information system is to be designed. Thus for any process that is to "filter out" inputs that have erroneous or other special values or else violate security criteria, it may be desirable to have two separate outputs. We may refer to an out-elementary process of this kind as an *out-elementary filter process (oef* process). Any information process can be constructed from a set of out-elementary processes and out-elementary filter processes. For this reason we find it desirable to use the term "elementary process" as meaning a process that is either an out-elementary process or an out-elementary filter process.

Often several distinct *e* processes may be able to produce a specific *e* message. Thus before a decision has been made as to which specific process to use, the *class of all possible e* processes that might produce the specified *e* message should be associated with the precedence bundle of this *e* message (as well as of the corresponding *e* concept). It is practical to introduce a name for this class of *e* process and we shall use the term "*e* computation." Thus the precedence bundle (Fig 2.18) will have to be associated first with a computation, *comp(A)*, for example, and then a specific process, *proc(A)*, has to be selected before implementation

$$\text{proc(A)} \in \text{comp(A)}$$

that is, proc(A) is a member of the set comp(A) of possible processes that could compute A. The concept of *e* computation (elementary computation) is useful not only to improve the theory but also from the practical point of view of project planning. For example, sometimes the system designer wishes to develop a certain ambitious process (A) which, however, requires some development work. It may be impractical to make the whole project dependent on whether the development turns out successfully or not. If the system design is based on comp(A), meaning

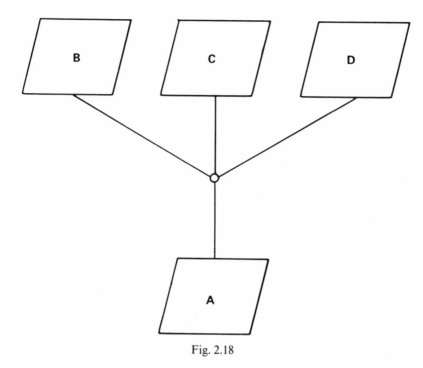

Fig. 2.18

that any process ϵ comp(A) will be usable in the system, the designer may start the project with a simple version of comp(A)—that is, a simple proc(A) and later on replace it by another version.

EXAMPLE 1: Suppose A is a sales forecast and B, C, D are, respectively, sales history, the development of the branch of the market and the economic development in general, then comp(A) will have to consider these three factors in one way or another. We may choose as the first version to consider only B, the sales history, using a statistical forecasting method, programmed for a computer. As a second version we may plan to add some modification to the statistical forecast, based on judgment of the general economic trend, whereas a third version, planned for the future, might be to add a statistical computation for the branch development.

If we choose the first version, this implies that we estimate the precedent "sales history" to be sufficiently significant and the other two precedents to be not sufficiently significant. This sort of judgment should, of course, be made by those persons in the organization who may be expected to have the best knowledge of the relations involved. Alternatively, it may be possible to acquire statistics and then to use statistical methods to compute estimates for the significance of each of the suggested precedents; or we may decide to design the system so that it will collect such statistics.

In-Elementary Computation (*ie* Computation). *ie* Process

Often an out-elementary computation (an *e* computation associated with an out-elementary process) can be partitioned into a set of *e* computations that have at most two *e* concepts as their precedents. We may call such an *e* computation an *in-elementary computation* (or *ie* computation). Similarly, we talk of in-elementary processes (or *ie* processes).

The reason why we have to allow for two precedents of an in-elementary computation is that for a computation to produce new information out of one *e* message, it needs the additional information from at least one other *e* message. The latter may be of the same kind as the first precedent (in which case we have only one precedent *e* concept) or it may be of a different concept.

> EXAMPLE 2: The *e* computation discussed above (see SF in Fig 2.19) may be partitioned into in-elementary computations (see SF1, SF2, and SF3 in Fig. 2.20). It may, for instance, be decided to implement SF1 by a computer program whereas SF2 and SF3 are done manually; SF2 and SF3 may, however, be supported by information provided by the information system.

It may not be necessary in the systems analysis to break down processing subsystems (modules) to in-elementary computations (*ie* computations). It may well be sufficient to stop the breakdown when *e* computations (out-elementary computations) have been defined, or even earlier. This, of course, will be determined by the analyst from case to case. When the design of the processes is to be taken on, however, it will usually be suitable to break down to in-elementary computations and in-elementary processes.

System-Design-Motivated Precedents and Processes

In addition to the information precedents associated with the object system (the intended information) the process that is to implement an intended precedence bundle calls for some additional precedents of its own. Thus, obviously, the process needs a program. In addition to this the process design is always subject to a set of constraints that have been imposed on it for economical or technical design reasons. It must then

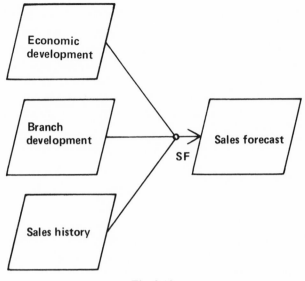

Fig. 2.19

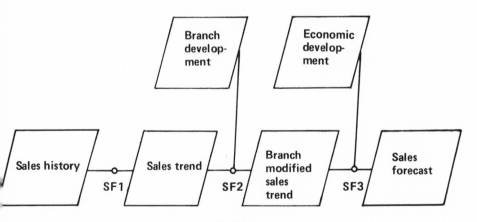

Fig. 2.20

77

have information about these constraints in order to ascertain that the process input is compatible with these constraints (Fig 2.21).

Thus in order to be able to check input data the process must have data about the prescribed input data formats. In order to retrieve data the process needs data about how data are stored, and so on. Thus we see that a process which is to handle data about the object system will need additional data (thus additional precedents) that inform about the structure of the data system itself. This is sometimes called "metadata." Likewise, in addition to needing processes associated with the precedence bundles for the object system, additional processes are needed to perform different sorts of data management operations.

Data Processes in the System

The information precedence relations that are specified in the object system–oriented stage of information analysis are associated with relations or interactions assumed to exist in the object system. When we implement an information system as a data processing system, we will usually have to introduce data processes that generate such relations among the data as correspond to the precedence relations. Thus to each information precedence bundle associated with the object system we will usually have a data process. However, other processes will also be needed in the system. Thus, for instance, for each permanent file in the system a set of file maintenance processes will have to be introduced—or a set of generalized processes will be used that will service several files. For example, each file needs a function that stores incoming messages. Other functions or processes, which delete or change file records, belong to the maintenance function. When we design consolidated files, we may also need to have consolidating processes in the system that will take individual records as input and put them into the consolidated files.

Thus when we come to define the processes, the precedence bundles obtained in information analysis define some processes but additional processes are then required by system design decisions.

Succedence Analysis

Precedence analysis is the right tool in the stage at which we are trying to find out what to have in the system. There are two reasons for this: (a) To determine the right information to have in the system we must start with the output that is needed or desired and then ask for the precedents; and (b) when we have defined information that is needed it makes sense, in general, to ask what other information could be used to produce it. It usually does not make sense to ask what all the potential uses (that is, the succedents) are in the system of the information defined.

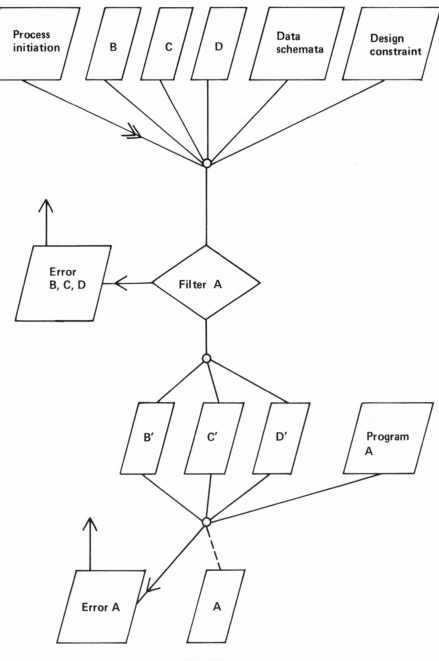

Fig. 2.21

In a later stage when we have defined the information to be available in the system, we will usually find it more natural or useful to ask for the succedents of certain information. Then, however, we are able to determine the succedents of any information kind or message through formal operations upon the documented precedence structure. For instance, this is directly obtained from the rows of the precedence matrix P^{00} or from the columns and rows of the incidence matrix E^{10} established during the information analysis for the system.

2.3   TWO MAIN CATEGORIES OF INFORMATION

Operative Information and System Information

Each time we are to perform an information processing operation we need some data that inform about the task at hand, be it a computation, a decision, or the guidance of a practical operation. For instance, if the process is to control the shipping of an article, we need information about what article to ship, how much, and to whom. In another example if we are to compute $\sqrt{x} = y$, we need to be informed about the value of x in order to perform the computation. We may refer to this kind of information, which is specific to an operation, as *operative information*. The important characteristic of operative information, from an information system point of view, is that it has to be procured anew for each individual information process execution. However, every information process has some other information precedents which, although they necessarily are to be available to the process, need not be procured anew for each execution but can be used repeatedly. Such precedents are thus not operative information. We may refer to them as *system information* because they may be stored and made available by the information system. The distinction between operative information and nonoperative information (system information) is basic to economic design considerations in information systems because not all information precedents of a process need to be input from outside for each execution. This raises the question as to how often the distinct information precedents that are system information, stored in the data base of the system, can most economically be updated or replaced by new information.

EXAMPLE 1: Suppose we have established that

$$y(o,t) = \sqrt{x(o',t')}$$

or the value of y at object o in time t can be computed as the square root of the value of x at object o in time t; ($y(o,t)$ and $x(o',t')$) are e messages, as can be seen. Suppose further that the square root is to be computed by the algorithm

$y(o,t)2 = $ sqrt $(x(o',t'),\epsilon)$
sqrt (x,ϵ)
$y = \frac{1}{2}(1 + x)$
If $y = \frac{1}{2}(y + x/y)$
if abs $(x - y^2) < \epsilon$ *then go to* It
stop

Here we see three distinguishable kinds of information: x is the operative information that specifies the operation to be performed by the square root algorithm; ϵ is a control parameter or directive parameter that controls the amount of work done by the algorithm; and the precision of the result $\sqrt{x,\epsilon}$ guides the process, step by step.

In the specific example above it is natural to regard x as "being processed," that is, changed by the process; ϵ as controlling the process although not being processed itself; and, sqrt, finally, as the program of the process. It should be observed that these distinctions may not always be as clear cut. The control parameter may be changed by the process and may also be regarded as part of the program. However, the important thing from a system design point of view is not whether there is a clear logical distinction between the information kinds involved but what the timing of their respective updatings should be. The intuitive classification that we could well make in the example will often be a natural one and may aid the designer in doing the timing estimates, and may aid our understanding of the subject. In the example it is obviously natural to regard x as the operative information which gives the "measures" for the task of the individual process execution and to regard ϵ as a control parameter or "precision goal" for the process. ϵ may be expected to be invariant for computations using a family of x values and thus to be provided anew fairly infrequently, whereas "sqrt" may be regarded as almost invariant (not quite correctly).

Directive Information

In the simple example studied above (sqrt) we had two kinds of system information, invariant over a certain amount of time, the control parameter ϵ and the program "sqrt." Both are seen to be means for directing the processing of the operative information $x(o',t')$. This suggests that in searching for the less varying information precedents of a process (and, hence, of the output of the process as well), we may look for information that is of a *directive character*. Note that it is not very critical whether what we regard as directive information is correctly referred to as such or not; the important thing is to determine all the information precedents that are of a nonoperative kind in order to determine their economic frequency of updating. The characterization as directive is merely a means for aiding the search. Each information kind will, of course, after having been pointed out as nonoperative, be studied as to its economic frequency of updating.

EXAMPLE 2:
  Object information:
    ordering of replenishment of inventory
    (estimated frequency: 100 times per week)
  Information precedents
    shipping ordered (trigger)
    order information
    inventory level
    deduction from inventory
    predicted delivery lead time (replenishment)
    cost of inventory holding
    cost of shortage of inventory
    predicted demand
    ordering cost
    objective
  Operative information precedents
    shipping ordered (trigger)
    inventory level
    order information
    deduction from inventory
  Directive information precedents
    objective
    cost of shortage
    cost of inventory holding
    predicted delivery lead time
    predicted demand
    ordering cost

Of the directive information precedents some may obviously change much slower than the others. As the estimation of the economic updating frequency for each information kind must necessarily be very crude, it may be satisfactory to classify them into just a few distinct classes, each of which has a certain period of updating.

Object information	estimated
ordering of replenishment of inventory	frequency
Operative information precedents	
shipping ordered (trigger)	100 times per week
order information	
inventory level	
deduction from inventory	
Directive information	
predicted delivery lead time	1/4 per week
predicted demand	
cost of shortage	
cost of inventory holding	1/20 per week
cost of ordering	
objective	1/50 per week

CONCLUSIONS

In Chapter 2 we discussed the precedence relations that may be defined between distinct messages or information kinds. We found the precedence relation to be an important one for the description of information systems as well as for guiding the information analysis. The precedence relations in an information system give rise to system matrices of some distinct kinds which may serve as formal description for the information structures of the system as a whole.

We also discussed the information processes needed in the system. To that end we defined some types of elementary processes. We observed that a data process will typically be required to implement each "precedence bundle" defined from the information needs of the object system. We observed also that, in addition, there will have to be further data processes, not corresponding to object system needs, which implement processes for data restructuring specified during the data design stage subsequent to information analysis.

REVIEW QUESTIONS

1   Explain, or give examples of, the terms "intramessage relations" and "intermessage relations".

2   What is a precedence bundle of an information unit A? What are the initial elements and the terminal elements of this bundle?

3   What are the advantages that can be taken from the insight that a

precedence analysis can be done without going into the details of the associated data process?

4 What information (that is, what e concepts) is represented by the matrices P^{00}, E^{10}, and M, respectively?

5 Describe the concepts "e process," "oe process," and "ie process." What is the relation between the concepts "e process" and "e computation"?

6 When a data process is designed to implement an information precedence bundle, the process will have other inputs and outputs than those specified by the precedence bundle. Which are they?

CHAPTER 3

DATA TRANSPORT IN A SYSTEM

In *Theoretical Analysis of Information Systems* (Lange-fors, 1966) the general concepts of *process grouping* and *file consolidation* are introduced. The illustrations given there were mainly selected from serial files and batch processing. In this chapter we contrast the effects of these operations on direct processing (transaction processing) versus batch processing. We also discuss the effect of grouping of processes that have distinct processing periods.

Systematization of the process grouping makes it interesting to study how the construction of programs for grouped processes might be formalized when the process programs, to be included in a group, and the system structure (matrices) are given. An example of this kind, worked by Nunamaker et al. (1972), is briefly discussed.

In discussing processes we, of course, introduce the dynamics of the system. However, we restrict ourselves to the "stationary aspects" of processing, that is, the main stream of events. On this level some overall architectural decisions have to be made prior to decisions concerned with the control of events. The latter aspects are not treated here.

3.1 INTRODUCTION

Data Transport and Physical Access Blocks

When data that are stored in secondary store (file storage) are to be used by a process (or by a terminal user), they have to be retrieved and *transported* to main memory (and possibly back again to file storage). Usually this data transport operation is extremely time consuming as compared with the processing in the computer CPU. Thus system design has as one of its main problems to reduce data transport. The basic structural difference between the functioning of a file storage and the main storage is that in accessing data in the file storage we get a block of many data terms, regardless of whether a single term or many terms are to be used. In main memory we fetch individual data terms. Thus data transport is influenced by what size of the access block is chosen (when there is a choice) and how the block space is utilized. (It should be noted that in some systems it is possible to transfer parts of access blocks to main memory. This can be used to save file volume by using long physical blocks and yet save buffer space in main memory.) The data transport involved in the fetching of a block is the storage time (head movement and rotation waiting time) plus the time to transfer the block (or, possibly, part of it). The design question is whether data terms or, rather, elementary entries, can be stored in each block in a way that reduces the number of block accesses. The block transfers are one per access, so once the block size is fixed, reducing accesses will reduce transfer in the same proportion.

Usually the block has a size that can carry several *e* entries. Thus several *e* entries will be stored in a block. To reduce data transport we try to store such *e* entries in the same block that is used in the same process or "run." The choice, of course, is whether to store several *e* entries of the same *e* file together (record blocking), or to store together *e* entries of several distinct *e* files (consolidation), or, of course, a combination of these.

The Data Transport with a Process

The data transport with a process varies greatly with the processing mode. The mode of processing is either a matter of choice by the system designer (or, possibly, by the data processing administration), or it is determined by the characteristics of the application itself or of the model used for the problem solution. This aspect of the mode being determined by the application is often forgotten. From the *processing point of view* we may distinguish between (a) *direct processing* (often called "transaction" (driven) processing) and (b) *linear batch processing*. There is a third mode of great importance, but too often ignored, known as *structural processing*. All of these may exist in a *multiprogramming* or in a *monoprogramming* environment.

From the *application point-of-view* we have (a) *small single jobs*, (b) *collection of small, separate jobs*, and (c) *larger jobs*.

DIRECT PROCESSING. When a transaction record that arrives is immediately allowed to trigger the process (or set of processes) that it calls for it is *direct processing*. Direct processing typically leads to a relatively large amount of data processing for the process because the data and programs called for by the process may have to be retrieved from anywhere in the system, as it cannot be known in advance which transaction will arrive next and which process will arrive next ("random access").

Direct processing is often called "real-time processing," but we consider this a misuse of terms. Thus "real-time" suggests "quick enough to be reasonably synchronized with the real-life operation concerned." Direct processing typically involves a small number of disk storage accesses each of which takes around 50 milliseconds; so direct processing may be a matter of seconds or tenths of seconds. This is real time in most business applications but would be too slow to be real time for a fast physical process. On the other hand a company goal-setting process may be real time if it produces results four times a year and would, hence, not require direct processing.

LINEAR BATCH PROCESSING. The term "linear batch processing" means collecting a batch (queue) that can then be arranged so the processing run will take one transaction after the other in such a way that needed file records (or data base entries) can be retrieved (once only) from a sequence of nearby physical positions. Typically, the larger the batch, the smaller will be the average physical access distance between the retrieved records and the greater will be the probability that subsequent records are stored in the same access block.

When the size of the batch goes down to one transaction, the batch process may (or may not) change to a direct process. In batch processing the program transport also is reduced in that the programs of the run can be resident in main memory during the run.

EXERCISE 1: What will be the effect (and how strong may it become) on the transport savings from using batch processing if we introduce multiprogramming?

EXERCISE 2: What are the factors that influence the interference between two batch processes or between a batch process and a direct process when the two are run concurrently?

SKIP LINEAR PROCESSING (SKIP SEQUENTIAL). In a linear batch processing in which a pseudo-direct-access file storage is used, we may skip all file records between the active ones. We may then talk of "skip linear" and in the special case in which the linear process is a sequential one we may say "skip sequential."

STRUCTURAL PROCESSING. Structural processing involves several data base records that have to be retrieved and processed (even when one single transaction initiates the process) in more or less complicated ways and in which the same record may be involved more than once. Contrary to linear batch processing, in structural processing it is, typically, not possible to arrange the transactions and file records so that a simple chain of retrievals can be utilized. The structure of this processing and its record retrievals and transports are determined by the structure of the application and therefore significant improvements of retrieval and transport may be possible through suitable arrangement. Thus when structural processing is involved, this fact often has strong effects on how the file should be organized.

Structural processing is common in production scheduling and in engineering systems computations, for instance.

SMALL SINGLE JOBS. Small single jobs are those that can be handled after the loading of all needed records and programs into main memory. "Small" thus depends on what size of main memory we expect. However, many jobs are small enough to be "small" with respect to most computers and some are large enough to be "not small" for any computer. Of course, a small single job will typically lead to a direct processing.

COLLECTION OF SMALL SEPARATE JOBS. We have a collection of small separate jobs when we have several transactions each of which calls for a small process and when there is no interrelation between the individual small jobs that calls for any restrictions in the order in which the jobs are processed. It is obvious that when a collection of small single jobs is concerned with the same file, we can always obtain a linear batch process by taking the single jobs in the collection in that sequence in which the file records involved are physically stored. This is true as long as we have means for ordering the transactions in the same sequence regardless of whether the file records are in a sequence according to some term value or are stored at random.

The fact is that many processes, notably in business applications, are small separate jobs, which makes it possible to take advantage of the linear batch processing that is so common.

EXERCISE 3: Show that batch random* is a batch linear but not a batch-sequential process.

LARGER JOBS. Larger jobs are characterized by the fact that though it is possible to break them down into a set of smaller processes, the latter are not independent and cannot be executed in an arbitrary order. Thus we see that for larger jobs we cannot take it for granted that they could always be processed in a linear batch mode. Indeed this is seldom the case. We may conclude that it may be highly misleading to talk of data processing as consisting of only direct or batch processing operations as is often done.

We can see that it is of great interest for processing-retrieval efficiency to be able to find out, given a "larger job," whether it is possible or not to organize it into a linear batch job. Also if it is not possible to achieve a linear batch process, it is of interest to know whether a "nearly linear batch process" is feasible and would be efficient. We discuss this problem next.

3.2   PROCESS STRUCTURE AND PRECEDENCE STRUCTURE

K-Progressive and K-Linear-Progressive Process

The problem of whether a larger job can be arranged into a linear process (or nearly so) was studied by one of the authors in a lecture given at Regnecentralen, Copenhagen in 1962 (Langefors, 1966). He introduced the concept of a K-progressive process, meaning that the process can be broken down into subprocesses for each of which the size of its

---

* "Batch random" is a term sometimes used to refer to processing a batch of transactions against a randomized file. It is made into a linear process by sorting the transactions into random order of the file, using the randomizing procedure also for the transactions. See Nijssen (1971).

current process set (working set) is at most equal to K and where no data are input more than once. (We could also say that the process is incremental with increment equal to K.)

The complete current process set is the set of data and program statements that must be input at any one time into a process to enable it to proceed enough with its execution to allow the deletion or output of some data or programs, thus making room for further input of the next current process set, and so on.

The concept of a K-progressive process and current process set is closely related to the concept of "working set" (Denning, 1968).

If the process is K progressive and the *memory covers* K (that is, if available memory space $\geq K$), then the process can be run as a linear process if supported by a file storage that can, at each stage, provide it successively with its current process set.

EXERCISE 1: Show that the run which is a collection of small separate jobs is a K-progressive process for some value of K with respect to the files involved.

If the memory space available is $\geq K$, then a K-progressive process can be run as a linear process *if* the files involved are sorted to the proper order. Note that if the file is not sorted to the proper order, then the process cannot be made linear by sorting the input batch if the process is a *general* K-progressive one. Thus if a file is involved in one process that is a general K-progressive process and in other processes that are collection runs, then all can be made linear by suitable sorting of the file as required by the general K-progressive process and of the other batches to match this order. If two or more processes are associated with the file and require distinct file orders, then all processes cannot be made linear, even if they are K progressive.

K-Progressive Process and Application Structure

What makes the concept of a K-progressive process interesting is that it is also related to the underlying application structure or model structure by data transport requirements. Thus it may act as a bridge concept which sometimes makes it possible to estimate data transport work from a knowledge of the object system structure.

It is, of course, useful to be able to determine early (before programming) whether a process can be made progressive and what K value is needed. It is also important to know whether it can be made linear or not. If it cannot be made linear K progressive because memory space is then $< K$ and if the space is near to K, can this be used to design the process as "nearly linear," thereby reducing the data transport? The latter may be very large in a nonlinear process.

The Importance of the Larger Jobs and Structural Processing

The "larger jobs" and "structural processing" situation is not as rare and unimportant as the data processing or data base literature suggests (by ignoring it). Although operations data in business data processing are mostly of the small job kind the planning, decision making, designing, and problem solving situations are not. Also semantic-oriented data base usage leads to a need for more structured processing, just as has always been the case in advanced engineering applications. Thus the need of file organization that is generated by structural processing is likely to be an important area in information architecture.

EXERCISE 2: If we are given a long, prescribed sequence of operations, each with a known service time, and given a required end time, then we can compute the required starting times. This

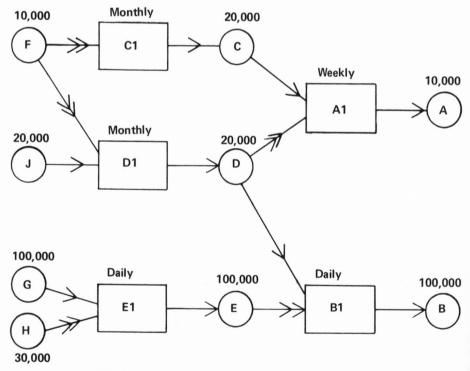

Fig. 3.1   Example of a batch processing system.

computation can be seen as a collection of small, but not separate, jobs. Thus it cannot be run as linear in any arbitrary order. Show that this is a K-progressive process and thus can be made linear in some order.

3.3 THE RESOURCES REQUIRED BY A PROCESS

Individual Resources

The incidence matrix E^{10}, or the coincidence matrix M, for the system (or the appropriate subsystem) contains some information that is basic to the determination of the amount of resources a process will require for one execution or for all executions during a batch run. These resource requirements are, in turn, information precedents for the estimates of cost and turnaround time for the processes. Because E^{10} gives this information for each process, as well as for the interplay between processes, it also gives information to support decisions on how to organize the possible cooperation between processes. To illustrate this let us look at an assumed row of an incidence matrix:

	A	B	C	D	E	F	G
A1	-1		1	1			

(assume A = C′ = updated C)

FILE UNITS. We see from this row for process A1 that the process requires four file units, one for the program for A1 and one for each of the files A (output) and C and D. The file units will typically be disks, or drums, or magnetic tape handlers. Only in the latter case will the number be important.

A file may sometimes be stored in main memory if it is very small, but we usually assume that when we use the system matrices in the design stage (contrary to the earlier information analysis stage), the columns of E^{10} (or of M) correspond to files on file storage.

FILE OPENING. The files A, C, and D are to be opened and closed if we have a *batch run* and may or may not have to be opened and closed if we have a *direct* process. If the files are on tape, the opening–closing involves tape reel mount and dismount. This operation may also be involved if removable disks are used. In any case, file opening will also require some CPU work to allocate file buffers in main memory and to fill the buffers.

SPACE IN MAIN MEMORY. For each file, buffer space will have to be reserved in main memory. Buffers may be in multiple versions. For instance, four or more buffers may be allocated to a pair of tape files, one of which is the output of an updated version of the other, in order to allow simultaneous reading and writing on files and processing at the same time. There will, of course, also have to be memory space for the process program.

CPU TIME. Of course, CPU time is involved in the process execution (or process executions of the run). In addition quite a lot of CPU time is required for the data handling. Thus interrupt handling, administration of file buffers, moving and packing of data between buffers, determination of addresses in file storage, conversion of input and output, storing and operating system work of other kinds all have to be counted in addition to the cycle stealing normally accounted for in estimates of this kind. (Many of the factors mentioned are usually forgotten, so CPU load caused by data transport is often severely underestimated.)

DATA TRANSFER CHANNELS. Data transfer channels are loaded with transfer of data blocks from or to all the files (A, B, and C in the illustration) and the swapping of the program as well, in the *direct-processing* case. (Of course, the program may be represented as one of the input files in E^{10}.) In *batch processing* programs swapping is negligible unless automatic paging or a similar technique of virtual memory is used to work with a small main memory, in which case swapping may be of importance. One transfer for each input record and two transfers for records that are output to be stored on disks or drums will be normal.* In addition there may be transfers of file directory records.

ACCESS CHANNEL, ROTATION TIME. For files that are stored on rotating storage, such as disks or drums, a waiting time equal, on the average, to half the rotation time will be normal. Again this will occur once for each input record access and for the program and twice for each file update output.* In addition it may also occur for file directory accesses.

---

* There will be an additional transfer if "reread as a write check" is used. Also, there may be an overhead of extra access operations in cases of "overflow" when a record does not find space in the block with its computed address.

ACCESS CHANNEL, HEAD MOVEMENT. For files that are stored on moving head storages, times for head movement will also have to be added to the fraction of the rotation times. These times may be highly dependent on the location of the new record to be fetched in relation to the last access location of the file storage unit. In (early) design stages it is often necessary to use some reasonable* average time for head movement. This will always be the case when the head mechanism is simultaneously shared with other programs.

Total Resource Requirement of a Process

All the resource components mentioned influence the total requirement posed by a process. The result, however, is usually more complicated than just a sum of the components. Furthermore the total results (in terms of total time, total CPU load, memory space, and so forth) are combined from these components in different ways depending on the environment and the mode of operation. Thus in order to do the total estimate in each case, we are usually interested in each individual component.

All of the resource components mentioned, except memory space and the CPU time for the execution of the processes themselves, are influenced by the way we organize files and processes. In other words, CPU load by each individual process is an individual function, whereas all the other components are system factors that are influenced by the cooperation of the distinct files and processes in the system. This is to say that it is the resources used up by the *data transport* that are influenced by the way we configure the system. (This includes CPU and main memory load associated with the transport.)

Effect of the Number of Data Channels

The time for data transports may be strongly dependent on whether there are one or more communication channels between the file units and the central processor. Thus if more than one channel is available, a serial file-updating process may cut the transport time in half by allowing the simultaneous operation of outtransport of one file record, processing of the next record, and intransporting the record thereafter. This requires multiple buffer areas in main memory, however. In connection with a disk storage, for example, multiple channels may shorten the time for retrieving a record in cases in which the access blocks are so large that the time for transfer interferes with the next access operation.

---

* Bad design may systematically lead to delays longer than the unweighted average. This is to be considered in choosing the "reasonable average."

3.4. DETERMINATION OF THE DATA TRANSPORT

The calculation of the amount of data transport will depend on the type of processing. We illustrate the transport analysis for the two extremes: direct processing and periodic batch-sequential processing.

Data Transport Associated with Single Transaction Direct Processing

In Fig. 3.2 when we want to calculate the data transport for a process A1, based on the row A1 in the incidence matrix E^{10}, we add two auxiliary rows v_d and a_d. The row v_d contains entries, which give the average *transfer volume* of one record of the file associated with the respective column including the *transfer volume* of the associated file directory records. At preliminary design stages the transfer volume would be estimated from the transfer size, using some approximate volume factor. The row a_d contains the corresponding magnitudes for the access work required for a file record, to which we again add the work

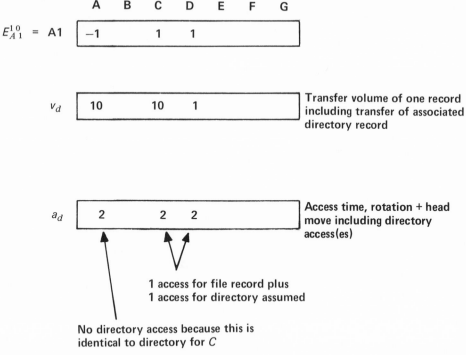

Fig. 3.2

required by the associated file directory records.* The reason that we use two distinct rows, rather than a single row containing the sums, is that although both entities (transfer and access) may be measured in the same unit, that is, time, they may be changed separately by separate design decisions. For instance, the transfer for one record will be changed if we change the block size, whereas the access work is unaffected by this.

$$\text{data transport} = |E_{A1}^{10}| \cdot v_d^T + |E_{A1}^{10}| \cdot a_d^T$$
$$= (10 + 10 + 1)\hat{v}_d + (2 + 2 + 2)\hat{a}_d = 21\hat{v}_d + 6\hat{a}_d$$

Here we have used v_d and $\hat{a}_d$ to be average times for the transfer of one access block and the access of one block, respectively. Thus the data transport time is not added into one single value until values for $\hat{v}_d$ and $\hat{a}_d$ have been specified. In this way we make it possible to recalculate easily the transport time if, for instance, the size of the access block is changed because this changes $\hat{v}_d$ and nothing else.

Next let us do this kind of calculation for the whole system described by the incidence matrix E^{10} in Fig. 3.3. The column to the right of E^{10}, which we have marked "Trigger," indicates which records are the ones that trigger the respective processes. For instance, it is indicated that the processes A1 and B1 are triggered by the records of the kind D. From the trigger vector we also see that there are 10,000 records of the kind D in the time period chosen as our reference period. Thus A1, for example, will be triggered and executed 10,000 times during the reference period. This means (as can be seen from the row A1 of E^{10}) that an A record will be output by A1 10,000 times in a period and, hence, 10,000 C records and 10,000 D records will be input to that process during the period. We can enter this information into the incidence matrix by multiplying all entries in a row of the matrix by the number of triggering records, according to the trigger column to the right of and the number of records per period column below the E^{10} matrix. The resulting matrix we denote by $\mathbf{E}^{10}$ in Fig. 3.4.

We do the analysis here as if each direct process would occur alone. In real systems the triggering transactions usually arrive in such random sequences that queuing effects occur. This introduces the need to consider the queuing effects on the values of v_d and a_d using simulation studies or queue theory.

---

* If the file directory is itself represented as a file by the incidence matrix, the transfer volume of its records may be represented separately in v_d and so should not be included in the v_d value for the file.

	A	B	C	D	E	F	G	H	J	Trigger	Number of records per reference period
$E^{10}=$ A1	−1		1	1						D	10
B1		−1		1	1					D	10
C1			−1			1				F	12
D1				−1		1	1		1	F	12
E1					−1		1	1		H	15

x 1000 = $\overline{a}$

v_d	10	1	10	1	2	10	2	1	1
a_d	2	1	2	2	1	2	1	1	1

(of exercise)

Fig. 3.3

EXERCISE 1:
Show that

$$\mu_T = \alpha_T \cdot \mid E^{10} \mid$$

where α is the vector obtained by replacing in the trigger vector each record name by the corresponding number of records with that name in a reference period.

We can now calculate the total data transport in the system during a reference period.

$$
\begin{aligned}
\text{data transport} &= v_d \cdot \mu + a_d \cdot \mu \\
&= (100 + 10 + 220 + 32 + 50 + 240 + 54 + 15 + 12)\hat{v}_d \\
&\quad + (20 + 10 + 44 + 64 + 25 + 48 + 27 + 15 + 12)\hat{a}_d \\
&= 733\hat{v}_d + 265\hat{a}_d
\end{aligned}
$$

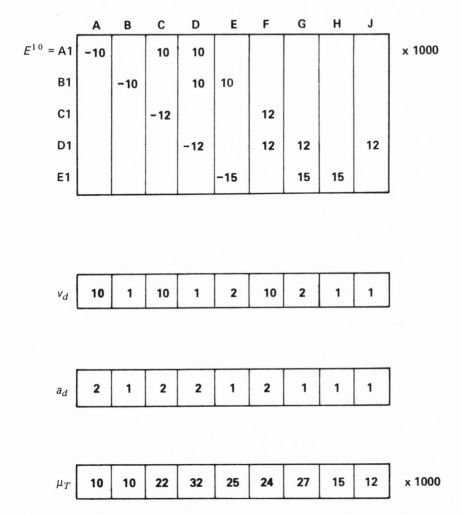

Fig. 3.4   The row μ_T contains the column sums of $|\mathbf{E}^{10}|$ and represents the transport multiplicity vector for records, that is, the number of records to be transported to or from the CPU during a reference period.

PROGRAM TRANSPORT. We notice that one of the files that is input to each process and thus one of the columns (or some of them) of E^{10} may be programs for the processes. *In direct processing, where the individual processes are triggered at random*, the program will usually have to be input from file storage just as any of the data records involved. On the other hand there may be some positive probability that the same program will be involved in two or more subsequent processes and thus the program transport may be less than one per process execution, on the average. It is also common to have direct (or on-line) applications when all transactions are concerned with the same program, all (or most) parts of which may be stored at the same time in primary storage, for example, in an on-line order entry system. Then the program transport may be negligible and hence left out of the matrix E^{10} (Langefors, 1966, 1973).

Data Transport in Periodic Batch-Sequential Processing

Let us see how this calculation of data transport becomes modified if we assume a periodic batch processing. We may do this analysis in different ways. One is to use a model that is as close as possible to the one used above for direct processing. This has the advantage of bringing the distinct processing modes into the same model, which may enhance the understanding of the whole area. Another is to use a somewhat modified model that is adapted to the specific characteristics of batch processing and may therefore be somewhat simpler. We shall choose the first alternative.

The effect of using batch processing is (a) to reduce the need to transport the programs for each process execution (or each transaction), and (b) to reduce the amount of file data transport per file record involved in each process execution (*each file record hit by a transaction*).

Note that this effect of "batching" to reduce "access distance" (for example, head movement) is destroyed if other processes (batch or direct) are allowed to use the same read/record head inbetween. Thus in batch processing there will be no programs among the files represented by matrix columns, as the program transport will be negligible.

Further the triggering of the individual processes will be replaced by a schedule triggering the batch runs in prescribed periods. Thus the trigger vector (α) will be a column that contains a figure for each process specifing how many batch runs there will be in a reference period. For example, if the reference period is one week, a daily run may have 5 in the trigger column and a monthly run of $1/4$.

In the representation of the batch processing in Fig. 3.5 we use a vector "number of records per run" instead of one for the reference period. We notice that the numbers in this vector will be the average

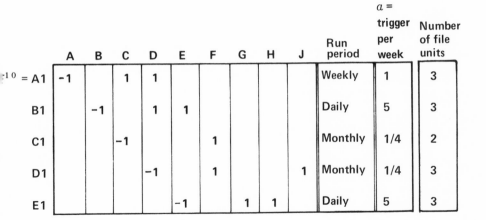

	A	B	C	D	E	F	G	H	J	Run period	$a =$ trigger per week	Number of file units
E^{10} = A1	-1		1	1						Weekly	1	3
B1		-1		1	1					Daily	5	3
C1			-1			1				Monthly	1/4	2
D1				-1		1			1	Monthly	1/4	3
E1					-1			1	1	Daily	5	3

v_d

12	2	12	2	3	12	3	2	2

(v_d assumed to have been modified by record gap effects)

	A	B	C	D	E	F	G	H	J	
Number of records per run	10	100	20	20	100	10	100	30	20	×1000

	A	B	C	D	E	F	G	H	J	
File transport volume	120	200	240	40	300	120	300	60	40	×1000

Standing files G, E (=G'), B (=E'=G'') = 100,000 records
Standing files C = 20,000, D '' = 20,000, J = 20,000

All files used in more than one process are standing files

	A	B	C	D	E	F	G	H	J
$\mu_T = a_T \cdot |E^{10}|$ =	1	5	1 1/4	6 1/4	10	2/4	5	5	1/4

= Number of file transports per reference period

Fig. 3.5

101

number of transactions during a run period for the transaction files, and the total number of file records for standing files.* If the files are on a pseudo-direct-access storage, for example, disks, a_d of Fig. 3.4 will be replaced by a_d/b (b is the blocking factor which is the average number of records per access block).† Furthermore if the files are on tape, we have to increase the values in v_d by amounts that take into consideration the interblock gaps on the tape. Thus if g is the transport size of the gap, the increment will be equal to g/b. In Fig. 3.5 we assume that such increments have been introduced into v_d'. By multiplying the transfer volume per record as indicated in v_d' by the corresponding elements in the column "number of records per run," we obtain the "file transport volume," which indicates the estimated transport volume for each file.

To obtain the total transport in the system represented by E^{10}, for one reference period, we have to compute the number of transports for each file during a reference period. Thus we have to multiply each figure in E^{10} by the number of runs for the associated process during a reference period. These numbers of runs are indicated by the vector α which gives the number of run triggerings during a reference period. Thus the vector giving the number of file transports per reference period is obtained as $\alpha_T \cdot |E^{10}|$.

Finally, the system transport is computed by multiplying each file transport volume by the corresponding element in $\alpha_T \cdot |E^{10}|$ and summing. We assume the processing to be in sequential mode.

$$\text{data transport} = (\text{file transport volume}) \cdot \mu$$

or

$$\text{data transport} = (1{\cdot}120 + 5{\cdot}200 + 5/4{\cdot}240 + 25/4{\cdot}40 + 10{\cdot}$$
$$300 + 2/4{\cdot}120 + 5{\cdot}300 + 5{\cdot}60 + 1/4{\cdot}40)\hat{v}_d$$
$$= (120 + 1000 + 300 + 250 + 3000 + 60 + 1500 + 300 + 10)\hat{v}_d$$
$$= 6540{\cdot}100\hat{v}_d$$

EXERCISE 2: Do the corresponding calculation of system transport assuming that "skip sequential" batch processing is used; that is, only those file blocks that contain hit records are accessed.

EXERCISE 3: The technique of using *virtual memory* is to let the programmer feel that he has the same file storage available for

---

* Thus if the run period would be doubled, there would be twice as many transaction records per run but the same number of standing file records.
† For instance, if there are 10,000 records in a file and it is stored by putting 10 records in each block, there will only be 1000 block access operations.

addressing as he would have if it were the main memory. The programming logic is thus made independent of the size of the main memory. What is the effect of main memory size on program execution time (a) in direct processing? (b) in sequential batch processing? and (c) in a combination of direct processing and batch processing?

3.5. INFLUENCE OF PROCESS GROUPING AND FILE CONSOLIDATION ON TRANSPORT

The Effect of Grouping Two Processes and of Consolidating Two or More Files

In designing the system we are interested in minimizing the total resource consumption over a period of time and hence of studying means for reduction of data transport (and response times) in the system. Among such means are *process grouping* and *file consolidation*. We discuss the effect of these devices very briefly in this section. Process grouping will be studied more deeply later in the chapter. File consolidation and other means for file organization have chapters devoted to them later.

DIRECT PROCESSING. A look at E^{10} and processes A1 and B1 in the illustrations used above, Figs. 3.3 and 3.4, shows that a record of file D has to be accessed and input to both of these processes for the execution of each individual process. Thus we see that if we would *group together the processes* A1 *and* B1, so that both would be executed while the D record is in main memory, then one input of D would be saved for each record of D. Thus in direct processing, 10,000 accesses and transfers are saved for the reference period, as D triggers A1 and B1 and there are 10,000 D records per period, in the example we have been using.

It is possible in this case of direct processing to input the programs for A1 and B1 one at a time, so that the memory space for application programs need only be "max (prog A1, prog B1)," assume 200, as indicated in the rightmost column at the side of $E^{10}_{(A1,B1)}$ below. The 10,000 accesses are determined by the fact that both processes A1 and B1 are triggered by the D records (column to the right of E^{10}, Fig. 3.3) and, according to the bottom row, below E^{10}, there are 10 times 1000 records of D in a reference period (Fig. 3.4).

When we decide to group two processes (for example, A1 and B1) together into one grouped process, the incidence matrix E^{10} for the new system thus obtained has the two rows (associated with A1 and A2,

respectively) replaced by one single row (process A1, A2) as indicated
below.

	A	B	C	D	E	F	G	H	J	Trigger	Space for program
$E^{10}_{(A1,B1)} = (A1,B1)$	-1	-1	1	1	1					D	200

PROCESS GROUPING IN BATCH PROCESSING SYSTEMS. A sequential
batch mode grouping of processes will have a similar effect. However,
certain complications arise if the processes grouped have different run
periods. (This we shall look into later.) Now, however, not only will
process grouping save one record transport for each processed record
but also for all other records in the standing files involved. This is
expressed more simply by observing that all the file transports, indicated
by elements in E^{10}, are saved when certain associated processes are
grouped. Thus for instance we see from E^{10}, or from Fig. 3.5, that if we
would group the runs B1 and E1 together, then we would save one daily
output of the file E and one daily input of E. Thus 10 transports of E
would be saved in a reference period of one week. Also, if E1 and B1 are
grouped together, the file E could be avoided altogether.

File Consolidation

Now that we have seen that by grouping processes together we may
reduce data transport, and may even eliminate files, and also have seen
that this may be represented by combining rows in the incidence matrix
E^{10}, let us see what kind of system modification would correspond to
combining columns in E^{10}. We shall now look into the details of these
system modifications.

Of course, the columns of E^{10} are associated with files or file records
(or with i concepts), so a combining of columns must be associated with
a combining of files or records, that is with *consolidation of files*. Again
the effect of this modification will be somewhat different in different
processing modes, so again we have to consider (at least) *the two extreme
cases: direct processing and sequential-batch processing*.

It is easy to see that if we consolidate the files C and D the number
of file units for A1 would be reduced from 3 to 2. Notice that this
reduction is often associated with a *proportional reduction of the file buffer
area* required in main memory (because we will often have a constant
block size chosen to reduce the effect of block gaps satisfactorily).* This
reduction of file units may be important if the files are on magnetic tape

---

* Note the possibility of skipping irrelevant parts of blocks through channel
programming in some systems.

but may be negligible (in itself) if files are on disks, as there may be any number of files on one disk unit. (It is important that the reader remember that when in our extremely simple example we talk of consolidating two files, we may well be regarding 50 *e* files in a realistic case as in Example 1).

EXAMPLE 1: It is common for a personnel file in a company to have 100 to 300 distinct terms in each record corresponding to roughly the same number of consolidated *e* files. It is also common that in each process only a few of these *e* files (or data terms in each record) are used in each processing run, so that a lot of data are transported as dead weight. Consideration of the effects of data transport in a systematic study of how to consolidate files might lead to having a number of distinct person files, as separate (if on tapes) or as linked (pseudo consolidated) if on pseudo-direct-access storage. Each such file might contain between 10 and 50 *e* files.

For tape files the resulting data transport might not be much changed. There might be an increased transport time (clock time) when the two files C and D were scanned simultaneously, using two separate channels, but in a realistic case with, say, 50 *e* files, there would not be enough channels to make this effect very strong and most likely it would be negligible. There would also be a slight reduction in total file volume because identifying terms (primary keys) might only be stored once for the consolidated file. Again, in realistic cases this effect would not be too significant. On the other hand, consolidation of the C and D files would mean transporting each of them with processes using only one of them. Thus in B1 and D1 the file C would be transported without being used and in C1 the file D would thus be a *dead-weight* transport. In real cases this effect is likely to be significant, too.

There are other effects of a decision to consolidate files that may be significant. This is because we usually have either to add a separate process that will perform the consolidation of the files (or corresponding processes that will have to be grouped) or we have to consolidate other files as a consequence, that is, those that are the other versions of the files considered. We can illustrate this by looking at Fig. 3.1. If the files C and D are to be consolidated into a file C·D, we would have to insert a consolidation process before A1. This consolidation process would input C and D and output C·D. Alternatively, we would have to group the processes C1 and D1 in such a way that C1·D1 would output C·D. This, however, would imply the additional grouping of the consolidation process together with C1·D1. In fact, such a grouping will always be very attractive for the great amount of data transport that it avoids.

A different situation is encountered if we consider the consolidation of the files D and E in Fig. 3.1. Here the consolidation of two files calls for additional consolidations. Thus in a typical system, with the structure shown in Fig. 3.1, the file D would be an updated version of file J; that is, D would be a file of an i concept which we may denote by $c(J)$. This is clearer if we use the file name J' instead of D.

Similarly, the files G, E, and B would probably be distinct files of the same i concept $c(G)$, say. We replace the name E by G'' and B by G'. Now consolidation of D and E will bring about a consolidated file that contains one file component of the i concept $c(J)$ and one file component of the i concept $c(G)$. This consolidation will also introduce the consolidation J·G. If we assume that process D1 is run before process E1, we would obtain the system of Fig. 3.6.* On the other hand D1 is only a monthly process, so it is likely to be more effective to group E1 with B1, which is a daily process like E1 itself.

It is seen that the consolidation J·G ($\approx$D·E) increased the system transport to almost double the amount. On the other hand the reduction that could be achieved by process grouping is then also greater.

The system can also be described by the incidence matrix E^{10} and associated rows and columns (Fig. 3.7). In determining v_d in Fig. 3.7 we simply have taken the sum of the record sizes of the component files. This usually gives too large a figure as the consolidation often reduces the number of data terms.

The E^{10} (Fig. 3.7) indicates that a grouping of D1 and E1 would not eliminate the outtransport of J'·G as J'·G is also an input to process A1. However, it is possible to use J'·G'' instead of J'·G as a precedent for A1; so it may in fact be possible to eliminate the file J'·G altogether by grouping D1 and E1.

In sum, then, consolidation of magnetic tape files will often be required in order to save file units and buffer space but it will probably be at the price of dead-weight transport.

In *batch-linear processing using pseudo-direct access storage* the saving of file units may lose its advantage. The possible saving of buffer space may remain but it will be reduced because the use of multiple, alternate

---

* Note that the need to assume a certain order of processing is caused by the representation we use. It is desirable not to make such decisions on order at this early stage before analyzing the consequence of alternative orders. Also, if direct processing is used, the order may have to be random.

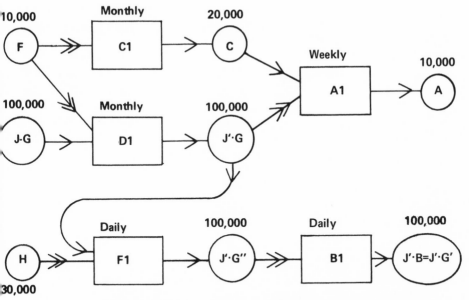

Fig. 3.6   The system of Fig. 3.4 after consolidation of D($=$J$'$) and E($=$G).
The consolidated files J$\cdot$G and J$'\cdot$G$'$ are a consequence of the
consolidation J$'\cdot$G. It was assumed that the 20,000 records of J
would join with records of G. (The file J$'\cdot$G as a precedent process
Al could be replaced by J$'\cdot$G$''$ or by J$'\cdot$G$'$.)

buffer areas is of much less effect with such storages. As a consequence
this processing environment appears to be of little use in file consolidation.

In skip sequential (using pseudo-direct storage) the dead-weight
transport would seem to disappear because a whole block has to be
transported with a record. Thus unused data would be transported with
the block in any case.

However, if we consolidate the records of C and D (Fig. 3.5), a
block would contain fewer (C,D) records than pure C or D records. This
will reduce the probability that several records in the batch being
processed in a run would hit the same block. This loss in efficiency will
be larger, the larger the batch. For very large batches we have the
batch-sequential processing discussed above and, again, there would be
little, if any, advantage in consolidating. Instead if the batch is very
small, we approach the direct-processing mode. Here the probability of
hitting more than one file record in the same block will always be nil, so
in this case the saving in some process by consolidating records, which

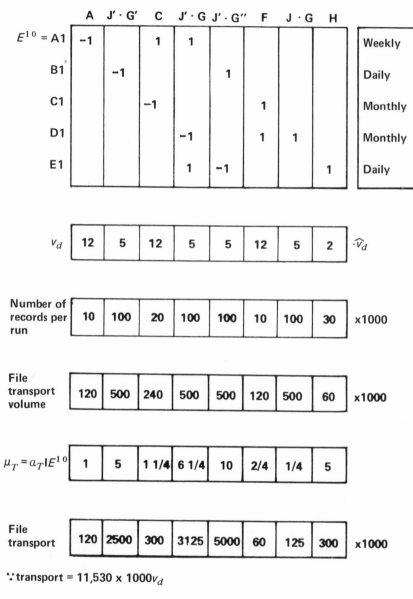

$E^{10} =$	A	J′·G′	C	J′·G	J′·G″	F	J·G	H		a	
A1	-1		1	1					Weekly	1
B1		-1			1				Daily	5
C1			-1			1			Monthly	1/4
D1				-1		1	1		Monthly	1/4
E1				1	-1			1	Daily	5

v_d	12	5	12	5	5	12	5	2	$\widehat{v}_d$

Number of records per run	10	100	20	100	100	10	100	30	×1000

File transport volume	120	500	240	500	500	120	500	60	×1000

$\mu_T = a_T l E^{10}$	1	5	1 1/4	6 1/4	10	2/4	1/4	5

File transport	120	2500	300	3125	5000	60	125	300	×1000

∵ transport = 11,530 × 1000v_d

Fig. 3.7

108

are common input to that process, will not be upset by such losses. As a consequence we see that in direct processing or in skip sequential with small batches we may consolidate file records to save data access work.

In total, consolidation will be of interest when tape files are used or when skip sequential with small batches is used. The latter case includes direct processing as its low extreme.

EXERCISE 2: What would be the column in E^{10} (Fig. 3.5) that would replace columns C and D if these were consolidated?

EXERCISE 3: How will the effect of process grouping on system transport be affected by file consolidations?

Effect of Pseudo Consolidation

When the files are on (pseudo-)direct-access storage, there are more possibilities for consolidating files than by the *record-collection* or by the *record-consolidation* types possible on tape files. These new types we call *pseudo consolidation*. For instance the files B, C, D, and E may be pseudo consolidated as shown in Fig. 3.8. We shall devote some full chapters to the problem of organizing the files, including consolidation or pseudo consolidation as well as the directory files or other name-to-address mapping devices.

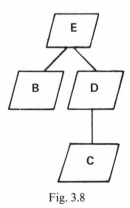

Fig. 3.8

EXAMPLE 2: *e* files associated with the object class A: *e*1, *e*2, *e*3, *e*4, *e*5, *e*6, *e*7

(a) *c* files | e1,e2 | | e3,e4 | | e5,e6,e7 |

(b) The three *c* files associated with A. These are pseudo consolidated together, that is, to access any record within, say, [e3,e4] the system will have to access first the block A.

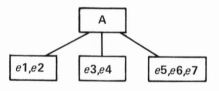

(c) A second, alternative pseudo consolidation. In this design, to access a record in [e5,e6,e7] the system will have to access first the block A and therefore the corresponding record of the file [e3,e4]. This record will contain a pointer to the record in [e5,e6,e7].

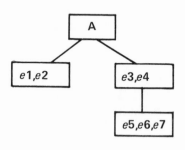

(d) A third pseudo-consolidation example.

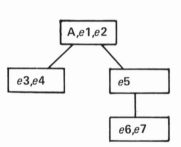

(e) Third entry. For example, the third entry may have the form in which *p5* is the property of the object A3, represented in the *e* file *e5*.

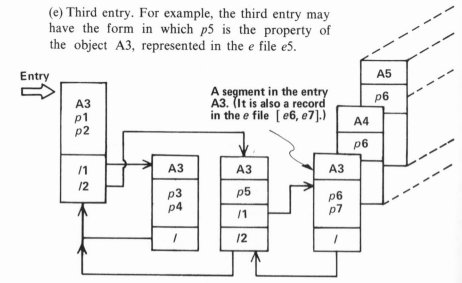

EXAMPLE 3: The *e* concept
    1 order(customer, article)
is a binary relation and is an information kind such that any message instance of it informs that a certain customer ordered a certain article at a certain date. The records of corresponding *e* file will, typically, occur as parts of "order lines," that is, are contained, each in a line of a sales-order document.
An associated *e* concept may be
    2 quantity(order transaction)
where the associated object class "order transaction" is equivalent to the *e* concept "order(customer, articles)" because any message instance of the latter identifies an order transaction. Hence we may replace quantity(order transaction) by
    3 quantity(order(customer, article))
It is seen that the "object part" of a record of the *e* file of (3) is a complete record of the *e* file of (1) (see section 3.1). It may have the form:
    [*customer C*, ordered 5 pounds, article A, date D]
and it may now appear as part of an entry under the object "customer C", that is, it may be consolidated with some other "customer file." The *e* concepts (1) and (3) may be transposed (see Chapter 4) to
    1′order(article, customer)
and
    3′quantity(order(article, customer))
and may be, alternatively, consolidated with some other "article file."

It will often be efficient to have both of the transposed versions in the system, one consolidated with a customer file and another consolidated with an article file.

3.6 CONDITIONS FOR PROCESS GROUPING AND FILE CONSOLIDATION

We have seen that process grouping and file consolidation may be used as design modifications to save data transport or other resource requirements. To use this design method we need to be able to determine not only the effect to be expected but also the logical conditions under which such modifications are possible.

The logical conditions for process grouping and for file consolidation are both very simple in principle. This does not mean, however, that it is quite simple to apply them. For process grouping it is easy to see that we have the conditions given below.

Precedence Condition for Process Grouping

Two processes cannot be grouped together if there is a precedence relation of higher than the first order between them.

That this condition is a necessary one is easy to see. Thus if one process, A1, say, has another process B1 as a precedent of higher than the first order, then there exists a third process C1, which is an immediate precedent of A1 and has B1 as one of its precedents. Thus A1 cannot be executed immediately after B1 and the two cannot be executed as one grouped process (Fig. 3.9).

Memory Condition for Process Grouping

Two processes can be grouped together if enough space is available in main memory to handle the programs of both, together with a program that coordinates them.

This condition is less strict than the first one. "Enough space" may simply mean to have space for a part of the program of the grouped process that is large enough to handle the program execution, even if this calls for swapping segments of the program from auxiliary storage. This is, however, only "enough" if in this way there still is a saving of data transport; that is, if the swapping of program segments implies less data transport than the file transport saved by the process grouping. As we have seen this may easily be the case in direct processing. On the other hand, in a typical batch-sequential operation this memory condition for grouping will often amount to requiring that there is space in main memory for the whole grouped process program to be resident in main memory during execution. The reason we mention this effect as a condition for grouping—rather than one among other effects to consider by means of design calculations—is that in all cases it will be necessary to consider explicitly the question of memory space when deciding whether or not to group processes. Thus before performance calculation

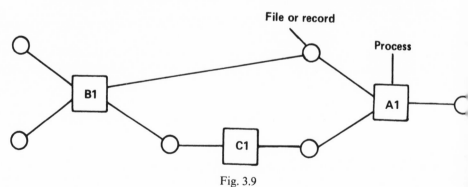

Fig. 3.9

can be done, to test different design alternatives, we must determine the amount of memory to use for grouped programs that will be assumed. The alternative grouping strategies include:

1. Grouping to the extent that all program segments of the group can be placed in memory (no swapping). This then means to study, for each memory size, distinct feasible groupings for that size and to repeat this for a number of possible memory sizes.

2. Grouping more than can be covered by memory. This means that swapping does occur. In this case several memory sizes, calling for different amounts of swappings, are studied. Again this is repeated for a series of memory sizes.

Condition for File Consolidation

Files can be consolidated if their records (or entries) contain the same identifiers or "object parts" (or "primary keys")—that is, if the files inform about the same objects, and if they may be stored in the same sequence.

This condition is obvious because the consolidation of files—by record consolidation, by record collection, or by record linkage (pseudo consolidation)—means that all terms associated with the same group of identifying terms (identifying the objects that the records inform about) are connected to this group by some data structural means.

EXERCISE 1: In the way programs come to be designed in our approach, through grouping of more elementary process programs, the advantage of the virtual memory technique is partly lost. What is lost and what remains?

EXERCISE 2: On-line programming, in which the programmer develops his program sitting at a terminal in direct communication with the computer, is sometimes rejected by programmers on the argument that the technique is disadvantageous by requiring programs to be broken down into small pieces. What will be the effect of using systematic program design, in which programs are constructed by grouping, in this situation?

The *e* concepts that are associated with distinct object classes may, nevertheless, have their *e* files consolidated if objects of one class are referred to in the property part of the other *e* file. This is still in accordance with the condition for consolidation given above. For instance, the *e* concepts

1. employee(department)
2. job(employee)
3. room(employee)

may be represented by the consolidated file

4. [department, employee, job, room]

An entry of (4) may have the form
department # date
employee #, job, room
employee #, job, room

$$\equiv$$

where the number of subentries "employee #, job, room" is variable and equals the number of employees in the respective department.

In this case it is seen that each entry of (4) contains a subfile (one or more entries) of another file [employee, job, room] which, in turn, is a file that is obtained by consolidation of (2) and (3).

It would be natural to refer to this kind of file consolidation as an *hierarchical file consolidation.* Of course, several hierarchical levels of consolidation are feasible.

More will be said about file consolidation, as one of several operators of file structuring, in Chapters 4 and 6.

Analysis of the Precedence Condition for Grouping

Although the precedence condition for process grouping is quite simple in form, it may take quite a lot of analysis to check for any pair of processes as to whether the condition is fulfilled or not. This can be done by searching through a graph of the system, or the incidence matrix E^{10}, or the information precedence matrix P^{00}, or the process precedence matrix P^{11}. Search of the matrices is fairly difficult if done manually but can easily be programmed for a computer. This is one of the reasons we may want to use formal systems descriptions and use computer-aided systems analysis and design.

As we know from system algebra we may also compute the precedents of the order i by iterated multiplication i times with the precedence matrix P^{11} (or P^{00}). The condition then means that A1 and B1 cannot be grouped if

$$A1 \in \mathscr{P}^{(x)}(B1) \qquad \text{or} \qquad B1 \in \mathscr{P}^{(y)}(A1)$$

where $x > 1$ and $y > 1$.*

---

* See Langefors (1966) for an extended illustration of this.

In general it will be faster to use a search algorithm than to use iterated matrix operations. On the other hand the latter may be possible to perform using standard matrix algebra programs. (This will only be the case if programs for large system matrices are available.)

3.7. TWO BASIC SITUATIONS FOR PROCESS GROUPING

There are two basic situations in which process grouping is of interest. Grouping has distinct effects in each of these two situations and in general the situation can be seen as a combination of these basic ones. It is therefore of interest to look at these two basic situations first.

The Process Bundle

The process bundle is a situation in which one file (or record) (F, say) is a triggering precedent of two or more processes (Fig 3.10). Thus for each record of F there will be an execution of each of the successor processes (F1, F2, and F3 in Fig. 3.2). If the processes are separate, then F has to be transported into each of them and hence if i of them is grouped together then $i - 1$ transports of F are eliminated. This is true for direct-processing and batch-processing modes alike.

The Process Chain

The process chain is a situation in which distinct files or kinds of records trigger distinct processes, each one of which is a succedent of the other in such a way that each pair of processes has a file in common, which is output from one and input to the other (Fig. 3.11). It is seen that in the chain the distinct processes may have distinct run periods, contrary to the bundle. It is then necessary to know precisely what happens to the processing of the longer period processes when they are grouped with more frequent ones. In this situation there is a great difference between direct processing (and skip sequential) on the one hand and batch-sequential processing on the other hand. In direct processing, grouping of processes in the chain would only save transport in those cases in which the triggering transactions of the distinct processes happen to hit the same records of the common files and, in addition, happen to arrive simultaneously. This does not appear to be very probable in general (unless the triggering transactions are, themselves, produced by processes having a common trigger, that is, belong to a bundle.) Thus this kind of situation does not seem to make process grouping very interesting. In batch skip sequential the probable saving may be higher but still, perhaps, often negligible, unless the batch sizes are large in comparison to the file sizes (a large hit ratio.)

In a batch-sequential processing mode, however, process grouping

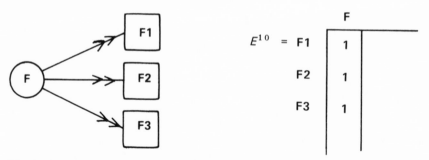

Fig. 3.10   Process bundle. (Double arrowhead used to indicate that the precedence relation is a triggering one.)

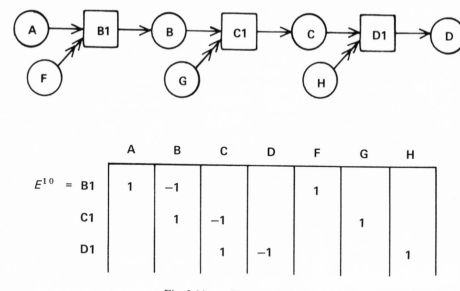

Fig. 3.11   Process chain.

may be very effective in the process chain situation, at least for those processes that have the same specified run periods. In this case each file that is output from one process and input to the succeeding process has to be transported out and in for each run period. *If such a file is not needed elsewhere* in the system, the grouping of its precedent and succedent processes would save both an output and input transport of the file and, in addition, would eliminate the need for the file unit and associated block buffers (if the processes have the same run period and, of course, if the grouping conditions are satisfied).

If such a file is needed elsewhere, its output transport is not saved by the grouping, as it has to be output also from the grouped processes. This will be the case, for instance, if the successor process (for example, D1) is run n times for each time of the predecessor (C1), in that then the intermediate file C must be output from C1 in order to be used for the $n - 1$ subsequent runs of D1.

We may conclude that the process bundle is the main system structure in which process grouping is of interest.

Effect of Different Processing Periods on Grouping of a Process Chain

In a process chain structure such as in Fig. 3.11 the typical case would be one in which A, B, C, and D appear as different updated versions of the same master file. If, for instance, the reference period is one day and if the transaction batch F comes once a month, G once a week, and H once a day, we may have (1/20, 1/5, 1) number of runs per period. If we would, for instance, group all three processes B1, C1, and D1 together into one process (B1, C1, D1), then this has to be run daily—that is, once per reference period—if no data production is allowed to be delayed because of the grouping. Then in 1/20 of the runs F would be added to the batch of transactions H, and in 1/5 of the runs G would be added. The file transport associated with F, G, and H would thus not be changed by the grouping. The master file would be transported twice per reference period (one input and one output daily) after grouping, whereas before grouping it would be transported 2 $(1 + 1/5 + 1/20) = 2/25$ times per reference period. It is seen that in the kind of system structure assumed here, probably the typical one, the difference in processing periods did not cause any complications in the analysis of the effect of process grouping. This was because when, for instance, the weekly batch process C1 was grouped with the daily process D1, the grouped process was still only run once a week, whereas during the other days the process C1 of the group would be skipped. (It is seen that in grouping processes we shall expect to have to add program modules that will handle this program administration.) A similar result would be obtained, however, if after the grouping, the process C1 would also be run daily while treating only that fraction of the batch G that was generated the day before. In both of these cases the processing work of each process as well as the intransport of the transaction batches remain unchanged by the grouping together with processes having distinct processing periods. (In the former case, however, memory space might be saved by not keeping the program C1 resident during such runs when it is not executed.)

If the grouping of a weekly process, such as C1 with a daily process D1, will lead to inputting the whole of G each day, rather than once a week (a less likely design), then the grouping will result in five intransports of G per week, rather than one. This, of course, will lead to a reduction of the transport saving obtained by the grouping, or perhaps the result may then be increased transport.

3.8. COMPUTER AID TO PROCESS GROUPING DECISIONS

Computations to Aid the Design Decisions Regarding Process Grouping
After it has been determined by analysis (or computation) which processes are possible to group, with respect to the precedence condition, we have to determine which processes are possible to group, given a certain available program space in main memory, and a certain swapping or nonswapping strategy. (This will then be repeated for a series of distinct memory space assumptions.) We thus want to compute the transport saving that may be obtained through different, feasible process groupings. A natural way of doing this analysis is to compute the effect of the possible grouping of two processes at a time, which are allowable for grouping. Thereupon we may study what grouping of the grouped pairs with single processes or with other pairs may still be allowable, and so on. Notice that the best solution is not necessarily the one that is obtained by first doing the most efficient grouping in pairs and then the most efficient grouping into three groups, or four groups, and so on. Thus what is wanted, and will come in the future, is "optimization" algorithms. However, until this is available, when we want to obtain an understanding of the problem, we can work with intuitive design decisions and use computations to aid with them.

EXAMPLE 1: In the system shown in Fig. 3.12, and Fig. 3.13, if we assume all files to have equal transport volumes, we see* that the

---

* Note that this is more easily seen from the matrix than from the graph.

most efficient grouping pair is A·B, as it saves three file transports
(a,b,c). A·C, A·D, and B·C save two transports, B·D saves one, and
C·D saves no transport. It is easy to see that the grouping of the
"best pair," A·B, does not belong to a best solution if the problem is
to find the best grouping into pairs of processes. Thus if we would
group A·B, which saves three file transports, we must group C·D,
which saves nothing. This solution thus gives a total saving of three.
Instead the solution B·C and A·D saves four transports.

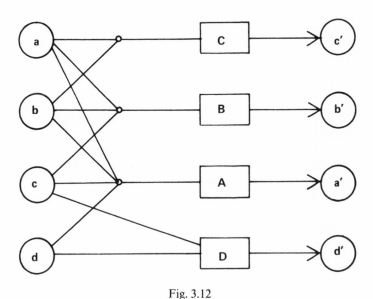

Fig. 3.12

	a	b	c	d	a′	b′	c′	d′
E^{10} = A	1	1	1	1	−1			
B	1	1	1			−1		
C	1	1					−1	
D			1	1				−1

Fig. 3.13

EXAMPLE 2: Batch processing, sequential files on tape (no skip sequential). In Figs. 3.14 and 3.15 we have a bundle of processes, B-Q-R, and a chain E-P-A-Q-A'-S-A''.

If we group, for instance, the processes R and Q, we save one intransport of file B', that is, we save a transport equal to 50 per reference period. If we group, for instance, Q and S, we save one intransport of A', thus the saving is 100. This is seen in that the grouped process Q·S will input B and A once per period whereby A' is output (to be used in the subsequent four runs of Q·S) and at the same time is used in the process S together with D' and C of that run. In the next four runs D' and A' are input together with the actual C file of the run. Note that if the process S would have had the same run frequency as process Q, then the grouping Q·S would have eliminated file A' altogether and the saving would have been 200.

In Fig. 3.16 we have illustrated how the system might look if we group processes Q and S. The only file transport that is changed by the grouping is that of file A'·A' is output once per reference period, as before, but is now input four instead of five times. The process program for Q·S will have to know that it will skip Q the second through fifth run during each reference period, and the operator or operating system will have to know that Q·S will have distinct input and output files during the first run in a reference period against those of the subsequent four runs in the reference period. In Fig. 3.16 we have assumed that the program will sense whether the operator (operating system) has mounted B and if so, it will run Q and S, else it will run only S. We have also indicated that the program will verify that A (rather than A') is mounted each time that B is mounted. The notation we used in the box for Q·S in Fig. 3.16 should be self-explanatory in view of our comments. We have indicated by means of double arrowheads that C is triggering for process Q·S; that is, the process Q·S is started each time that a transaction of type C is input. In Fig. 3.17 E^{10} contains enough of the information for the calculation of data transports as a design aid. It does not, however, contain all the information needed as a specification of the programs for the processes nor that which is needed by the operator (or operating system). This, however, is information that should not be present in the overview documentation (graphs or matrices), as it is only needed when we study individual processes or groups of processes. Thus when we use E^{10}, for example, as an overview aid to find out processes that might be suitable for grouping, we can retrieve local information about each process whenever necessary to study the effects to be expected from grouping.

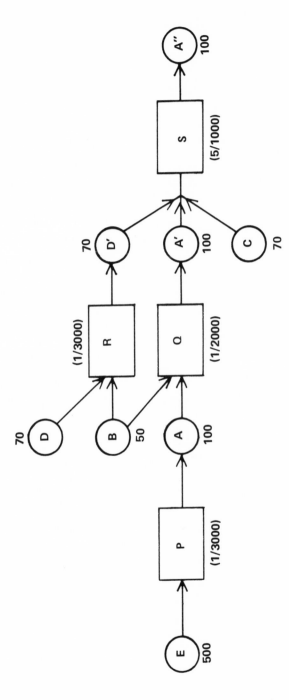

Fig. 3.14 Batch processing. The figure below a file symbol (circles) indicates the transport volume of the file. The pair of figures below a process symbol (box) indicates the number of runs per reference period and the program memory space.

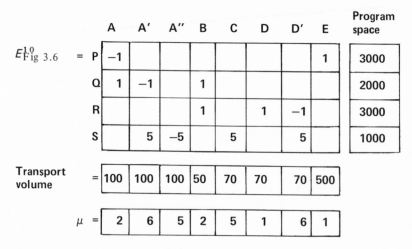

	A	A'	A''	B	C	D	D'	E	Program space
$E^{10}_{Fig\ 3.6} =$ P	−1							1	3000
Q	1	−1		1					2000
R			1			1	−1		3000
S		5	−5		5		5		1000

Transport volume =	100	100	100	50	70	70	70	500

μ =	2	6	5	2	5	1	6	1

Transport $= 13 \cdot 100 + 100 + 12 \cdot 70 + 500 = 2740$

Fig. 3.15   Incidence matrix E^{10} of the system in Fig. 3.14.

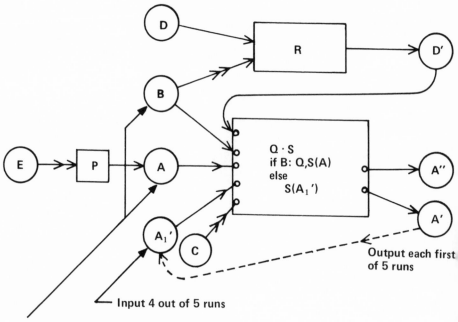

Input in that 1 out of 5 runs
when A_1' is not used as input

Fig. 3.16   Processes Q and S grouped. A' is denoted by A_1' when used as input. It is sometimes necessary to use two distinct symbols for A' in its two roles, for example, as in E^{10}, in Fig. 3.17. Double arrowheads indicate triggering information precedents.

122

		A	A′	A″	B	C	D	D′	E	A′₁	Program space
$E_{\text{Fig 3.8}}^{10}$	= P	−1							1		3000
	Q·S	1	−1	−5	1	5		5		4	3000
	R				1		1	−1			3000

Transport volume	=	100	100	100	50	70	70	70	500	100

μ =	2	1	5	2	5	1	6	1	4

Transport $\quad = \quad 12 \cdot 100 + 100 + 12 \cdot 70 + 500 = 2640$

$A′_1$ = file A′ when used as input

Fig. 3.17 $\quad E^{10}$ for the system of Fig. 3.16. (Note that the number of runs per reference is not just indicated for each process but has to have distinct figures in the row Q·S.)

Figure 3.16 can be represented in an incidence matrix E^{10} (Fig. 3.17) with supplementing vectors in the known way. Figure 3.16, instead, contains some additional information that we have not yet shown on how to formulate in the matrix-vector way. We shall return to this point later.

EXERCISE 1: Do the calculation of the effects of possible groupings for a system similar to Fig. 3.14 but where all processes have the same run frequency (five runs per reference period).

How to Represent the Results of Transport Computations for Process Grouping

We have seen that it is possible to use formal computations to obtain estimates for data transport of different system designs using matrix calculations or equivalent schemes under certain conditions (amended where appropriate with calculations of the effects of queues in the system). Thus a computer can be used to do such calculations for distinct design alternatives (process groupings.) It is thus of interest to find out how the result of such calculations can best be presented to the designer to aid him in inventing new alternatives to analyze or in selecting among those already calculated. Likewise if we would have the design process automated, using some design algorithm, it is again of interest to find out how to arrange the results so as to enable an efficient analysis by the algorithm. We shall study, briefly, one such device.

To compare distinct groupings of pairs of processes (or pairs of groups of processes) we may use a matrix M that has one row and one column for each process (or grouped process). In each position in this matrix we may insert either one of two alternative kinds of entry. In one alternative we shade (or cross over) the whole entry to indicate that the two processes associated with the entry may not be grouped. In the other alternative we insert two numbers. One of these indicates the amount of saving of data transport that would follow if the associated processes become grouped together. The other number indicates the memory space needed to accommodate the program of the grouped process.

In Fig. 3.18 we have shown M of the system in Fig. 3.14. The entry (Q,S) of M, for example, says that grouping the processes Q and S would save a transport equal to 100, which follows from our computations above (Figs. 3.16 and 3.17). In addition it informs that a memory space of 3000 is needed to store the grouped program Q·S. We have filled in the other cells of M from intuitive computations based on Fig. 3.14. It is seen in Fig. 3.18 that the grouping Q·S is the most favorable one in that it is best in both factors. It leads to the biggest transport saving and yet requires the smallest memory space. Note, however, that it may, nevertheless, not be the best choice because the grouping operations that are thereafter possible may be inferior (see Example 1 of Section 3.8). It is this kind of complication that makes mathematical design models desirable. However, in a manual design process this kind of information is of great interest to the designer.

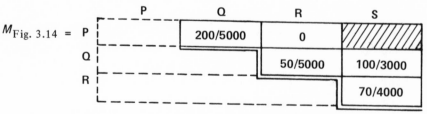

Fig. 3.18 M matrix for the system of Fig. 3.14.

3.9. THE CONSTRUCTION OF GROUPED PROCESSES

When we group processes together, what we have in mind is to keep programs, which implement the abstract processes associated with suitably interrelated information precedence bundles, simultaneously available. These processes are thus kept as resident in main memory or swapped in (and out if they are not of reentrant type) as transactions call for them when arriving. Of course, it may not be efficient to group processes if the programs in the group will, as a result, be swapped extensively, as then the data transport spent on program swapping may outbalance the saving in file data transport caused by the grouping.

When several complete programs are grouped together, the individual input and output procedures and checking procedures are replaced by one common I/O set for the whole group. It is more natural to approach the program construction in such a way that the individual process programs are implemented as separate procedures, each of which implements the abstract program associated with one of the precedence bundles in the group (or equivalently one of the output information in the group). The input and output and error procedures are then constructed for the group and so is an administration module for the whole group.

Data that are only intermediate between two processes in the same group will, as discussed earlier, not appear as files in the grouped system. Such information kinds are only cared for by a data area local to the process group in which just those records of these files are stored that are needed for each individual execution. We illustrate this with a small system as illustrated by the incidence matrix E^{10} (Fig. 3.19). As can be concluded from E^{10} the processes perform the following:

D: Updates the inventory file from receiving reports
E: Splits the batch of customer transactions into two kinds
F: Splits the batch of warehouse transactions into two kinds

Below E^{10} we have (in Fig. 3.19) shown the row in the new incidence matrix that would be obtained if we would group the processes D·F or E·F or D·E·F, respectively.

Figure 3.20 is a graph representation of the system (only the part containing processes D and F). In the block for the process F we have indicated the condition for the splitting of the batch of transactions. In Fig. 3.21 we have described the system as it might look after grouping the processes D and F.

In Fig. 3.22 we have described the process programs for the

	Inventory	New inventory	Receipts	Customer transaction	Customer payments sum	Customer order	Warehouse transaction
E^{10} = D	1	−1	1				
E				1	−1	−1	
F			−1	−1			1

D·F	1	−1		−1			1
E·F			−1		−1	−1	1
D·E·F	1	−1			−1	−1	1

Fig. 3.19

processes D and F as well as the program for the grouped process F·D. Note the close similarity between Figs. 3.22 and 3.21. These programs are written under the assumption that E^{10} is also available.

In this example it is obvious that what is changed when F and D are grouped is that in F *"output:* Receipts" and in D *"input:* Receipts" are eliminated. This was exactly what was to be obtained by the grouping. Instead it is, of course, necessary to add the test *"if* code *of . . . ,"* as this is needed to administer the combined process. It is seen that in this case, at least, an automatic construction of the grouped process F·D, given the processes F and D, might be feasible (as suggested by Langefors, 1966).

The process descriptions above are assumed to be available together with E^{10}. Thus it was not necessary to specify, for instance, for process D that it has two input files, "receipts" and "inventory", and one output, "inventory'", as this is seen from E^{10}.

The reason we did show *"input* receipts" in *D* was that thereby "receipts" was shown to be the trigger. When we write a normal program, for instance a COBOL program, we cannot (yet) assume that the compiler will have the information E^{10} available. Thus in a COBOL program we have to add some further information about the process

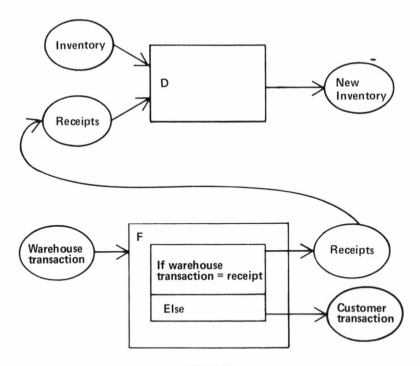

Fig. 3.20

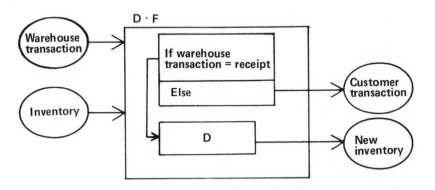

Fig. 3.21

127

D

    input: Receipts
    perform: Update inventory

F

    input: Warehouse transport
    if: Code *of* warehouse transport = R *then*
               output Receipts
    else: *output* Customer transport

F·D   *input:*   Warehouse transport *and* Receipts
         if: code *of* Warehouse transport = R *then*
                  Update Inventory
         else: *output* Customer transport

Fig. 3.22   Process descriptions.

design. We show below a set of COBOL programs for the processes D,F and D·F as well as for D·E·F (Nunamaker et al., 1972).

Some work has been done to develop programs (Fig. 3.23) for the automatic construction of program for grouped processes (Nunamaker et al., 1972).

PROCESS D

OPEN   INPUT   OLD-INVENTORY-FILE,   RECEIVING-REPORT-FILE,
    OUTPUT UPDATE-INVENTORY-FILE.
LABEL.   READ RECEIVING-REPORT-FILE AT END GO TO CLOSER.
    PERFORM UPDATE INVENTORY-FILE.
    GO TO LABEL.
CLOSER. CLOSE ALL FILES.

PROCESS E
    OPEN INPUT CUSTOMER-TRANSACTION-FILE, OUT-PUT CUSTOMER-PAYMENT-FILE, CUSTOMER-ORDER-FILE.
    READ CUSTOMER-TRANSACTION-FILE AT END GO TO CLOSER.

Fig. 3.23   COBOL program (From Nunamaker et al., *Processing Systems Optimization through Automatic Design and Reorganization of Program Modules,* Purdue University Press, by permission.)

(Continued)

     IF CODE OF CUSTOMER-TRANSACTION EQUAL 'P' THEN WRITE CUSTOMER-PAYMENT-REC FROM CUS-TOMER-TRANSACTION

     ELSE WRITE CUSTOMER-ORDER-REC FROM CUS-TOMER- TRANSACTION.

     GO TO LABEL.

CLOSER. CLOSE ALL FILES.

PROCESS F

     OPEN INPUT WAREHOUSE-TRANSACTION-FILE, OUTPUT RECEIVING-REPORT-FILE, CUSTOMER-TRANS-ACTION-FILE

LABEL. READ WAREHOUSE-TRANSACTION-FILE AT END GO TO CLOSER.

     IF CODE OF WAREHOUSE-TRANSACTION EQUAL 'R' THEN WRITE

     RECEIVING-REPORT-REC FROM WAREHOUSE-TRANSACTION ELSE

     WRITE CUSTOMER-TRANSACTION-REC FROM WAREHOUSE-TRANSACTION. GO TO LABEL.

CLOSER. CLOSE ALL FILES.

Fig. 3.23   (Continued)

By combining and reorganizing Processes D and F into one module, the following integrated module is generated (Fig. 3.24).

MODULE D-F

     OPEN INPUT WAREHOUSE-TRANSACTION-FILE, OLD-INVENTORY-FILE, OUTPUT CUSTOMER-TRANSAC-TION-FILE, NEW INVENTORY-FILE.

LABEL. READ WAREHOUSE-TRANSACTION-FILE AT END GO TO CLOSER.

     IF CODE OF WAREHOUSE-TRANSACTION EQUAL 'R' THEN UPDATE INVENTORY-FILE ELSE WRITE CUS-TOMER-TRANSACTION-REC PROM

     WAREHOUSE-TRANSACTION. GO TO LABEL.

CLOSER. CLOSE ALL FILES.

Fig. 3.24   Integrated module generated by combining and reorganizing Processes D and F.

The ability to combine processes D and F (eliminating file F′) and E and F (eliminating file F″) does not guarantee that both files can be eliminated by grouping processes D, E, and F; that is, certain program variable dependencies existing between processes D and E may prohibit the reorganization of the total grouping. However, if such dependencies do not exist, then processes D, E, and F may be combined and reorganized to produce the resultant module (Fig. 3.25).

MODULE D-E-F

OPEN INPUT WAREHOUSE-TRANSACTION-FILE, OLD-INVENTORY-FILE, OUTPUT NEW-INVENTORY-FILE, CUSTOMER-ORDER-FILE,
CUSTOMER-PAYMENT-FILE.
LABEL. READ WAREHOUSE-TRANSACTION-FILE AT END GO TO CLOSER.
IF CODE OF WAREHOUSE-TRANSACTION EQUAL ′R′ THEN UPDATE-INVENTORY-FILE ELSE
IF CODE OF WAREHOUSE-TRANSACTION EQUAL ′P′ THEN WRITE
CUSTOMER-PAYMENT-REC FROM WAREHOUSE-TRANSACTION ELSE
WRITE CUSTOMER-ORDER-REC FROM WARE-HOUSE-TRANSACTION.
GO TO LABEL.
CLOSER. CLOSE ALL FILES.

Fig. 3.25

EXERCISE 1: Write COBOL programs for the system of Fig. 3,14 and for the grouped process B1-A1 of Fig. 3,16.

3.10 DESCRIPTION OF THE CONTROL STRUCTURE

The incidence matrix E^{10} defines the connections between the processes and the information precedence structure of the "whole" system. It does not define the program logic or the dynamic process initiation conditions. This is not usually desirable as it would complicate the description and thus reduce the overview provided by E^{10}. Instead E^{10} contains the process names, and these serve as "name pointers" to descriptions of process logic, so the information is there. However, we change perspective when we go over from the overall system (or subsystem) design to the process design. At that stage we can use E^{10} to select such processes as may be of interest to group together, and the associated files or *e* concepts. This makes up a small part of E^{10} so that, at this stage, it becomes feasible to combine the process descriptions with E^{10}, thus displaying more of the information relevant to process design in one document (or document group). This, for instance, is of interest for the construction of grouped processes (Section 3.9).

When we want to combine process description with the incidence matrix, the decision table suggests itself. The combination of decision tables with information precedence structure can be done in a very natural way (Langefors, 1973). However, it will often make it necessary to split the processes into subprocesses which are controlled by logical conditions. This will, for instance, always be true for elementary filter processes. These always contain a logical filter part and two distinct output parts.

The combination of E^{10} and the process description is, of course, already established in Figs. 3.20 and 3.21. What we have to do, mainly, is to replace the "if" statements by a decision table. To do this for the process F, for instance, we split F into three parts: the "filter part" F0 and the "output parts" F1 and F2 (Fig. 3.26.) We set up in Fig. 3.27 the incidence matrix corresponding to Fig. 3.26. The incidence matrix EC has been given three properties not found in the common uses of E^{10}. These modifications stem from the fact that the normal E^{10} does not exhibit the control structure (just as in Fig. 3.20 where we had to add the block containing the "if" statement). This is the reason we chose the notation EC rather than E^{10}. One modification is that in EC the output of F0 could not be simply denoted by a minus sign because the value produced by F0 will determine which of two distinct output messages *Trig1* or *Trig2* will be output. The second difference is that it is assumed

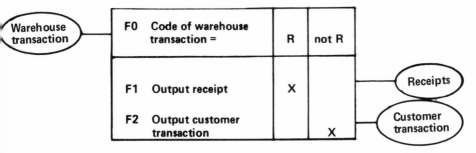

Fig. 3.26

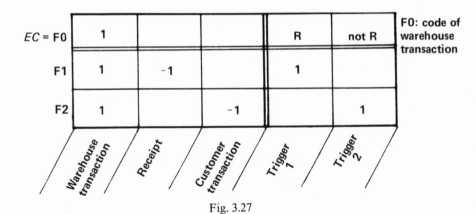

Fig. 3.27

that what is made known through the matrix is that the input indications of *Trig*1 to process F1 and of *Trig*2 to F2 have a triggering function. This could have been indicated by replacing the 1 by another symbol or group of symbols. In *EC* this was done instead by using italics for the information names *Trig*1 and *Trig*2.

The third difference is that for the "filter subprocess" or control subprocess name *F*0 we also used italics to indicate its special character which also implies that its input indication (1 for "warehouse transaction") is to be taken as a triggering input.

As a further illustration we set up *EC* for the whole system of Fig. 3.20. We also change the basic assumption and assume that, contrary to above, the process F will be run for the whole file "warehouse transaction" before process D gets started—rather than running on a transaction basis. Thus we illustrate that this control problem can also be displayed. The latter change implies that we need to add another control subprocess to F, which we denote by F01; F01 will check whether the whole file "warehouse transaction" has been handled.

In EC of Fig. 3.28 we had to add another pair of conventions, thus, for example, in the column for Trig3 we have 1 for the row F1 and a 2 for the row D to indicate the sequence, saying that first process F1 is to be triggered and then process D.

To read Fig. 3.28 we note that the processes *F*0 and *F*01 have names in italic and, hence, they are control processes. It follows that they are triggered by their input which, in both cases, is "warehouse transaction". Thus when a record of warehouse transaction arrives (thanks to some control external to Fig. 3.28) F01 and F0 are to be executed. If the output of F01 is N, then either of the processes F1 or F2 is initiated, depending on the value of F0(that is, R or not R). If F01→Y (yes) then

	Warehouse transaction	Receipt	Customer transaction	Inventory	New inventory	Trigger 1	Trigger 2	Trigger 3	Trigger 4	Code
$EC = F0$	1					R	not R	R	not R	Code
F01	1					N	N	Y	Y	Warehouse transaction= Last warehouse transaction
F1	1	-1				1		1		
F2	1		-1				1		1	
D		1		1	-1			2	2	

Fig. 3.28

F1 or F2 is executed, whereupon D is initiated. The facts that "receipt" is to be rewound (and possibly resorted) and then process D runs for the whole file inventory are not explicitly displayed in EC of Fig. 3.28 just as such control information is normally left out of E^{10}. This information can be made explicit in EC by adding more control processes, and the associated rows of EC, and more control columns.

EXERCISE 1: Develop the EC for the same subsystem as in Fig. 3.28 but with transaction-controlled processing also of process D, rather than batch processing as in Fig. 3.28.

EXERCISE 2: Develop EC for the whole system of Section 3.9.

EXERCISE 3: Expand EC of Fig. 3.28 to display also the control mentioned just above.

Means for describing the control conditions in separate control matrices have been worked out by Nunamaker et al., (1972) and by Sölvberg (1972). The combined incidence and control matrix EC, shown here, was developed from an idea by Christer Jäderlund (1974).

CONCLUSIONS

In information systems design, contrary to design of separate data processing runs, we have to decide on data and file structuring and, to a lesser extent, on process structuring as part of the "whole system." This can, of course, only be mastered by concentrating on main system structure aspects. This is thus one instance where dynamical details must be left for later, more local, considerations. In this chapter we studied the system matrices, such as the incidence matrix E^{10} (together with some supplementary rows and columns giving "size information") as a tool for providing the necessary overview to support some qualitative and quantitative estimates upon which early structuring decisions are made. We discussed two main structuring operations, file consolidation and process grouping, and the effect of these on some structural "stream properties" such as data transfer and data access streams. We also very briefly looked at how programs for grouped processes can be systematically obtained from programs for the individual processes plus some structural and dynamical information regarding the interfacing of the processes in a group. In this connection we saw how the incidence matrix could be expanded to contain also some control information, thus developing from a tool for describing stationary phenomena to a description of dynamical control events. Recent contributions to the area of this chapter are given in Bubenko (1973), Nunamaker et al. (1972), and Solvberg (1972). Earlier work was presented in Langefors (1966).

REVIEW QUESTIONS

1. There are three distinct modes of processing data. What are they? Each of these may exist in either of two distinct environments. What are they?
2. Describe the common misuse of the term "real-time processing."
3. The data transport associated with the use of a (pseudo-) direct-access file storage can be defined in two components. What are they? How are they computed by means of the incidence matrix E^{10}?
4. File consolidation can be done in two ways that are distinct on the record level. Describe these two. What is meant by "pseudo consolidation"?
5. What are the complications connected with process grouping when the processes have distinct periods?

CHAPTER 4

ELEMENTS OF FILE SYSTEMS OR DATA BASE STRUCTURING

To design file systems the designer needs to know many things. For example, he should be throughly familiar with a catalogue of distinct types of file structures, together with some of their relative advantages and disadvantages. In the previous chapter we obtained some insight into a few basic structuring possibilities and the interplay between these and such phenomena as data transport (including transfer and access). In the present chapter we study more distinct file structures and try to get some systematized feeling for their possible variations and interrelations. With this as a background the designer should be able to outline some reasonable file-structuring alternatives when facing an actual system design problem. He will then have to make a choice of one of these alternatives or choose a good new one, or a good combination as a result.

4.1 FILE SYSTEMS DESIGN

Data that are stored in the system to provide stored information to distinct users are organized into files, that is, collections of entries representing messages of the same kind (same i concept). To locate the entries of a file, either for storing or for retrieving actions or processing, there must be one or more *directories* for each file. To organize the file system is thus to organize a collection of *directory–file pairs*. File system design thus involves three main features: (a) structure of file entries—the storing and fetching of data in an entry; (b) structure of files—the construction of files as collections of entries and directories; and (c) directories—any devices for determining the location of a file entry.

Each of these features is a complicated one. Fortunately, it is possible to study one of them at a time, but to design the system we must have a good understanding of all its features. The design problem is to organize so as to obtain balance of retrieval time in distinct processing modes—for example, direct processing and batch processing—and of space, cost, and security.

Structure of File Entries

RETRIEVAL OF ENTRIES. To retrieve a specific data entry of a specific file, or to store an entry, in the system we have to enter the "name of the entry," or a description of it, to the appropriate directory–file pair. The retrieval mechanism of the system thus will (a) locate the appropriate directory–file pair, and (b) perform a directory decoding on the entry name (or description) to produce the location of the entry.

In Fig 4.1 an illustration is presented of how a retrieval request, which specifies the entry name B, is brought to the directory for decoding. The directory (or, rather, the retrieval mechanism using it) points to the location of the file entry B. For generality the file entry B is indicated as a very general structure, consisting of several contiguous *segments*, such as X, Y_1, and Z_1 in the diagram. The file structure may be of many distinct kinds. On the one end of the spectrum there is the traditional file structure with each entry formed as one contiguous record and with these records stored in one contiguous file area, ordered to sequence of increasing or decreasing values of the entry names (Fig. 4.2). In this case the directory only has to point to the location of the label record of the file (which may itself be regarded as part of the

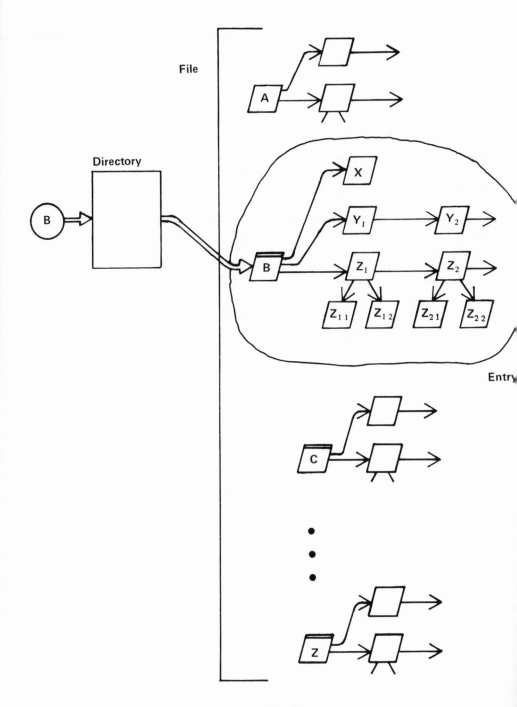

Fig. 4.1a

138

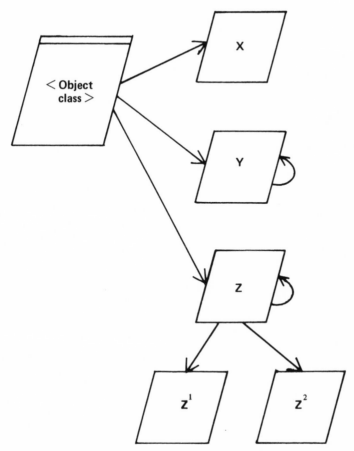

Fig. 4.1b Graphical description of the entry type of which B in Fig. 4.1a is an occurrence.

directory). Only sequential search over the main file is available for retrieval in this design.

On the other end of the spectrum is a design in which the entries are scattered around the file storage with each entry consisting of a set of distinct subentries, in several hierarchical levels. The lowest level usually contains small, contiguous segments. Figures 4.2 through 4.7 illustrate some different, possible file structures.

In all the distinct file structure designs, shown in Figs. 4.2 through 4.7, and many more, the directory always has the function of pointing to the location of a specified entry. We shall see later that the directory also may be structured in many different ways.

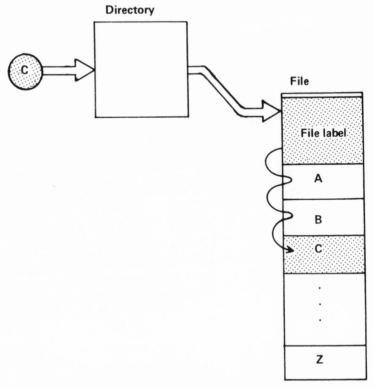

Fig. 4.2   Sequential (contiguous) file search to entry C.

PROBLEMS OF DESIGN. It should be obvious from Figs. 4.1 through 4.7 that there is a large number of distinct ways to organize data structures into entries belonging to any specified object (or object–property combination) or to any specific property. We shall see later that there are still more possible configurations. All these entry structures have distinct characteristics which make each of them suitable in certain situations of retrieval or processing and for a certain choice of hardware. To design an information system thus means to select for each file an entry structure that is efficient for the combination of all the data processing tasks involving the file and for the equipment to be selected for the whole system as well as for the individual files. In addition there is also the problem of selecting a good set of *retrieval mechanisms* or *directory structures* for the distinct files and processing tasks. Finally, the entry structures to be selected also have to be adapted to the structure of the storage units and the processors. For instance, the entry structures

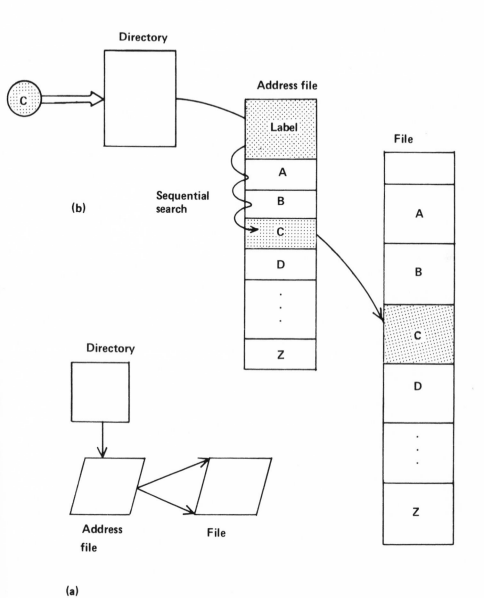

(a)

Fig. 4.3   Sequential file with sequentially searched address file.

141

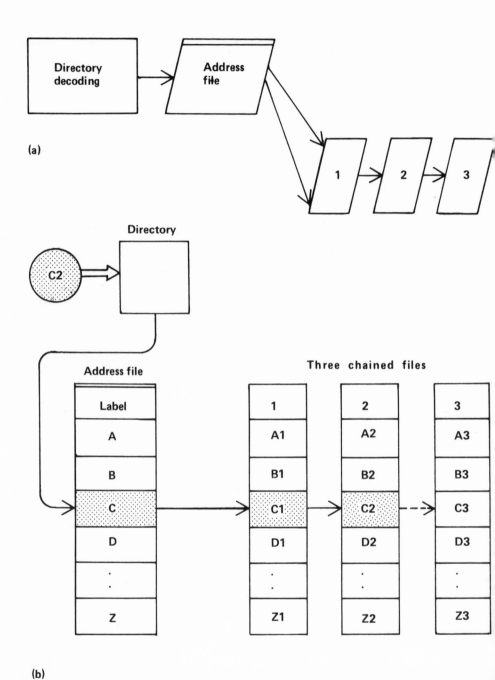

Fig. 4.4   Three chained sequential files with sequential address file (thus four chained files in total).

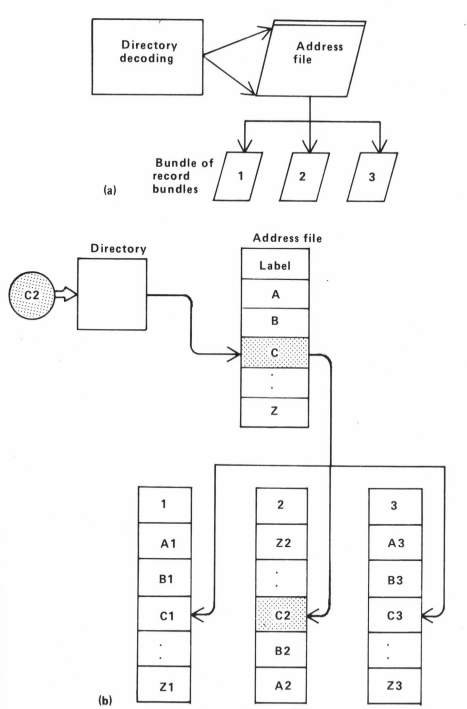

Fig. 4.5   Three bundled sequential files, of which one is sequenced in converse order, with sequential address file.

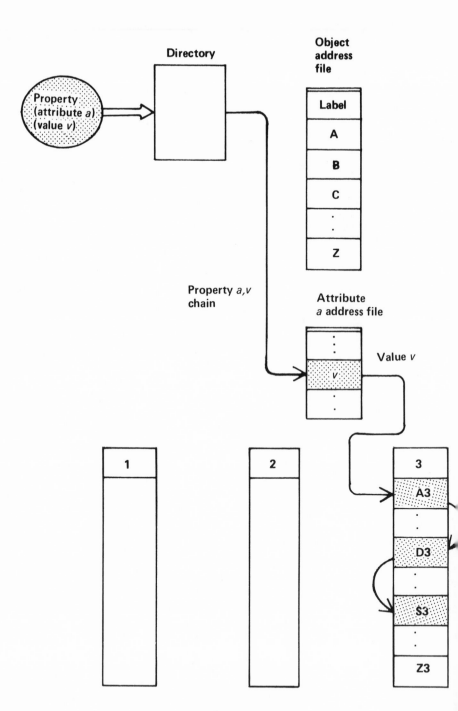

Fig. 4.6a

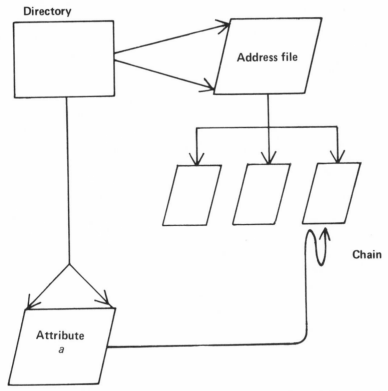

Fig. 4.6b   Simplified diagram of the type of structure of which Fig. 4.6a is an occurrence.

are to be adapted to the access blocks. It is not hard to see that the total design problem is an impossible one if we try to solve it piecemeal in connection with programming of the individual applications or processing "runs." Indeed, such a complicated design problem can only be handled in a reasonable way by using the basic principle of system design. Fortunately, it is possible to reach reasonable decisions on entry structures and file structures as well as directory structures against assumed *classes* of equipment (such as sequential storage, pseudo-direct-access structures of two to four different performance classes) while leaving details of the internal structures of the subentry records (bits and bytes) to be decided later when selection of actual equipment has been made. Thus we see that a stage of *architectural work* has to precede detailed *construction* such as selecting equipment, constructing data term structure, and doing programming. Two main areas of the architectural stage are *file structuring* (deciding on entry structures and relations between entries) and *directory structuring*.

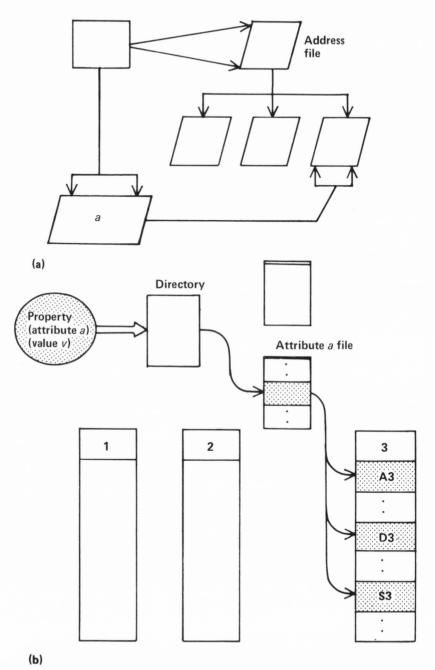

Fig. 4.7   Three bundled sequential files with sequential address file.

In Figs. 4.1 through 4.7 we have given illustrations of some possible (and fairly typical file structures) although the directory was always left as a "black box." We shall now proceed to illustrate some possible directory structures. In this way we obtain a broad idea of what is involved in structuring the whole system of *directory–file pairs*. It is, of course, likely that after studying possible selections of file and directory structures separately, we will have to study combinations of directories and file structures before final architectural evaluations and decisions are made on the directory–file structure.

The architectural stage, like all architecture, must also do a careful study to adapt the system to the needs of people and, indeed, to *design it* for the needs of people.

Survey of Kinds of File Entries

DEFINITION 1: An *object entry* is all data about a specific object o_i in which o is the class of objects and i is a member index in the class; thus o_i is a member of the class o.

DEFINITION 2: An *e entry* is the data of an e message; the data are about one property (the attribute–value pair) of one object at one time (interval) or about one relation between two or more objects.

DEFINITION 3: A *consolidated entry* (*c* entry) is all data about an "aspect of an object," which consists of a group of e entries that are consolidated or pseudo consolidated (all data about an object or instance of a *c* concept).

EXAMPLE 1:
  Object class: o
  Attributes of *c* concept: a,b,c,d,e
Thus the e concepts are (o,a), (o,b), (o,c), (o,d), and (o,e) or, for example, (o,e,o) if e is a relation.
  c concepts (assumed) : (o,a,b,c) and (o,d,e) or (o,d,e,o)
o_δ, is assumed to have been introduced as a name for the *c* concept (o,d,e).
An object entry o_i may have the form given in Fig. 4.8.
We assume here that the record o_δ is required to be retrievable directly by the name o_δ as well as by o_i.

DEFINITION 4: An *object set entry* is a set of object entries linked to a "set entry header" associated with a name given to the set entry.

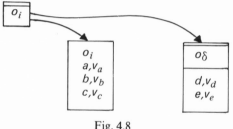

Fig. 4.8

EXAMPLE 2:

1. Set entry connecting all object entries having the property (a,v_a), for example, (weight = 130 pounds)
2. Set entry connecting all object entries having "Be" as the first part of their name. ("Be" is the name of the group.) This is a case in which the directory (decoding) is incomplete so that the entries in the set must be analyzed before a specific name is found (for instance, an entry named "Bertram").

Structure of Directories, an Overview

DIRECTORIES AND RETRIEVAL REQUESTS. Whatever file structure is selected by the designer, a directory* has to be provided to locate each file entry requested. A number of different directory structures are possible and most of them can be used in combination with most of the file structures. However, details of a directory of a certain kind of structure may be different depending on the file structure chosen.

There has to be a *central directory* (or "system directory") which directs each retrieval request to the appropriate *file directory*. For each file there has to be one or more different directories, depending on the kinds and frequencies of retrieval requests that are expected for the file. Each retrieval request must specify exactly which information is wanted; that is, each individual elementary entry to be retrieved must be specified. This can be done either by naming the file together with object name, attribute name, and time for each e entry, or it can be done by merely specifying each individual e entry. The first alternative requires the user to know what file each e entry belongs to and thus causes some

---

* Note that we are using the term "directory" in a very broad sense here in order to avoid having to mention many distinct terms such as address calculation algorithm, address file, and so on. They are all means for locating a file or a file entry.

difficulty for the user and leads to severe complications whenever the system has to be reorganized. It has the advantage, though, of calling for a slightly easier directory decoding.

The second alternative, easier for the user when forming enquiries or application programs, calls for a slightly more complex central directory in the system which directs enquiries to the directory of that file which contains the *e* entry requested for further directory decoding. Alternatively, the directory may just refer the enquiry to the entry of the object identified by it and then a search is made on the file entry to find the attribute looked for.

We may say that the two alternatives correspond to using enquiries that are either *file oriented* (in that they specify the appropriate file entry) or are *infologically oriented* in that they specify the elementary message to be obtained while ignoring the data design. We can also see immediately that the central directory must contain a file of data that informs us in which files the *e* entries are stored. How they are embedded in the file entries may be described in the file directories (or, possibly, in the file).

In Fig. 4.9 we have illustrated how the enquiry about an *e* message e_1 is presented to the central directory and is, by this directory, directed to the proper directory (assumed to be the directory A_b) for the file A. The directory A_b in its turn locates the entry A_i of file A, which contains the *e* entry associated with the *e* message e_1. In Fig 4.9 dotted lines indicate that the central directory "reaches" all file directories and that each directory associated with a file "reaches" all entries in that file.

TWO MAIN KINDS OF DIRECTORY. We use the term "directory" in a very general sense here: A directory (the central one or a file directory) is either a *computation algorithm* which transforms a "name" into a storage address or is an address file (or a set of such files). It will, typically, point to an area of storage that contains a group of entries of a file or of an address file associated with the file, rather than to a specific entry. Thus the directory decoding will often have to be followed by a search through a group of entries in an address file or a main file. Thus the use of a file directory can be seen as a means for reducing the work of searching the address file, which in turn is a means of reducing the file search.

It follows from what we have said that a directory could be an address file that points to areas in a main file or in its address file. Because such a directory file contains only descriptions of areas, each of which is associated with a file entry, it is smaller than the main file (or the address file of the main file), so search in it takes less work. This search can then be reduced still further by using a second-level directory file that points to areas in the first-level directory file. Directory

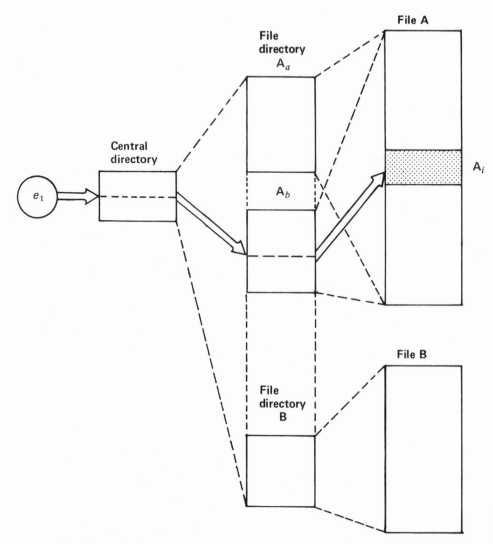

Fig. 4.9   Retrieval of entry A_i from file A as an answer to a request of e message $e1$. A_i is assumed to contain the e entry $[e1]$ representing $e1$; A_a and A_b are distinct directories for the file A.

150

decoding of a file directory would thus require search of the small second-level directory file and one area of the first-level directory file only.

Directory file search may be still more reduced by introducing more levels of directory files so that the file directory is seen to be a hierarchy of directory files. A further reduction of search time by means of a hierarchical structure is obtained by putting the upper-level files in faster memories before doing a decoding operation. With our general definition directory search may also be a combination of address computations and address file searches.

DIRECTORY HIERARCHY AND NAME HIERARCHY. The fact that efficiency of search often calls for organizing the directory as a hierarchy of address files has an important relation to the question of how to identify the objects in a system. Thus identification of objects and identification of data entries about the objects tend to have a similar structure for search efficiency reasons and for logical or conceptual reasons. This suggests that the designer will find it natural to consider handling these two problems in combination. Each entry in one hierarchical level of a directory file points to a number of entries of the file at next lower level, and each of these, in turn, points to several entries further down, and so on down to a number of file entries. Thus each entry on a high level commands a larger set of file entries than one on a lower level. Accordingly, there are fewer entries on a higher level in the directory. This is in accordance with properties of names or identifiers of objects and entries. Thus in order to be able to differentiate among many entries, the name must contain many characters. A fraction of the name, having a few symbols, may thus be sufficient to identify an entry of a directory file in a high level. As an extremely simple example we might consider a case in which the first letter in a name identifies the entries in the highest-level file of a directory. Another example identifies the request for retrieval of an *e* entry. To identify an *e* entry we will have to specify all its (conceptual) terms or, subject to suitable system design, all terms except one. The latter is fundamental to information retrieval from a data base (see also Structure of File Entries in Section 4.1).

Formal Definition of the File Concept

We hope that the preceding part of this chapter has given the reader an intuitive feeling for the file concept and the problems and possibilities in connection with directory–file structuring and design. In this section we shall take a slightly more formal attitude toward the issues under discussion. In practical design work it may not be necessary to know the formal definitions of concepts like "file" and "entry," although they may help to avoid confusion in the communication between different designers. On the other hand if practical file design work is going to improve, good file design theories are needed, and in the formation of such theories formally precise concepts cannot be dispensed with.

FILES, ENTRIES, TERM GROUPS, AND SEGMENTS.

DEFINITION 5: A *file* is a triple $<x, y, z>$ in which
1. x is a set of *entries*, each of which is an ordered set of (data) *terms* representing a message belonging to a particular message type, or i concept, and each of which is uniquely identified within the file by the data contents of a subset of its terms, called the *entry point* (term group), or the (primary) *key*, of the entry;
2. y is an *entry description* describing how the terms of the entries of the file should be rearranged in order to conform to the *normal format* for representing messages with file entries—the normal format is assumed to be common to all files belonging to the same file system or data base;
3. z is an *access algorithm*, which, given the data contents of a particular entry point, delivers for further processing the complete entry or any specified e entry, or set of e entries, identified by the particular entry-point value, and edited in accordance with the *normal format* mentioned in (b)—the access algorithm should also be able to retrieve, for successive processing, *all* the entries of a file, as the result of one request, in which the entry-point values of the file do not have to be explicitly given.

There is a representative relationship between the datalogical concepts "file," "entry," and "term," and the infological counterparts, which are "message type," or "i concept," "message," and "reference," respectively.

The entry description and the access algorithm of a file are parts of the *directory* of the file. However, the directory, as we have described it in previous sections, may also contain several other parts; parts that are shared by several files. The directory of a file may even contain parts that are themselves files in the same right as the (main) file. Such files, directory files, also contain entries representing messages belonging to a particular i concept; they have their own entry descriptions and access algorithms. Very often a set of directory files and a main file together form a particular kind of structure, a so-called $\alpha\beta$ complex. The design of $\alpha\beta$ complexes will be further discussed in Chapter 6.

The access algorithm of a file may be very sophisticated, with different subalgorithms corresponding to different search strategies to be used in different situations. In Definition 5 we stated as a minimum requirement that the algorithm should be *somehow* capable of retrieving any identified entry of the file as well as *all* the entries of the file. The former requirement may be thought to imply that the file has to be allocated to a direct-access memory. This is not true, however. An algorithm may consist of a lot of *steps*, and these steps may involve, for instance, a partial serial scan of a file. Naturally, much more *efficient* algorithms for retrieving single entries may be designed if it has been decided that the file will reside on a direct-access memory. Other operations, which the steps of the access algorithm of a file may involve, are table look ups and hashing, or scrambling, of identifiers.

DEFINITION 6: A *term group* is a subtuple of (not necessarily adjacent) terms of a file entry that together represent a conceptual reference (see Structure of File Entries in Section 4.1). The individual terms of a term group will usually represent sub-references of the reference represented by the term group as a whole.

EXAMPLE 3: Consider an entry
    1. $<t_1,t_2,t_3,t_4,t_5,t_6>$
where
        t_1 = CAR REG NO
        t_2 = ABC 123
        t_3 = COLOR
        t_4 = YELLOW
        t_5 = TIME
        t_6 = JAN 1970
The entry (1) is supposed to represent the information (*e* message) that a certain car has a certain color at a certain point of time. It is obviously practical to be able to talk about the term groups
    2. $<t_1, t_2>$ = the object term group
    3. $<t_3, t_4>$ = the property term group
    4. $<t_5, t_6>$ = the time term group
as entities in their own right.

EXAMPLE 4: The data representation of the Swedish civic registration number could be regarded as a term group

5. $<t_y, t_m, t_d, <t_x, t_s>, t_c>$

where

t_y = year of birth
t_m = month of birth
t_d = day of birth
$<t_x, t_s>$ = birth number
t_s = sex
t_c = check digit

DEFINITION 7: An *entry segment* is a subtuple of adjacent terms of a file entry. For each entry one or more segments should be defined in such a way that each term of the entry belongs to exactly one segment.

The segment concept will be needed in the file-structuring discussions to be carried out in Chapter 6. The idea is that entry segmentation* should be a prerequisite for mapping (allocating) different parts of one and the same entry into different storage blocks of a memory. Thus whereas the terms of a particular segment should be mapped into contiguous storage positions, different segments of an entry may be spread out all over a memory, or even over different memories. Naturally, however, the access algorithm of the file has to be able to retrieve all segments of all entries.

Term groups and entry segments are two different kinds of term structures. The term "group structure of an entry" is a reflection of the infological microstructure of a message. By grouping the terms of an entry the designer can make it easier for himself and others to survey the infological contents of the entry. When a designer proposes to split an entry into several segments, he should give datalogical, efficiency oriented reasons for this.

In Fig. 4.10 the diagram technique introduced by Bachman (1968) has been used to illustrate the relationship between the concepts defined in this section.

---

* Note that what is usually referred to as a "segmentation" of an entry (or "record") is, from a systematic construction point of view, a set of consolidations. Each segment consists of a set of *e* entries from *e* files that have been consolidated. The connecting of the segments to a file entry then corresponds to a "pseudo consolidation" of the set of consolidated files. See also Section 3.5.

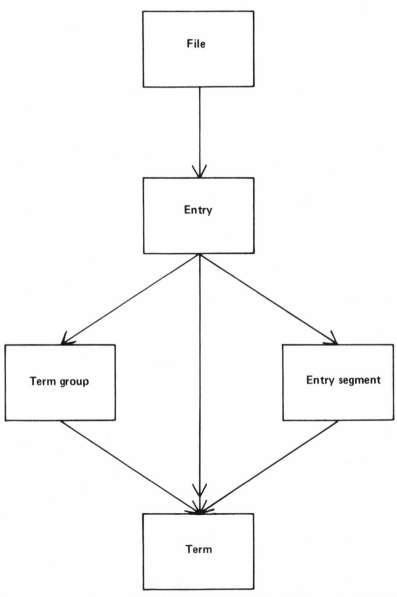

Fig. 4.10   "Bachman relationships" between concepts. Each arrow represents a relationship between two kinds of entities. The direction of an arrow represents the fact that an occurrence of one kind of entity consists of zero, one, or more occurrences of another kind of entity.

155

DIFFERENT KINDS OF FILES. We shall define three basic kinds of files—object files, property files, and relational files—each of them characterized by the kind of entity referred to by the entry points in the file.

DEFINITION 8: An *object file* is a file whose entry points refer to objects or $<$object, time$>$ pairs.

DEFINITION 9: A *property file* is a file whose entry points refer to properties or $<$property, time$>$ pairs.

DEFINITION 10: A *relational file* is a file whose entry points refer to tuples $<R, o_1, \ldots, o_n>$, or $<R, o_1, \ldots, o_n, t>$, where R is an n-ary object relation, $o_1, \ldots, o_n$ are objects, and t is a time.

Naturally, all three kinds of files are subject to the general file definition given in Definition 5. Thus any object, property, or relational file should be equipped with an entry description and an access algorithm fulfilling the requirements (b) and (c) stated in Definition 5. For *access algorithms of relational files* we state here the *additional requirement* that they should accept as input not only complete entry points,

$$<R, o_1, \ldots, o_n> \quad \text{or} \quad <R, o_1, \ldots, o_n, t>$$

but also *partial entry points* that result from suppressing at least one and at most n object references in a complete entry point. As output the access algorithm should deliver all entries in the relational file whose entry points coincide with the input entry point as to the components that are not suppressed in the latter.

As can be seen from the definitions we have left the door open for a time term to be part of the entry-point term group of the entries of all kinds of files. We have chosen to do so because it may sometimes be desirable to be able to establish files in which different time versions of the same message type occur in different entries of the same file. This issue will be further discussed in Chapter 6.

We have defined elementary messages (*e* messages) as the "atoms" of information. We have also defined basic classes of information, called *e* message types, or *e* concepts. The datalogical counterparts of *e* messages and *e* concepts will be called *e* entries and *e* files (see Structure of Directories in Section 4.1) respectively, and they are defined in the following way:

DEFINITION 11: An *elementary file entry*, or *e* entry, is a file entry representing an *e* message.

DEFINITION 12: An *elementary file*, or *e* file, is a file, each entry of which represents *e* messages belonging to one and the same *e* concept.

In view of our earlier discssion of three basic kinds of files, we also realize that there are three basic kinds of *e* files, namely, (a) elementary object files, or *object e-files*, (b) elementary property files, or *property e-files*, and (c) elementary relational files, or *relational e-files*.

The reader may have noticed that our definitions of *e* file and *e* entry do not logically imply that all entries of *e* files are *e* entries. As a matter of fact the entries of property *e* files will mostly be non-elementary, or consolidated, *c* entries. Consider, for example, the property *e* file representing the *e* concept $<$PERSON,AGE$>$. The entries of this property *e* file will have the structure

$$<\text{AGE}, a, o_1, \ldots, o_n, t>$$

where $<$AGE, $a>$ is the entry point, and where $o_1, \ldots, o_n$ refers to objects having the property AGE $= a$ at time t. Obviously this entry represents a message that is a consolidation of n elementary messages

$$<o_i, \text{AGE} = a, t>, \qquad i = 1, \ldots, n$$

In an object *e* file each of these *e* messages would have been represented by a separate *e* entry, each of them identified by a unique object reference, but in a property *e* file this cannot be done because of the requirement stated in Definition 5 that each entry point should uniquely identify one entry. Sometimes even object *e* files may contain *c* entries. Suppose, for example, that we choose to represent the relational *e* concept

$<$BROTHER, PERSON, MALE PERSON$>$

by an object *e* file. This file would then have the following structure with entry points underlined:

$<$<u>PERSON, JOHN</u>$>$, $<$MALE PERSON, SAM$>$, t;
$<$MALE PERSON, AL$>$, t;
$<$<u>PERSON, ED</u>$>$, $<$MALE PERSON, DAN$>$, t;

<PERSON, EVE>,   <MALE PERSON, DAVE>, t;
                 <MALE PERSON, TOM>, t;

.
.
.

Note that the corresponding set of e entries

<PERSON, JOHN>, MALE PERSON, SAM>, t;
<PERSON, JOHN>, MALE PERSON, AL>, t;
<PERSON, ED>,   MALE PERSON, DAN>, t;
<PERSON, EVE>,   MALE PERSON, DAVE>, t;
<PERSON, EVE>,   MALE PERSON, TOM>, t;

.
.
.

is not a feasible file, because the entry points do not uniquely identify their entries. We shall sometimes use the term *quasifile* for a set of entries with nonunique entry points.

4.2   INTRODUCTION TO FILE STRUCTURING

Examples of e-File Structures: Sequential Files

The traditional file structure is the *sequential file*. This design was strongly influenced by the use of types of file storage (magnetic tapes, punched tapes, punched cards) that favored sequential handling of data in the files. A sequential file is assumed to be stored in a set of *storage blocks* or *access blocks*: areas of storage handled as units so far as data access and transfer is concerned. The file itself is a set of data entries, one entry for each object or concept. The data terms of an entry are stored in a contiguous arrangement and such entries are called *records*. The records are ordered sequentially according to the value of a specific term or term group in the record. This term (group) is the *key* or the *name* of the record and is usually likewise the *name* of the object that the record informs about. Usually the size of each record is smaller than a block, so that a number b of records is stored in the same block. We may then say that the *blocking factor* is equal to b. (It may also happen, in some systems, that records are larger than blocks so that a record is stored in more than one block.)

Notice that we have described two logically distinct objects: (a) the unallocated file, a set of data entries, and (b) the set of storage block areas into which the file entries are mapped when the file is allocated. (See also Chapter 6.)

Scattered Records File

Sometimes it is more practical to allow the file entries to be stored as records that are scattered around the file storage or sequenced in varying ways so that the records of a file can occur in distinct blocks in a more or less random way. A block may then contain records from the same file, in random order, or records from distinct files. This arrangement is possible when records can be retrieved by their block address.

One reason for using scattered record files is, for instance, to place the records in blocks, the addresses of which are computed by some algorithm, such as a randomization (or "hash coding") procedure. Another reason may be to store records wherever free space is available. In Figs. 4.5 and 4.6 we assume that it is also necessary (which may or may not be true) to store in each record the terms (object class, attribute) that identify the *e* concept, which was not necessary in the sequential file of Figs. 4.11 and 4.12. We may omit this by introducing some other means to link together the records belonging to the same file. Then, however, these links require link data (or reference data) to establish them. These data will either have to be stored in the records or in a special directory file associated with the *e* file.

The scattering of the records makes it necessary to have some mechanism (retrieval mechanism) that makes it possible to locate each individual record. Two basic ways of linking the records of the file together, as well as linking them to the file name, are possible. These are the bundle arrangement and the chain arrangement.

THE FILE AS A BUNDLE OF RECORDS. In *bundle arrangement* there is a file directory that contains location data which form links to all records of the file. These links are *address links*, or perhaps *name links*, giving the block address of each record or its name.

The entry shown in Fig. 4.18(a) contains some redundant terms because the term "identifier 3", $<$object class$>$, and $<$attribute$>$ of the main file entry were also necessary to have in the directory. A nonredundant entry is shown in Fig. 4.18(b). It indicates how some file data can be left out from the main file because that information is provided by the directory. This makes it more natural to regard the directory–file. In Fig. 4.18(b) we assumed it necessary or advisable to have a "return link" from the property subentry back to the directory or index subentry (which was located at "ind 3").

$$e_1: \quad p, a_1, v_1, t$$

$$e_2: \quad p, a_2, v_2, t$$

.
.
.

$$e_n: \quad p, a_n, v_n, t$$

(a)

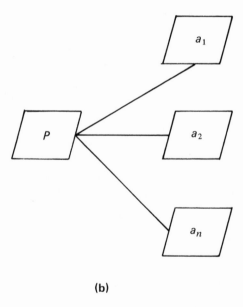

(b)

Fig. 4.11   (a) e files in which p is object class, a is attribute, v is value, and t is time. (b) Bundle of e files about object class p.

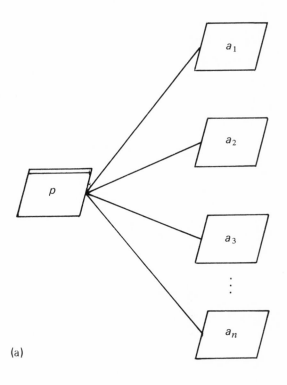

(a)

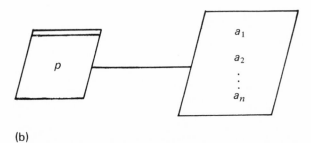

(b)

Fig. 4.12   (a) Bundle of e files (p, ai) accessible by p (identifier) that is, for individual p objects (the e files are pseudo consolidated for p; $a2$ is also directly accessible). (b) e files $[p,a1, \ldots p,an]$ consolidated to $[p,a1, \ldots ,an]$).

161

e File

File head ($<$ object class $>$ $<$ attribute $>$)

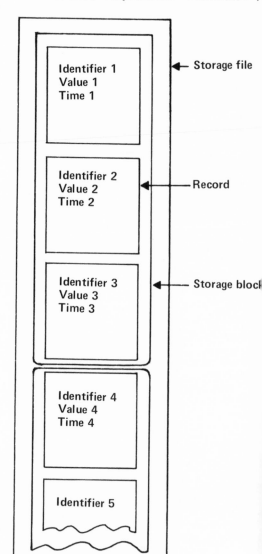

Storage file

Record

Storage block

Full entry for object
($<$ object class $>$ identifier
3) in this file:

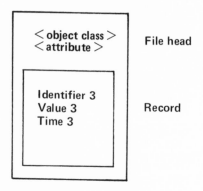

Fig. 4.13

162

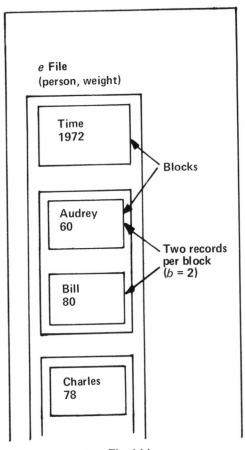

Fig. 4.14

Notice that the terms <object class>, <attribute> and identifier (id.) 3 in the property subentry of Fig. 4.18(a) together form a name link back to the directory subentry and thus form the counterpart to "address" "ind3" "in Fig. 4.18(b).

THE FILE AS A CHAIN OF RECORDS. In a *chain arrangement* the file directory contains a name or address link to one record of the file, and each record contains one (at least) data term that is a link (name or address) to the successor record.

It is obvious that the chain arrangement imposes "sequential properties" on the stored file. The arrangement of file records in a chain makes the records a sequential file with possibly scattered records. As

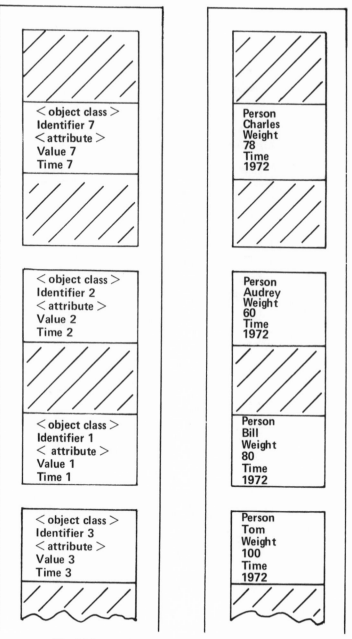

Fig. 4.15

Fig. 4.16

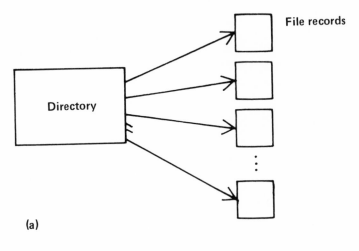

(a)

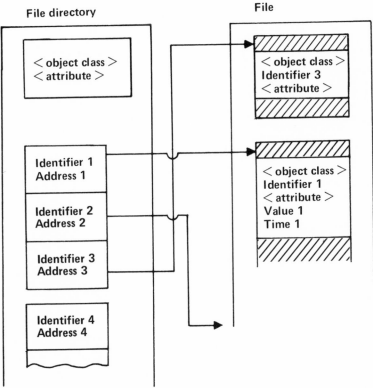

(b)

Fig. 4.17   Bundle arrangement. (a) Records form a bundle rooted by the
directory. (b) The directory file may, alternately, be regarded as
one file, the entries of which are record pairs.

165

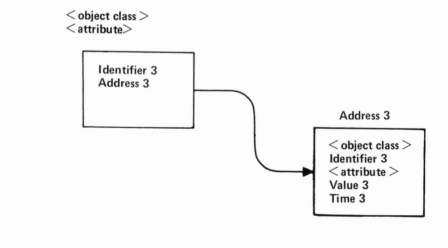

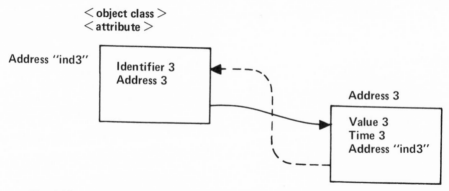

Fig. 4.18   (a) Entry 3 in a file consisting of a directory file and a main file.
             (b) Nonredundant entry.

block accesses will usually be required for each new record, even in serial processing, such a file will be much slower than one with a contiguous, sequential arrangement. It will, however, allow for a much easier insertion of new records than will a contiguous, sequential file. For this reason we may also use partially chained records, in an otherwise contiguous, sequential file as a result of insertions and, maybe, even deletions.

Scattered-Entries *e* File

It may be the case that the *e* entries are not stored as scattered, contiguous records, but their distinct terms are scattered (although this does not seem very likely). The entries themselves can thus, exactly as the files, have three basic kinds of arrangements: contiguous (record form), bundle, and chain. As an illustration we show in Fig. 4.19 the entry (person,Charles,weight,78, ...) in one possible chain form.

Transposition (or Inversion) of *e* Files

An *e* message of the *e* concept (person, age) will usually be regarded as *information about* the *identified person at the specified time*, telling the value of his age. This is to say that it will provide the answer to the question indicated by the question mark in

(person,person identification,age,?,time,value of time)

The information system may be assumed, for instance, as being able to interpret this question by regarding the underlined words (or words marked in some other way) as identifying the *e* file and then to retrieve the set of all entries in this *e* file having the specified value of "person identification"; whereupon it would select, out of this set, that entry which has the specified value of time. We may say that we have assumed a retrieval by name of an entry for which (person, age, person identifier, "time," value of time) is used as the *name* or *retrieval key*. We may also say that "person identifier" (plus time identifier if distinct time versions of entries are taken into the same file) is used as the entry name within the *e* file named [person,age].

> EXERCISE 1: Describe two different formats for putting questions to an information system. The identification of the file should be by other means than underlining some words. We make this explicit by referring to this *e* file as [person, age]$_{person}$ identification.

The *e* message of the *e* concept (person, age) can, however, be regarded alternatively as giving other information such as, for instance, *information about the specified age of a person*—telling who among the persons having this age, at the specified time, is the one associated with the "person identification value." Thus we are now letting the specified age be the object informed about.

When so regarded the single *e* message would only provide part of the answer to the question about which persons have the specified age at the specified time: (person,?, age,value of age,time,value of time). The full answer to this question requires retrieval of all those entries in the *e* file [person, age] that contain the specified values of age and time. Notice that this time the retrieval-by-name function of the system (as assumed

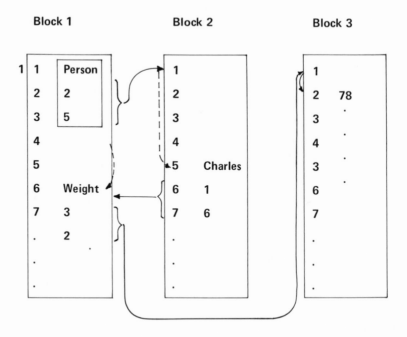

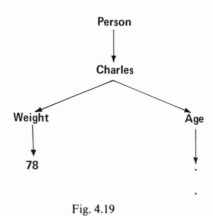

Fig. 4.19

above) would only be able to identify the *e* file; it would not now be provided with the names of the entries containing the answer. Thus if no further devices are introduced, it would be necessary to scan the entire *e* file while testing each entry for its values of age and time. The *retrieval by property* which is thus now required (looking for entries with the specified age property) is seen to be more complicated.

It should be noticed that there was a special reason, which we introduced ourselves, why the retrieval by property (the age property in our illustration) was more complicated. The reason was, simply, that we assumed the *e* file [person,age] to be organized in such a way as to have "person identification" as the retrieval name (or key). Thus we assumed that all entries of the file having the same person identification belonged to the same set of data within the *e* file. Of course, we may instead decide to organize the file associated with the *e* concept (person,age) to have "value of age," rather than "person identification," as its name for retrieval. We would thus have the *e* file [age, person] if we are still assuming values or identifiers associated with the first term in the file definition bracket (here [age,person]) to be used as entry names for retrieval. We may, of course, even decide to have both kinds of file organization for the *e* concept (person,age), but then we must have two *e* files—[person,age] and [age,person]—associated with the *e* concept (person,age). We may now also consider this as representing two distinct, though closely related, *e* concepts: (person,age) informing about persons their age and (age,person) informing about age those persons who have it.

The files [person,age] and [age,person] are distinct files, but they contain the same data terms and may be regarded as file instances of the same *e* concept (person,age). We may say that one of the files is obtained through a *transposition* (or *file inversion*) of the other:

$$\text{transpose [person,age]} = \text{[age,person]}$$

and

$$\text{transpose [age,person]} = \text{[person,age]}$$

or, regarding both *e* concepts and their file instances, transpose (person,age) = (age,person). In view of the formal definitions in Section 4.1, we realize that object files and property files are each other's transpositions, or inversions. For example, [person,age] is an object file, and [age,person] is the corresponding property file.

EXERCISE 1: Discuss the relation between our transposition of *e* files and the transposition of a matrix.

EXERCISE 2: How is concept transposition related to the pairs,
precedents/succedents
components/assembly, ("consists of"/"goes into")
father/son
flows/potentials in a system

As we have seen, transposition is a change in the organization of a
file which makes another term (or term group) in the file entries (or
records) act as the retrieval name (or key) in the retrieval-by-name
operation. Transposition may be obtained by rearranging the entries in
the file (resorting the file) or by changing the retrieval-by-name
mechanism. (This shows that the arrangement of the entries in a file and
the design of the retrieval mechanism both belong to the file organization.) Transposition makes a retrieval by a property available as one of
the system's retrieval-by-name functions. Of course, we will often want
to be able to retrieve file entries by the object name or, alternately, by a
property. As transposition is a complicated operation we will therefore
have to decide whether or not to have different transposed versions of a
file stored simultaneously in the information system. This will be one of
the major considerations of the file system design (see Chapter 6).

Retrieval Mechanism for an *e* File

To retrieve a specific *e* entry from a specific *e* file we need first to get
at the appropriate directory for the *e* file. The directory is identified by
the *e* concept (object class, attribute), for instance, (person,age) together

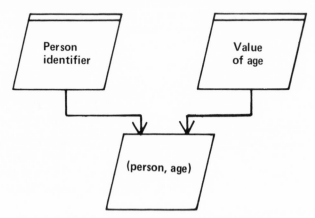

Fig. 4.20   Two transposed directory–file pairs corresponding to *e* concept
(person, age) and its transpose (age, person). One main file and two
directories.

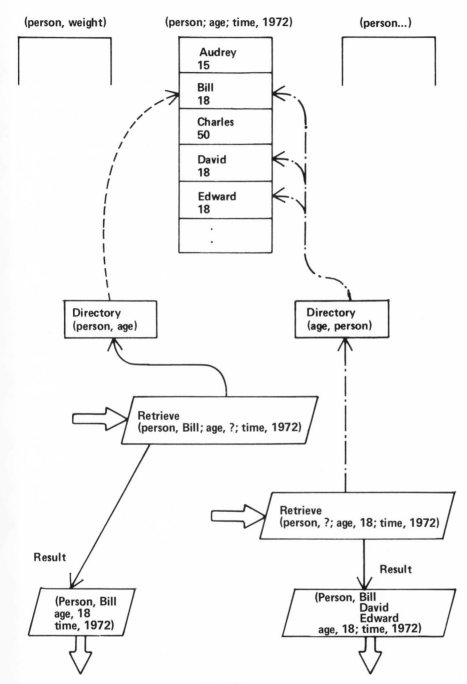

(person, weight) (person; age; time, 1972) (person...)

| Audrey 15 |
| Bill 18 |
| Charles 50 |
| David 18 |
| Edward 18 |
| . |

Directory (person, age)

Directory (age, person)

Retrieve
(person, Bill; age, ?; time, 1972)

Retrieve
(person, ?; age, 18; time, 1972)

Result

(Person, Bill
age, 18
time, 1972)

Result

(Person, Bill
David
Edward
age, 18; time, 1972)

Fig. 4.21

171

with the retrieval name to be used such as the object identifier or the value associated with the attribute such as "person identifier." Thus if the question is

(person,Bill,age,?,time 1972)

the underlined words may inform the system that the concept is (person,age) and that we want its time version, 1972. Further, as the person identifier is given in the question (Bill), the system also "knows" that it is the directory (person,age,time,1972) organized so as to have "person" identifier as the retrieval key that is to be used. We see that the retrieval operation, called for by the question, requires one first step which retrieves the directory of the proper directory–file pair. It is natural to assume that the system has a *central retrieval directory* which is a table containing all directory–file pairs existing in the system. It may be convenient to call any directory of a directory–file pair a *file directory*. Thus to answer a question the system finds from the question the proper directory–file pair identification, then searches the *central directory* to find the proper file directory and uses that directory to locate the proper entry of that file (or set of entries).

Consolidation of Sequential *e* Files

The elementary concepts (*e* concepts) to be represented by data stored in the system are determined by the tasks the system has to do. The designer then has to decide for each *e* concept whether it is to be represented as an object file (that is, in a retrieval-by-object-name form) or as a property file (that is, a retrieval-by-property form) or both. He also has to decide on which form of directory–file pair arrangement to use. Thus even at this early stage we encounter quite a few problems for the file system designer. There are many more problems to be tackled. We turn to one of them now: the problem of how to consolidate the *e* files into consolidated files or *c* files (see also Chapter 3).

Each *e* concept has to do with one class of objects. For each class of objects, such as "persons," there will usually be many distinct *e* concepts and corresponding *e* files. Thus if there are 20 distinct object classes and, on the average, 20 distinct attributes for each object class and if each *e* file would occur in both transposed versions ("object entries" and "property entries" in the file, respectively), then the central directory would have to inform about 800 *e* file versions. This is a lot, although not very hard, for a computerized system. However, if each *e* file version was stored on a separate file storage system, there would have to be 800 file stations. This is far above what would be reasonable if the file stations

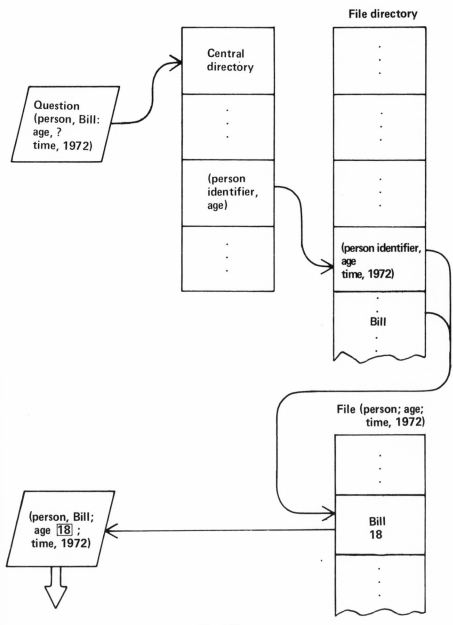

Fig. 4.22

173

were magnetic tape stations. Even if many tape files were stored on shelves, there still might be far too many tape stations required.

If the file storage system were instead a set of disks, the required number of 800 stations might not be prohibitive (they may be, for example, 800 cylinders) but there would still be some disadvantages in having each *e* file separately stored. The answer to this problem is to bring together several *e* files concerned with the same object class to form one consolidated file or *c* file. We have here another problem for the file designer: which *e* files to consolidate. To handle this design problem the designer needs to be familiar with different ways of consolidating files and the effects of each on the performance of the file system and on the entire information system.

One rather extreme way of consolidation is to consolidate all *e* files belonging to an object class into one single "object-class file" (or "object file"). For instance, we might have one single "person" file containing all *e* files giving different properties of persons.

A very extreme consolidation is obtained if we do not distinguish between distinct object classes but consider only "objects," regardless of their kind. We would then need only one single *"total" object* file for the object-identifier arrangement (that is, arranged for retrieval-by-object name). We would, however, still need one transposed file version for each property to which a retrieval-by-property arrangement is required. However, all these transposed versions can also be consolidated into one single, large, consolidated *"total attribute file"* by regarding each individual attribute (that is, each individual property class) as a member of one universal attribute class (class of property classes). Of course, a still more consolidated arrangement is conceivable: that of having the whole data base as one single file in which object names and property names both work as retrieval names.

Having talked very broadly about consolidation of files, we need to look at some concrete illustrations before we proceed with the theoretical discussion. To illustrate distinct ways of consolidating files, we shall need to consider distinct ways of designing directory–file pairs. It is natural to start with the traditional file design of sequential files as it was for those, being the traditional ones, for which concepts such as "file" and "consolidation" were originally defined. We then further study other types of file design and see how the concepts of "file" and "consolidation" had to be modified to cover these files. We finally encounter, of course, the question as to whether the old concepts are at all useful in the new, more general environment.

Suppose we have a set of *n* distinct sequential *e* files $(o,a_j, j = 1,2, \ldots ,n)$ all of which are associated with the same object class $[o]$. Suppose further, for the sake of illustration, that the *e* files are arranged to have their entries (records in this case as the files are contiguous, sequential) named by the object identifier. Thus if *o* denotes the object class and *i* denotes the identifier of the object *i* in the class [*o*], we may use $(o,a)_i$ to denote the *i* *i*th entry in the *e* file [*o,a*] corresponding to the *e* concept (o,a) associated with the attribute *a* and the class of objects *o*.

FILE CONSOLIDATION BY RECORD COLLECTION. If we want to take the *n* files $oa_1, oa_2, \ldots, oa_n$ together into one, consolidated file, which is still arranged for retrieval-by-object name, it is natural to do this by collecting all entries, from all *n e* files, which have the same identifier o_i (or *i*) to be stored together contiguously. We then may say that we have consolidated the *e* files by record collection or that we have a *file consolidation by record collection*.

$$a_{ij}:: = \text{value of } a, \text{ for object } o_j$$
$$i\epsilon \qquad 1,2,3, \ldots$$

$\text{file}(oa_1) = (oa_1)\{(1,a_{11})(2,a_{12})(3,a_{13}) \ldots \}$
$\text{file}(oa_2) = (oa_2)\{(1,a_{21})(2,a_{22})(3,a_{23}) \ldots \}$

.

.

.

$\text{file}(oa_n) = (oa_n)\{(1,a_{n1})(2,a_{n2})(3,a_{n3}) \ldots \}$
$\text{file}(o_{a1} \cup oa_2 \cup oa_3 \cup \ldots oa_n) = (0,a_n)\{(1,a_{11})(1,a_{21}) \ldots$
$(1,a_{n1})(2,a_{12})(2,a_{22}) \ldots (2,an_2) \ldots \}$
record collection

where oa_n is arbitrarily chosen as the name of the consolidated file; (oa_n) to the right of the equals sign symbolizes a "file label."

Notice that in $(1,a_{11})(1,a_{21})$ and so on, for instance, a_{11} and a_{12} are values and do not inform about which attribute they belong to. Therefore *either* the records must also contain the attribute names $(1,a_1,a_{11})(1,a_2,a_{21})$ *or* there must be a description of the meaning of the records in the record collection.

EXAMPLE 2:
  file(person,weight) = (person,weight){(Audrey,60)(Bill,80)
                                                  (Charles,78) ... }
  file(person,sex) = (person,sex){(Audrey,female)(Bill,male)
                                              (Charles,male) ... }
After consolidation by record collection:

file(person-weight ∪ person-sex) = (person,ws){(Audrey,60)
record collection   (Audrey,female)
        (Bill,80)(Bill,male)
        (Charles 78)
        (Charles,male) ... }

Notice that in this example to know, for instance, what 60 in (Audrey,60) means, we must go to the definition of the file:

file(person-weight ∪ person-sex)

presented in the left-hand side of the file expression. The system thus must contain information that is equivalent to this. Alternatively, each record must also contain the attribute name:

file(person-weight ∪ person-sex) = (person,ws){(Audrey,weight,60)
record collection   (Audrey,sex,female)
        (Bill,weight,80)
        (Bill,sex,male)
        (Charles,sex,male) ... }

In this case when each record contains the appropriate attribute name (the records are then often called "self-describing records"), it is not necessary to have records for all attributes of all objects. We have illustrated this by assuming no record to be present for attribute "weight" of Charles.

As the advantage sought by using consolidation by record collection is greater flexibility, which requires the form in which attribute names are stored in the records, this form must be regarded as the normal one of record collection files.

EXERCISE 3: What would correspond in COBOL to a file with record collections?

EXERCISE 4: Why would we choose to have a COBOL file using record collection?

FILE CONSOLIDATION BY RECORD CONSOLIDATION. In a file consolidated by record collection the record identifier has to occur in each record. Thus some data space is saved if the records in each collection are consolidated into one single record, as we would then have only one occurrence of the record identifier rather than n occurrences. In the examples above we would then have file($oa_1 \cup a_2 \cup a_3 \cup \ldots a_n$) = ($oa_N$){ ↑

$(1,a_{11},a_{21}, \ldots a_{n1})(2,a_{12},a_{22}, \ldots a_{n2}) \ldots$
$(n,a_{,ni} \ldots)$}

record consolidation

and

file(person-weight $\cup$ sex) = (person,ws){ ↑

(Audrey,60,female)(Bill,80,male)
(Charles,-,male) … }

record consolidation

In these illustrations we have assumed fixed-record formats (which are fairly common with consolidated records). Therefore the fact that we assumed no information to exist about weight of Charles had to be taken care of by inserting a symbol to indicate this in the position of the record where the value of the weight of Charles would have been placed.

EXERCISE 5: Work out the form of the file

[person-weight $\cup$ sex]

consolidated by record collection, using self-describing records (attribute names stored in the records).

4.3 RETRIEVAL AND UPDATING IN DIFFERENT KINDS OF FILES

Sequential Files

RETRIEVAL FROM A SEQUENTIAL FILE STORED IN SERIAL-ACCESS STORAGE. Retrieval from a sequential file in a serial-access store (such as a tape system) is by reading sequentially all records until a match is found, or it is clear that a matching record does not exist, between the name of the record (the key) and the name specified in the enquiry presented by the person or the computer program asking for information from the file. The retrieval-by-name mechanism in this case consists of the central directory, which specifies the location of the file—for instance, the disk track of the first record or the tape reel—and a procedure for reading sequentially the record names. Thus in this case we may regard the file label, usually occurring as the first record, as a very simple directory. It can be used in the retrieval mechanism for verification that the correct file is processed and, for instance, to inform about the size of the file. Also the record description (or descriptions) of the file could be regarded as belonging to the file directory.

To retrieve a single record we may have to scan the entire file. On the average we have to scan half of the file if each record has equal probability of being requested.

EXERCISE 1: It is often the case that some records are requested much more often than others. What would be the average proportion of the file scanned per single enquiry if the retrieval frequency of the records can be described by the 80 to 20 percent rule; that is 20 percent of the records are to be retrieved 80 percent of the time, and 80 percent of the records are to be retrieved 20 percent of the time? It is assumed that the records of the file are arranged into two subfiles which are stored one after the other on the file medium so as to minimize retrieval time.

Concatenated files, chopped files. When distinct files are stored on the same file storage unit, one after the other, we may say that we have the files *concatenated.* The reverse operation to concatenation might be called *chopping.* Chopping subdivides the file into two or more parts, each containing a subset of the set of entries in the file. (In contrast "file splitting" is reverse to file consolidation.) If n records are to be retrieved in the same operation, then on the average $1/n$th of the file will have to be scanned per retrieved record, assuming equiprobable record retrieval.

Often batch processing, or batch enquiry, is used to reduce the retrieval work per retrieved record. It may also happen that n records are retrieved for one single enquiry, for instance, and then, of course, again $1/n$th of the file is scanned per retrieved record. This saving is thus not because there is a batch of transactions but because there is a number of file records to be retrieved.

RETRIEVAL FROM A SEQUENTIAL FILE IN A (PSEUDO-)DIRECT-ACCESS STORAGE. If the sequential file is stored in a direct-access store or a pseudo-direct-access store (disk, for instance) retrieval can still be made by sequential reading of the file record names. Now, however, it is also possible to reduce the amount of file scanning by some sort of *interpolation.* We can then determine the distance of the name of the record asked for from the first record in the file, and the distance between the first and the last records. Based on a comparison of these two distances a location within the file is determined that would be suitable to use for starting the search. Based on the value of the identifier of the record at the location determined in the first step, a new interpolation operation can be performed or a serial search can be done.

In some situations binary search may be a good alternative to interpolation. This topic will be further discussed in Chapter 6.

UPDATING OF SEQUENTIAL FILE. Updating may only require the change of some data terms in some records. The file handling then required is the retrieval of the records concerned and the rewriting of them after they have been changed. Most sequential file systems of the magnetic tape variety do not allow writing in the middle of a file. For such systems the entire file is always rewritten after updating. Thus two versions of the same file are always scanned during updating (or changing) some records in this kind of system.

Updating may also require the insertion or deletion of records. *Deletion* may be done by actual deletion or by writing some kind of blank symbol into a record. *Insertion*, instead, always requires that all records, subsequent to the inserted one, be moved away to leave space if the file is still to remain a sequential one. If the file is on a magnetic tape system, which requires rewriting of the file, then the moving of records does not call for any extra data transport. If the sequential file is stored on equipment that allows writing into any block in the file (which is typical of disk storages and is available in a few magnetic tape systems), this facility cannot be made use of and part of the file must be moved if the file is to remain a sequential one. Thus in this system insertion may cause much more data transport than record changes or deletions. For this reason we may use instead a sort of *semisequential* file in which most records are stored in sequence but inserted records are stored in specific spillover areas. We will have to reorganize the file by moving records into sequence if too many records are in the spillover areas. In this type of file (semisequential file) a record to be inserted is stored in a spillover area and a pointer or *link* to this area is inserted at the place where the record should have been inserted.

Files with Record-Bundle Arrangement

RETRIEVAL BY NAME IN A FILE WITH RECORD-BUNDLE ARRANGE-MENT. In a file with a *record-bundle arrangement* the directory–file pair forms a bundle in the sense that the directory is connected to each of the file records by a retrieval-by-name mechanism. When provided with the name (key) of a record, the directory determines the address of the record (Fig 4.23).

The directory of a record-bundle file can be an address computation algorithm or it can be an *address table* or, more precisely, a *name/*

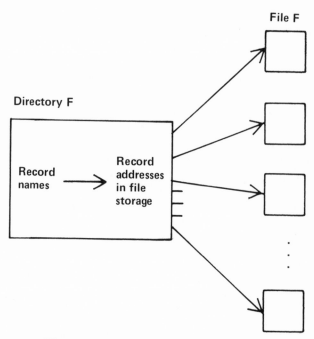

Fig. 4.23   Bundle of directory–file pair F.

record–address table (together with a table search algorithm). The address computation design leaves little control to the designer of where each individual file record is placed. The records have to be placed at the location of their computed address which usually is random within a specified area of storage (computation by *randomization* or *hash coding*). In this case there thus must be a scattered record arrangement of the file. The address-table type of directory gives the designer full control of where to place each individual record of the file. He may thus place the records in sequence of their record name values, in which case he will talk of an *indexed-sequential file*—more accurately, an *indexed-sequential directory (file pair)*.

It is also possible to obtain control of the placement of records in computed address design by inserting an *address file* between the computation algorithm and the file (Fig. 4.24). This means that the file directory is of the address-table type in which the table search algorithm has been replaced by an address computation algorithm which computes the address in the address table that corresponds to the name specified by the retrieval request. We may say that we have *indirect address computation* when an intervening address table is used and that otherwise

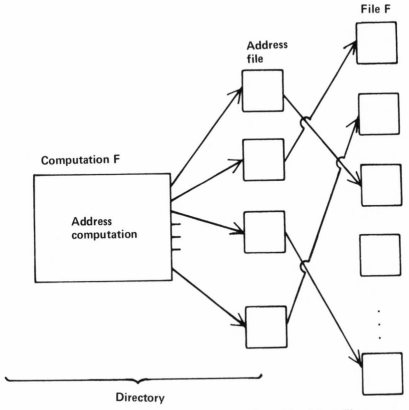

Fig. 4.24   Name to address computation with address file.

we have a *direct* address computation. Obviously, the address table is itself a file with as many entries as there are records in the file. Thus to perform a retrieval by name from the file by using a retrieval mechanism with an address table requires, as a first step, the retrieval of the entry with the specified name from the address table. This retrieval will be by search or address computation. For this to be better than retrieving by search in the file proper, the address table must be sufficiently smaller than the file. This will be the case only if the file is consolidated from a sufficiently high number of e files. However, retrieval by address computation may be faster for any kind of file, even for an e file. In Fig. 4.25 an illustration of a directory–file pair in record bundle form (*indexed file*) is shown. Figures 4.26(a) and 4.26(b) illustrate a directory–file pair of bundle form, in which the file is sequential (indexed sequential file).

Notice that in a directory–file pair in which the directory is an address table there are two records for each name, one of which is in the address table (or address file) and the other of which is in the main file. For instance, to the name o_3 correspond

$$(o_3, \text{adr } 3) \quad \text{and} \quad (3, a_{13}, a_{23}, \ldots a_{n3})$$

Thus in this case the directory–file pair consists of a set of record pairs or segment pairs. The record pair associated with a name o_i is thus the entry for o_i in the directory–file pair. This entry is a bundle, or chain, of two subentries, each of which is, in this case, a contiguous record.

RETRIEVAL BY PROPERTY IN A FILE WITH RECORD-BUNDLE FORM; ATTRIBUTE DIRECTORIES. In retrieval by property we ask for all records of a file that have a specified property, that is, a certain value for a certain attribute. For instance, to ask for all records of file oa_n which have the property (attribute, a_i; value, a_{ij}) is to request a retrieval-by-property operation. The result is to be a retrieval of all records in the file that have the property (a_i, a_{ij}). Obviously, the directory that determines the record address corresponding to each object name is of no help here. We would need to scan the whole file to do a retrieval-by-property operation. However, it is easy to see that a directory of the name-to-address type can also be introduced such that it enables property-to-address mapping. Thus in a directory for retrieval by property there will be an entry for each property (or attribute–value pair) exactly as there is one entry for each object name in the name-to-address directory. The entry will, however, generally contain several addresses, as there may be several records in the file that contain the specified property. (That there is usually only one address per object name in a name directory is because we usually, but not necessarily always, assume the name to be unique as a record name, or a record collecting name, in a file.)

The distinct properties will belong to distinct property classes, one for each attribute. Thus for each attribute represented in a file, we may have one directory. We may thus talk of attribute directories, in which each attribute directory is part of the retrieval-by-property mechanism that retrieves according to properties defined by distinct values for this attribute.

As an illustration we assume that in the file oa_N the records o_2 and o_3, and no others, have value p for attribute a_2 (Fig. 4.28).

The entry corresponding to a specific property in the pair (attribute directory a_2, file oa_N) is seen to be a bundle of subentries (segments in this case). For instance, the bundle shown in Fig. 4.29 corresponds to the property $(a_2 = p)$ in Fig. 4.28.

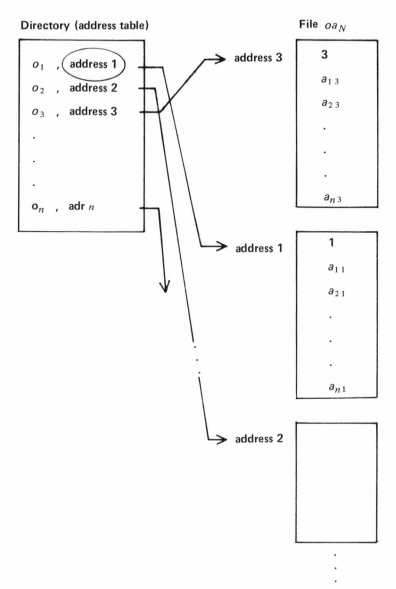

Fig. 4.25   Directory–file pair in record bundle form (nonsequential). A directory of address table kind, that is, indexed file.

183

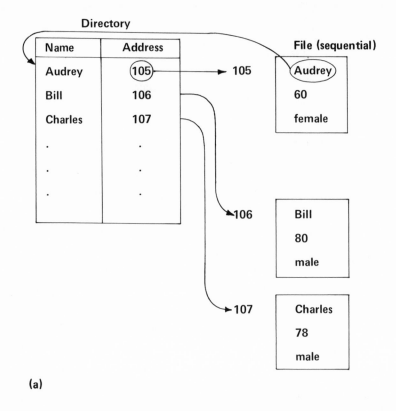

(a)

Fig. 4.26   (a) Directory–file pair in record bundle form (sequential). An indexed sequential file for (person $\cup$ weight $\cup$ sex). (b) Another form of indexed sequential file for (person $\cup$ weight $\cup$ sex). Names in file records replaced by address-to-name position in directory.

It appears now that there is some slight formal difference between retrieval by name and retrieval by property even when the latter is supported by a directory as well. Thus retrieval by name basically selects one file record, whereas retrieval by property selects a bundle of whole file records so that the latter appear as subentries in retrieval by property. Another, and more significant, difference is that the attribute directory cannot be a direct address computation (it may be an indirect one, using an intervening address file), at least not if the object directory of the same file is a direct address computation. Also in the attribute directory, name links may be used instead of address links.

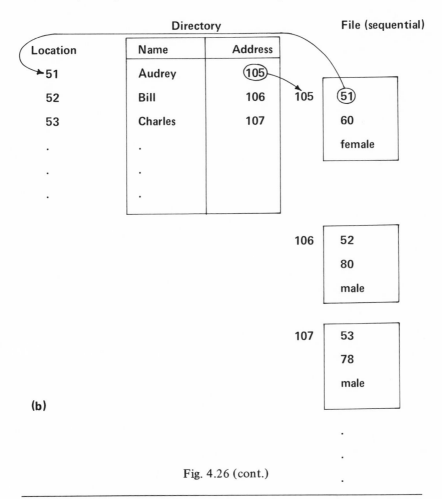

Fig. 4.26 (cont.)

EXERCISE 2: Why is it not possible to use name links in place of address links in a name directory?

EXERCISE 3: What changes are needed in the system of Fig. 4.28 if in one record the value of a_2 is changed? For instance, make the change $q: = p$.

EXERCISE 4: What changes are caused by a decision to relocate one file record (for instance, if record o_2 is moved from address 103 to 105) in the system according to Fig. 4.28 and Fig. 4.30, respectively?

TRANSPOSITION (FILE INVERSION). The introduction of an attribute-a_i directory is a transposition of the directory–file pair. This transposition

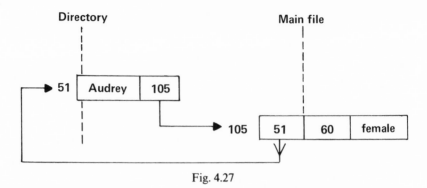

Fig. 4.27

could be said to be a *transposition by the attribute* a_i. Thus in a consolidated file we may have many possible transpositions, one for each attribute.

$$\text{transposition } (a_i/\text{directory}/\text{file}) = (\text{attribute } a_i \text{ directory})/\text{file}$$

The transposition by the attribute a_i may be obtained by introduction of the attribute-a_i directory only, leaving the file unchanged. If the file exists in one version and is associated with a name directory and also with an attribute-a_i directory, then we have two directory–file pairs corresponding to two transposed directory–file pairs.

To retrieve all records containing the property $a_i = a_{ij}$ will call for several block accesses in general, since the records will usually be in distinct blocks if the file is random or sequenced to object names. We can therefore speed up the retrieval by property $a_i = a_{ij}$ by restructuring the file, for instance, by arranging the file records in a sequence of the value of a_2. We would therefore obtain the most efficient transposition, in terms of time, for "transposed retrieval," by both adding an attribute-a_i directory and by resequencing the file. In other words most efficient transposition of a directory–file pair by attribute a_i calls for both transposing the directory (from name directory to attribute-a_i directory) and transposing the file (into one sequenced by values of a_i).

If we want to have both efficient retrieval-by-object name and retrieval by property $(a_i = a_{ij}, (\text{any}_j))$, we may have to have two distinct complete directory–file pairs (Fig. 4.33). Likewise, if the directory is a direct address computation scheme (randomization) and if we also want the directory–file pair transposed by attribute a_i to have direct address computation, then we must have two transposed file versions, each having the locations of records that the computation determines.

Attribute directory oa_N

Attribute a_2

Value	Links to records
ⓟ	101,103,
q	102
r	—
s	—
.	
.	
.	

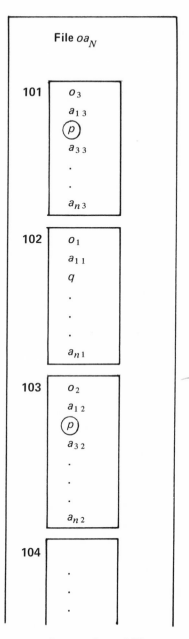

File oa_N

101
o_3
a_{13}
ⓟ
a_{33}
.
.
a_{n3}

102
o_1
a_{11}
q
.
.
.
a_{n1}

103
o_2
a_{12}
ⓟ
a_{32}
.
.
.
a_{n2}

104
.
.
.

Retrieve $(oa_N$, property $a_2 = p) \longrightarrow$ records o_3 and o_2 of file oa_N

Fig. 4.28   Retrieval by property, supported by an attribute directory. Retrieval of records in file oa_N which have value p of attribute a_2.

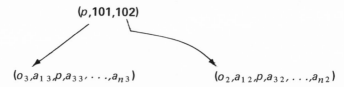

$(p, 101, 102)$

$(o_3, a_{13}, p, a_{33}, \ldots, a_{n3})$ $(o_2, a_{12}, p, a_{32}, \ldots, a_{n2})$

Fig. 4.29   Bundle of records which constitutes the entry for $(a_2 = p)$ in the (attribute a_2 directory)–(file oa_N) pair.

PAIRWISE (AND GROUPWISE) ADDRESS COMPUTATION. If the address of the block in file storage is computed from the value of object identifier o_i, then the location within the block may be computed from the value of a_{ij}. Transposition may then be obtained by computing block address from a_{ij} and location within block from o_i. Likewise it may be possible to form a combination of several (n) attribute–value pairs and compute the location of entries having n different properties in common.

If not all attributes relevant to a file are represented in each record, then we may also use the set of attribute directories to determine all records of the file that contain one value or another of a certain attribute (retrieval by attribute). This is determined from all record addresses contained in the attribute in question.

COMBINED SEVERAL-ATTRIBUTE DIRECTORIES.* We may, of course, want to have attribute directories for several attributes. As it costs memory space to store the directories, the important *design decision* will be to determine which attributes are to be provided with attribute directories and perhaps, also, the design decision as to whether or not to have transposed file versions for some or all of the attributes for which directories are provided. Having both the attribute directory and a special transposed file version for an attribute, in order to support very fast retrieval, can be costly of space. We would probably use address computation instead, with an associated transposed file version for such attributes for which very fast retrieval is required.

A directory consisting of a set of attribute directories together with a file oa_n is shown in Fig 4.34.

Files with Entry-Bundle Arrangement

ENTRIES IN THE FORM OF BUNDLES OF SUBENTRY RECORDS. In files that are stored in direct-access or pseudo-direct-access storage systems it is not necessary to have the file entries in contiguous form, that is, as records. Entries may be stored as bundles of subentries, usually bundles

* More on this will be presented in Chapter 6.

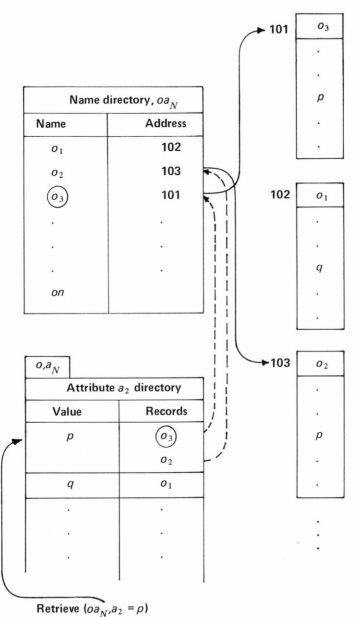

Fig. 4.30   Retrieval by property $(a_2 = p)$ from file oa_N using attribute directory with record name links.

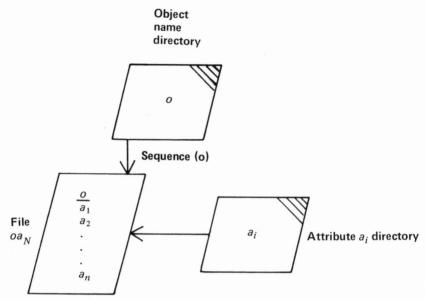

Fig. 4.31   Two transposed versions of the file oa_N using one main file and two directories.

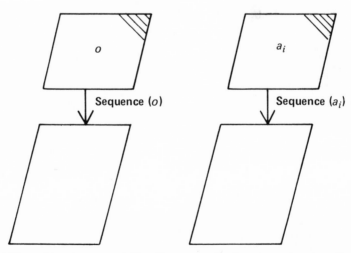

Fig. 4.32   Two transposed file–directory pairs for oa_{N1} using two distinctly sequenced main files.

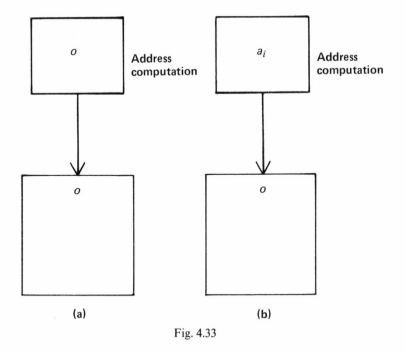

Fig. 4.33

of records. We may have a set of e concepts associated with the object class o. They may be oa_1, oa_2, ... ,oa_k,$oa_k + {}_1$, ... ,oa_n. We may consolidate these into two consolidated c concepts,

$$oa_k = o,a_1,a_2, \ldots ,a_k$$

and

$$oa_{KN} = o,a_{k+1}, \ldots ,a_n$$

We assume that we have two associated, consolidated files, consolidated by record consolidation as follows:

$$[oa_K] \quad \text{and} \quad [oa_{KN}]$$

The entries in the two files, associated with the object o_i may be

$[oa_K]_i$	and	$[oa_{KN}]_i$
o_i		o_i
$a_{1,i}$		$a_{k+1,i}$
$a_{2,i}$		$a_{K+2,i}$
.		.
.		.
.		.
$a_{k,i}$		$a_{n,i}$

Attribute directories

File oa_N

a_1

a_{11}	**102**
a_{12}	**101**
	104
a_{15}	$\vdots$

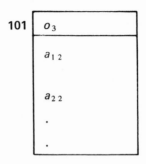

a_2

a_{21}	**102**
a_{22}	**101**
	103
$\cdot$	$\cdot$
$\cdot$	$\cdot$
a_{2t}	

$\vdots$

a_n

Fig. 4.34

We may regard this pair of records as the *entry o_i* in the system of files.

ENQUIRY CALLING *c* FILE ENTRY OR *e* ENTRY. To retrieve, for instance, $a_{2,i}$ (for the object o_i and specified time) we may either request the o_i record of the *c* file $[oa_k]$ or we may request the *e* entry $[o,a_2]_i$; that is, we may either request the file entry *i* or the specific *e* entry wanted. To retrieve $a_{1,i}$, $a_{2,i}$, and $a_{k,i}$, we may either request $[oa_k]_i$ or we may request the three *e* entries $[o,a_1]_i$, $[o,_{a2}]_i$, and $[o,a_k]_i$ for the specified time.

1. *If the retrieval is by the file record* $[oa]_i$ (a) we must know the file

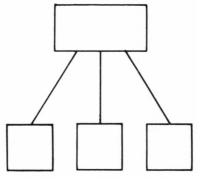

Fig. 4.35　　　Entry as a bundle of records (or segments).

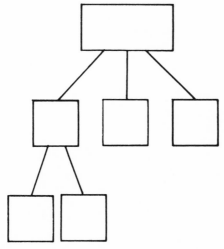

Fig. 4.36　　　Entry as a bundle of three subentries one of which is again a bundle.

name $[oa_K]$; (b) we must know that $[oa_K]$ contains all requested entries; (c) we must fetch the e entries from the file record; (d) only one directory decoding operation is required; and (e) only one block access is needed for fetching the file data.

2. *If the retrieval is by the e*-entry descriptions (a) the user is not required to know the names and content of the files; (b) the user need not fetch the e entries for the file record; (c) three directory decoding operations are needed; and (d) only one block access to the file is necessary.

If we want to retrieve, for instance, a_{2i}, a_{ki}, and a_{ni} for the object o_i, we will have to perform two *directory decoding* operations, one for each of the files oa_K and oa_{KN}, to determine the addresses of $(oa_K)_i$ and $(oa_{KN})_i$. We would then, in addition, have to perform transport (access and transfer) of both of these records. If, instead, we ask for a_{2i} only (or a_{2i} and a_{ki}), we would only have to do one directory decoding and one record transport operation.

We may consolidate the two files $[oa_K]$ and $[oa_{KN}]$ to obtain, say, $[oa_N] = [o, a_K \cup a_{KN}]$. In that case to retrieve a_{2i} and a_{ni} we would need only one directory decoding and only one block access (provided the consolidated record goes into one block). We would still need to transfer the same amount of data. In this case if we ask only for a_{2i}, we would need one directory decoding and one access (as in the case of two files); but we would now have more data transfer work, in that the record $[o, a_N]_i$ needs be transferred, instead of only $[o, a_K]$.

PSEUDO CONSOLIDATION. We may, instead of consolidation—which brings the records together into consolidated, contiguous records—introduce a sort of weaker association by the introduction of a header

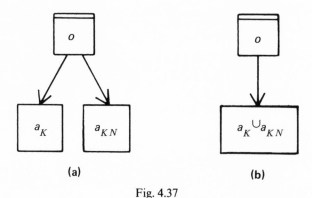

(a)   (b)

Fig. 4.37

record that contains links to the two records (Fig. 4.38). This means that we introduce a new file, containing the header records, a "header file," which links the two main files together into a "file bundle" as shown in Fig. 4.38(a). Each entry in the file bundle is a bundle of records. We may call this weaker kind of consolidation a *pseudo consolidation* or, more precisely, a *pseudo consolidation by bundling*.

To retrieve a_{2i} and a_{ni} would, in the file bundle, require only one directory decoding (provided address links are used) but three accesses and the transfer of both main file records plus transfer of the header (which may be negligible). (The extra access could have been omitted by making one of the main records also the header.)

To retrieve a_{2i} or a_{ni} would call for one directory decoding, two accesses, and one main record transfer (plus transfer of the header record).

EXERCISE 5: Discuss the retrieval work necessary in the chained design of Fig. 4.39 to retrieve a_{2i}, $(a_{2i} + a_{ni})$, and a_{ni}, respectively.

RETRIEVAL AND UPDATING IN PSEUDO-CONSOLIDATED FILES. Retrieval by name and retrieval by property in pseudo-consolidated files are similar to the case of consolidated files to the extent that the retrieval of the header can be done in exactly the same way. Notice, however, that because the bundles and chains are formed by links (usually address links), the distinct files in the file bundle may be *sequenced differently*. For instance, we might have $[oa_K]$ sequenced by o_i and $[oa_{KN}]$ sequenced by $a_{K + 1, i}$.

4.4 FILE-STRUCTURING OPERATORS

In this section we have seen many examples of how files may be formed and transformed. Among other things we have discussed phenomena such as file transposition, or file inversion, and file consolidation. Transposition and consolidation can be seen as examples of general *file-structuring operators*, formal tools to be used in the file system design work.

As was just said, we have only shown a few examples of the file-structuring operators and transformations that are possible with these operators. We have not tried systematically to find something like a minimal, complete set of formally well-defined file-structuring operators. However, it is our hypothesis that it should be possible to find such a set, thereby making it possible to describe the transformation of any set of e

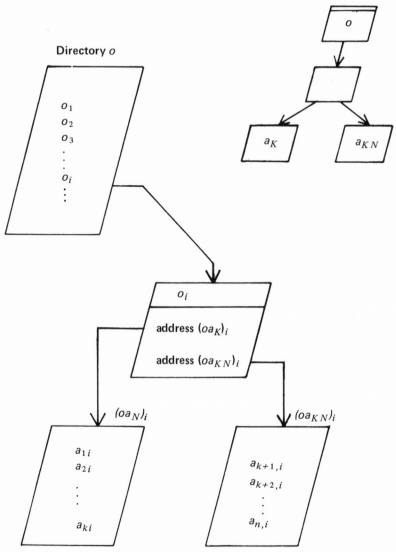

Fig. 4.38   Entry o_i in the bundled file pair $[o,a_k,a_{kn}]$. The entry in this case is a bundle of records $[o,a_k]$ and $[o,a_{kn}]$ are pseudo consolidated by bundling. (a) File bundle corresponding to the record bundle. The file is a bundle of entries which, in turn, are bundles of records.

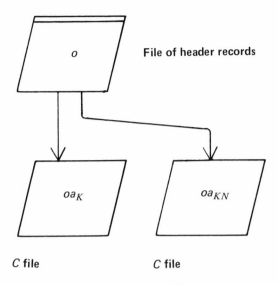

Fig. 4.38   (Continued)

concepts into any feasible file structure of practical importance by means of a sequence of these operators. There are several reasons why it is highly desirable that we be able to do this. One reason is that it enables us to solve any file-structuring problem in small, perceivable steps. With a clearly defined "language" for file structuring, it will also be much easier for the designers to communicate ideas among themselves and to document their analyses and decisions in a detailed and precise way. It might also be possible to build a comprehensive, normative file-structuring theory in terms of the elementary operators to be presented here, a theory that would be less partial* than most theoretical analyses are today because of the lack of a general, precisely defined framework. Moreover, such a general, formal framework will be absolutely necessary if computers are going to be able to solve total file-structuring problems, either at preoperation time, or dynamically as a regular data base maintenance task. In summary, a file-structuring language and theory based on the operators proposed below should be of potential value:

1. For individual file designers in problem-solving situations
2. As a communication tool for designers

---

* By a partial analysis we mean an analysis that concentrates on one aspect of the (file structuring) problem and more or less forgets about other aspects and possibilities.

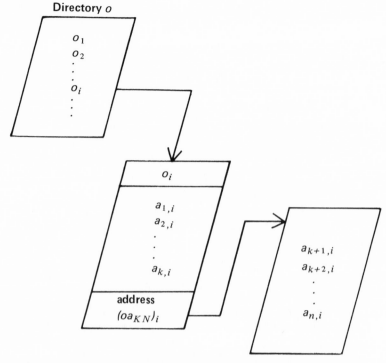

Fig. 4.39   (a) Entry o_i in the file pair o, a_k, a_{kn} consolidated by a chaining of
records for o_i. (b) Simplified diagram that corresponds to (a).

3. For documentation purposes
4. For the development of a general, normative file-structuring
   theory
5. In computer-aided design and redesign of file structures
6. In file maintenance efforts automatically controlled and performed by a data base management system

We shall return to the subject of file-structuring operators in
Chapter 6. Here we shall only enumerate the five basic categories into
which we have found it logical to classify the set of imaginable operators.
Together with the label of each category we have also stated a few
examples of operators belonging to the category.

File Establishment Operators
By means of operators belonging to the category of file establishment we decide that a particular e concept should be established as a

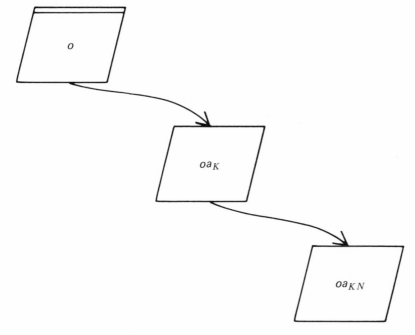

Fig. 4.39   (Continued)

particular kind of file. At "establishment time" the file is assumed to conform to some well-defined "normal format" (see Definition 5 in Section 4.1).

EXAMPLE 1:

Establish e concept x as a virtual file.

Establish e concept x as an object file (property file, relational file).

Transpose the object file x into a property file.

Intraentry Structuring Operators

Intraentry structuring operators transform the internal structure of the entries of a file into a format that somehow deviates from the "normal format."

EXAMPLE 2:

Entry compression
Reordering of terms
Entry chopping, or segmentation
Ordering of segments

Interentry, Intrafile Structuring

Operators belonging to the category of interentry, intrafile structuring are used to change the relationships between different entries of the same file. They leave the interfile structure invariant.

EXAMPLE 3:
Ordering of entries
Intrafile consolidation

Interfile Structuring

Interfile structuring operators change the relationships between different files.

EXAMPLE 4:
File consolidation
File overlapping

File Allocation Operators

By means of operators belonging to the category of file allocation the files are finally allocated to memory structures.

EXAMPLE 5:
Cluster formatting
Choice of addressing algorithm
Choice of synonym-handling algorithm

CONCLUSIONS

We found that most or all file structures and data structures can be obtained by a combination of three main forms: contiguous, bundle, and chain. In discussing file organization we found that we have to consider directory–file pairs instead.

The discussion was based on that of elementary files, e files, which are representations of e concepts. All other files appeared through consolidation of e files into c files in many distinct ways and during change of structure. It was found that an object e file, for example, plus a property directory could be replaced by an object file and a "transposed" (or "inverted") version of it at approximately the same expense of storage but with some performance gains. Hereby the insight that a file and its directory are, in many respects, inseparable was further strengthened by the finding that the *information* to be contained in a file is "partly" in its directory.

CHAPTER 5

DIFFERENT KINDS OF DATA BASE INTERACTIONS AND TRANSACTIONS

In this chapter we shall introduce and analyze the data base concept which tends to play an evergrowing role in the theory and practice of information systems architecture. We shall adopt what we call the "infological approach" to data bases. This means that we think of the data base as being primarily a black box reservoir of information, the ultimate purpose of which is to serve planners, decision makers, and other information consumers. Only secondarily do we think of the data base as a set of files with more or less complex data structures. We think that the needs and desires of the ultimate users of data bases and the "natural" structure of information should govern computer-oriented, datalogical design work in a much more fundamental way than is common practice today.

5.1 INTRODUCTION

The purpose of a data base is to receive, retain, and produce information, knowledge, about a slice of reality, S. We will call S the object system of the data base. The infological approach to data bases starts out from the assumption that S will often satisfy the following general description.

DEFINITION 1: S contains different kinds of objects. At any point of time every object in S possesses a set of properties. Some of the properties of an object are local; that is, they are independent of the existence and properties of other objects in S. Other properties of an object are relational; that is, they are dependent on the object's relations to other objects in S.

It is seen that this general description (Definition 1) of an object system rests upon four fundamental concepts which we have presented earlier in this book: object, property, object relation, and time. A fifth fundamental concept within the infological framework is "reference." In much the same way as objects, properties, object relations, and times are supposed to be the building blocks of the object system, references to object system entities may be combined into structured information, that is, messages, about the object system. References and messages are conceptual, nonphysical entities, which may, however, be represented by data and datalogical structures like file entries, files, and file complexes. Datalogical structures are allocated to memories and thus have to reflect both the infological structure of the represented information and the physical storage and access structure of the representing medium.

Thus the infological theory of data bases makes a clear distinction between (a) the object system, (b) information about the object system, (c) data representations of information, and (d) the storing and accessing medium to which the data are allocated. During the design of a data base, we have to define an efficient mapping of (a) into (d). According to the infological view, this task may be performed in a more systematic way and with more constructive assistance from the ultimate users of the data base if we subdivide the (a) → (d) mapping into the partial mappings (a) → (b), (b) → (c), and (c) → (d). While defining (a) → (b) we are only concerned with the infological aspect of the data base. Datalogical considerations are deliberately postponed to later design steps.

203

What we actually do when we define the (a) → (b) submapping is that we individualize Definition 1 with respect to a particular object system S' and a particular data base $DB(S')$. In principle this is done by telling what objects in S' are of interest, what properties these objects may have, what relationships may prevail between different kinds of objects, and by what names we want to refer to different object system entities. A statement of this kind will be called a *specification of the particular infological model IM (S')* underlying the data base DB (S'). Whereas Definition 1 is assumed to be valid for all object systems of all data bases, an *IM* specification will usually only be valid for one particular data base.

Infological theory does not uniquely determine one particular infological model IM (S') for a particular object system S'. If two different project teams were given the same specification task, they would be likely to come up with slightly different results. Thus the same slice of reality may be looked at through different "infological glasses." However, adherence to the infological vocabulary and syntax will make it easy for any project team member, or even for an outsider, to put the finger on the differences and to argue for one view or the other.

Neither the object system nor its data base reflection will usually be static. Instead there will be constant exchange of information, a constant communication, between the data base and its environment. We shall show in this chapter how much of the interaction between the data base and its environment may be described in terms of the same basic infological concepts as are used for the static description of the information contents of the data base. Among other things we shall discuss two infological structures, the $\alpha\beta$-retrieval query, and the $\alpha\beta\gamma$-retrieval query, which have turned out to be the fundamental constituents of virtually all transactions between the data base and its ultimate users.

For those who are to perform the computer-dependent, datalogical design of a data base, the infological "black-box view" will not be sufficient. However, it is highly desirable that the datalogical concepts and models, which computer-oriented designers use, are compatible with the infological framework. Only then will it be possible to "translate," in a systematic way, the external, user-oriented requirements, as they manifest themselves in a particular infological model, $IM(S')$, into internal, datalogical data base properties. In Chapter 6 we shall see how such a "translation" may be performed, provided that (a) the e concepts of the infological model have been specified together with (b) parameters like relative frequencies and response-time requirements of different kinds of transactions.

Via the concepts of *e* concepts and *e* files, which we have defined and discussed in earlier chapters, it is possible to extend the infological view of data bases in a very natural way so as to cover the computer-oriented, representational aspect of a data base as well. (This will be shown in Chapter 6. We shall see there how the specification of the infological model and the interaction pattern of the data base are to be followed by a series of datalogical design steps that are based directly on the results of the infological analyses.)

According to the extended infological theory the initial datalogical design step consists in a transformation of the set of *e* concepts of the infological model into a set of object, property, and relational *e* files. Then we apply formally well-defined file-structuring operators by means of which we may transform the initial file structure into a file structure that better fits (a) the expected infological pattern of the transactions which will hit the operative data base, and (b) the storage and access structure of available memories.

After a number of applications of the file-structuring operators, we will arrive at the file structure that is to be implemented. The final file structure, or file system, will contain a number of subsystems called "$\alpha\beta$ complexes," or directory–file complexes. The internal structure of such a complex may or may not conform to some well-known file organization technique. However, we will have designed our file system in a much less arbitrary and much more user-influenced way than is common today.

5.2 THE DATA BASE AND ITS ENVIRONMENT

The Infological Data Base Concept

At the present state of the art it does not seem to be possible to give a short definition covering all aspects of the complex data base concept. It seems justified and necessary for users, systemeers,* computer specialists, and information system researchers to have slightly different opinions as to what a data base really is. On the other hand if different categories of people are to be able to communicate constructively with each other in a data base design project, their respective conceptualizations of the data base have to be compatible, even if they are not

---

* It has been found convenient to use the single term *systemeering* (as in "engineering") to denote the combined analytical and creative task that is often referred to by the phrase "system analysis and design." Beside being convenient, the term stresses the integrated entirety of the task. Those who perform the task will be called *systemeers* (as in "engineers").

identical. We think that the infological view of the data base, as being basically a black-box reservoir of information, is a view that promotes the development of a relevant common kernel of ideas and attitudes among those who take part in a data base project. The infological data base concept will be discussed in this chapter. In Chapter 6 we shall show how the infological data base concept may be extended so as to cover datalogical design aspects as well.

The infological data base concept is based on the ultimate user's view of the data base. The ultimate user of a data base is an information consumer—a planner or a decision maker, for example—and to him the data base is an information source among other information sources. Thus from a user's view a data base may be regarded as a black box reservoir of information, the contents of which he is able to retrieve and process in more or less the same way as he is able to retrieve and process the information contained in his own frame of reference or in the minds of his fellow workers.

If we adopt the infological view of the data base concept, we realize immediately that the ultimate user of a data base is up to essentially the same interpretation and confidence problems as he is up to when he uses any artificial or human source of information that is external to his own mind. As always when an information consumer directly or indirectly uses an external source of information, the user of a data base has to question the retrieved information. The information may be more or less uncertain, and this in turn may or may not affect the solution to the user's problem. The information in the data base could be deliberately or inadvertently biased for some reason. The definitions, assumptions, and models underlying the information contents of the data base may not be what the information consumer believes them to be. Thus the user of a data base should not only request the information he needs to solve his problem, he should also request information about quality and other properties of the directly needed information. We shall refer to such information as *information on information*. Information on information is made up of messages, the object parts of which are themselves messages.

Information on information is one important category of *meta-information*. The latter concept also covers (a) information about the basic constituents of the particular infological model underlying the data base—for example, formal and informal definitions of attributes and object types; and (b) information about the data representations of the information contents of the data base—for example, file descriptions.

DEFINITION 1: Data representations of metainformation will be called *metadata*. Subsystems of data bases containing metainformation and data representations thereof may be called *metadata bases*.

A well-designed data base should stimulate the user to request metainformation. At least it should assist the user in his search for such information. We shall call these tasks "the semantic mission of the data base." This mission will be discussed further later in this section when we discuss the basic subsystems of the infological data base.

We gain several advantages by adopting the infological view of the data base as being a black box reservoir of information with which the information consumer communicates. One advantage, which is particularly important during the early stages of the data base goal-setting and design process, is that the interest of the designers is focused on nondatalogical problems such as the quality and interpretation problems mentioned above. Thus the infological data base concept could help the designers avoid the common mistake of jumping too soon into discussions about what file and data structures to choose, what programming language or software package to use, and other similar problems concerning the *internal* properties of the system to be designed and constructed. Before such datalogical problems are tackled, the *external* infological properties of the planned system should be settled as far as possible. In other words the designer of a data base, like the designer of any other system, should consider very carefully *what* the system should do before he devotes too much energy to "how" questions.

Figure 5.1 visualizes the data base black box, its environment, and the communication that is assumed to take place between the data base and its environment. Applying the black-box approach to the data base means that we do not care about the details of the data base subsystem structure. Instead we discuss input and output to and from the system, and the relations between input and output. The input emanates from the environment, and the output is delivered back to the environment. The environment of a system may be defined as the set of conditions that are relevant to but not under the control of the managers of the system. However, we have to be careful when we use such a definition in general discussions of data base design because what is under the control of the goal setters and designers will vary from one data base design situation to another. A data base is often a component in a broader information system, which may or may not be designed or redesigned in connection with the design of the data base. Thus in a practical situation the boundaries between the controllable main system and the uncontrollable environment should perhaps be drawn in a different way than is done in the subsequent discussion.

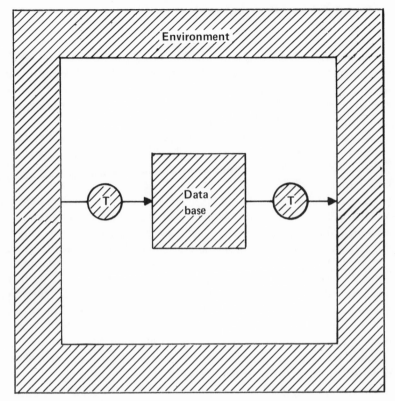

Fig. 5.1

The inputs to and the outputs from a data base will be called *data base transactions* with a common name. From an infological point of view the data base transactions are *conceptual messages*. From another point of view they may be regarded as data representations of conceptual messages, that is, as *data entries*. The latter view may be justified during late stages of the data base design process and during critical phases of implementation and maintenance.

The input and output transactions of a data base system usually appear in pairs: An input transaction causes the appearance of an output transaction. What kind of input transactions a data base should be ready to accept, what kind of output transaction a particular input transaction should result in, and how long the intervening processing may take in different situations are good examples of *external* properties of the planned data base. Thus they are good examples of problems that could and should be discussed in infological terms at an early design stage.

The Data Base Environment

Figure 5.2 is a revised version of Fig. 5.1 in which the data base environment has been broken down into eight subsystems. The arrows indicate the principal information and control flows between the environment and the data base and between the different environment subsystems. Each of the eight environment subsystems will be briefly described below.

OBSERVED AND CONTROLLED OBJECT SYSTEM. If we define the object system of a data base as the slice of reality that has significance for the existence and functioning of the data base, we see that all systems indicated by Fig. 5.2, including the data base itself and its designers, are

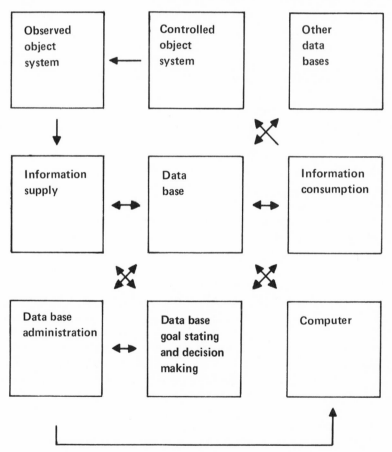

Fig. 5.2   Environment subsystems surrounding the infological data base.

actually parts of the object system. When we refer to the object system in two of the subsystem boxes of Fig. 5.2, we think of the object system in a more restricted sense, the *object system proper*, composing (a) the observed object system and (b) the controlled object system.

By the *controlled object system* we mean the slice of reality that is consciously affected by the decisions taken by the ultimate users of the data base on an information basis that is at least partially supplied by the data base.

By the *observed object system* we mean the slice of reality referred to by the nonmeta (see Definition 2) information in the data base.

Although the observed object system and the controlled object system may sometimes coincide, they need not always do so. Observations about one category of objects, say, enterprises, may very well be used in decisions primarily concerned with another category, say, persons. Even when the same object types are concerned, the information supply and consumption processes may affect different subsets of individual objects; for example, planning for a whole community may be based on information about the preferences of people belonging to a random sample.

The data base designer is faced with different kinds of design problems depending on the degree and character of overlapping between the observed and the controlled object system. We think here of design problems caused by the "free will" of the observed objects in situations in which the observed objects have the possibility of exercising influence over what information about them is reported via the information supply function to the data base.

Suppose that the observed object system and the controlled object system do not overlap. Then the observed objects will neither gain nor suffer from the decisions and actions based on the information contents of the data base. Thus it may be difficult to motivate the observed objects (persons or enterprises, for example) to assist the information suppliers, and this difficulty may be fatal if active cooperation is needed.

On the other hand if the observed object system and the controlled object system do overlap, then an observation on a particular object may more or less directly affect the service given to or the action taken against the very same object by the information consumption function of the data base environment. Naturally, in such a situation an object may be motivated to distort the observations reported to the data base.

EXERCISE 1: Suppose that you are to design an information system for a company, and that the primary task of this information system is to produce statistical reports about various activities within the company. Give examples of what kind of design problems you will encounter due to "the free will of the observed objects." How would you tackle the problems?

INFORMATION SUPPLY AND CONSUMPTION. The information supply subsystem comprises all kinds of resources and activities engaged in supplying the data base with information concerning the objects to be observed in order to facilitate decision making concerning the objects to be controlled. Thus the information supply function covers all processes, persons, and equipment engaged as follows:

Observing and measuring particular phenomena in the object system
Filling in questionnaires
Interviewing
Coding, that is, classifying or transforming the original observations into the categories of the particular infological model underlying the data base
Data registration, that is, representing the observations and the coded information by data messages
Transforming and transmitting data
Preliminary quality control of input information and data.

The *information consumption* subsystem comprises all kinds of resources and activities engaged in the utilization of the information in the data base. Thus the information consumption function covers all processes, persons, and equipment engaged as follows:

Identifying, operatively, information needs in the decision processes for which the data base has been designed
Formulating the information requests in terms of the particular infological model underlying the data base
Transforming the formalized information requests into data transactions, which are submitted to the data base
Receiving and interpreting the answers from the data base
Analyzing the answers, thus making them adequate for effective utilization in decision processes
Influencing and making decisions concerning particular aspects of the object system

In many data base environments the information consumption subsystem will be the function that interacts most frequently with the data base. The interaction between the information supply function and the data base will usually be frequent—the more frequent, the more dynamic the data base (see Data Base Dynamics in Section 5.2).

Depending on the level of ambition that is set for a particular data base, one and the same task—for example, coding, error elimination, or "intelligent analysis" of retrieved information—may be allocated to the data base system itself or to one of its environment subsystems. Sometimes the task may be most efficiently performed in "conversational mode" as a joint effort by the data base and its environment.

DATA BASE GOAL STATING, DECISION MAKING, AND ADMINISTRATION. Like most undertakings worth systematic study, the design, construction, and operation of a data base require some kind of *goal-stating and decision-making* function. This function, like the others, is a system of resources and activities. The most important resources within the goal-stating and decision-making function are, of course, the human resources. In this connection it is important to remember what is often stressed in modern organizational literature, namely, that those who really set the goals and make the decisions are not necessarily identical with the executives who have the formal authority to do so. The real goal setters and decision makers are those who have the power to establish or reject goals and to produce or resist change.

The data base goal-stating and decision-making subsystem will naturally be most active during the early stages of data base planning. When the data base has been designed, constructed, and put into operation, activity from this subsystem will only be required occasionally and mainly on initiative from information supply, information consumption, or data base administration. These activities may concern major infological extensions desired by the consumers, such as exchange of hardware equipment for technoeconomical reasons or for the sake of suppliers' or consumers' convenience. It is the task of the goal-stating and decision-making subsystem to pool and reconcile the interests of the other subsystems during all stages of the data base system.

The *data base administration* subsystem embraces all those planning, systemeering,* programming, operation, and supervision activities in *connection with the design, construction, and running of the data base* system that by formal or informal decisions have been delegated to it from the goal-stating and decision-making subsystem. Among other things datalogical and infological restructurings of the data base are carried out by this function. *Datalogical restructuring* may, for instance,

---

* See footnote, page 205.

be for changes of the file structure of the data base in order to speed up response times or save secondary storage, whereas *infological restructuring* will mean such things as the introduction or elimination of an object type or an *e* concept, or the changing of the secrecy status of a particular attribute. It should be noted that the data base designer himself is a part of the data base administration function, a circumstance that will inevitably complicate any attempt to arrive at an "objectively optimal" solution to a design problem or to "objectively evaluate" the performance of a particular data base.

THE COMPUTER. The computer subsystem of the data base environment comprises all devices devoted to the running of the data base (and possibly several other applications), as well as all people, processes, and so on engaged in managing and operating these devices. In principle the devices may be of any kind, even manual. Very often they will be components of an electronic computer system.

It may seem strange to separate the computer from the data base and regard it as part of the data base *environment*. There are several reasons for this, however. First, it is not at all certain that we may buy a new computer or substantially reconfigurate the old one at the same time as we design the data base. Thus the computer may very well be a condition that is relevant to but not under the control of the managers of the data base system, and then, according to the definition stated in Section 5.2 we should consider it a part of the system environment rather than a part of the system itself.

Second, the same computer system may have to be shared by several applications, of which the data base system to be designed is only one. Even if the data base designers in such a situation should have partial control over the computer configuration, it is convenient to consider the latter a separate system.

Needless to say the formal separation of the computer system from the data base should not stop us from integrating the design of the two systems whenever this is found to be desirable and feasible.

EXERCISE 2: We have said that both the computer subsystem and the data base administration subsystem are meant for the running of the data base. However, "run the data base" means different things within the two subsystems. Try to explain the difference.

OTHER DATA BASES. The nine system boxes in Fig. 5.2 may be grouped in the following way. The two upper left boxes represent the object system to be observed or controlled. The six boxes at the bottom of the figure represent the information system to be designed. The planned data base is a part of this system. Finally, the upper right box represents other data bases, belonging to other information systems, which are to be connected to the planned data base and the planned information system. The interaction between different data bases of such *a data base network* may run so smoothly as to give the information consumers the impression that they are interacting with *one* data base. The question then arises, why should we distinguish between "our" data base and the other data bases in the network, the *external* data bases? The reasons are similar to the reasons for separating the computer system from the data base (see above). Thus it is not at all certain that the external data bases and the external information systems to which they belong are to be designed or redesigned at the same time as we design "our" data base and information system. However, our possibilities of influencing the design of the other data bases are likely to be substantially less than our possibilities of influencing the design of the particular data base we have been explicitly asked to design.

Even if we have only partial influence on the environmental information systems and data bases with which "our" information system and data base will interact, we shall, of course, see to it that we make the most of any influence that we might have. Suppose, for example, that the data bases are to be run on the same computer. This means that the same computer subsystem belongs to the environments of several data bases (see Fig. 5.2). Then it is obvious that coordination and cooperation between the different information systems will be needed "for technical reasons." Once the cooperation activities have started, however, the parties involved may well discover that they all stand to gain much more from redesigning and integrating their information systems than they did by sharing only one particular resource, the computer. For example, it will probably prove advantageous to all parties if the data bases in the network are designed to utilize the same definitions of common infological entities, such as common object types and common attributes. The overall quality and timeliness of the information could often be improved if the different information systems are synchronized and updating activities are coordinated. Such synchronization and coordination are also likely to lead to savings, particularly within the respective information supply subsystems.

EXERCISE 3: Could there be any negative effects as to the quality of the information if different data bases are coordinated so that redundancies are eliminated and possible information contradictions are reconciled? If there are, should this stop integration of information systems, or are there other means for preventing the bad effects? What can the alert designer do?

Basic Subsystems of the Infological Data Base

Still regarding the data base from the ultimate user's point of view as basically a container of information, we shall try in this section to identify a few principal functions or subsystems of the infological data base. It should be stressed that the aim of this effort is primarily to provide a deeper *understanding* of the data base concept as such. In the next chapter we shall tackle the same analytical problem from a slightly different point of view, that of the designing computer specialist. Then other factors than pure infological intelligibility have, of course, to be considered as well. For example, this analysis must aim at a subsystem structure that facilitates construction (programming), operation, and maintenance of the planned information system. However, the infological understanding of the data base will no doubt guide the designer in his systemeering task, and it will certainly provide a sounder basis for the discussions and negotiations that take place between users, managers, designers, and other interested parties during the goal-setting process.

Now let us analyze what has to be inside the data base from an infological point of view. We have talked of the data base as a reservoir containing a set of information. What information? The set of messages that has been put into the data base minus the set of deleted messages might seem to be a strong candidate. But consider a data base that has been fed with the following *e* messages:

1. p is a well-known politician.
2. q is a famous actress.
3. p and r are brothers-in-law.
4. s is the fiancé of q.
5. r murdered s yesterday.

Five elementary messages have been put into the data base. Nevertheless it seems reasonable to claim that the data base contains other messages as well. For instance, it could be argued that the data base also contains the newsworthy *e* message,

6. Well-known politician's brother-in-law murdered fiancé of famous actress yesterday.

although this message has not been inserted into the base.

Thus we expect a data base to have not only a *reproductive* capability, that is, the capability of perceiving, retaining, and reproducing information on request, but we also assume it to have some *deductive* power. The origin of this deductive power, which has to be inside the data base itself, will be called the *data base schema*, or just the *schema*.

Messages that, thanks to the schema, are derivable from other messages in the data base need not themselves be *explicitly stored* in the data base. There are perfectly legitimate reasons, however, related to design goals such as retrieval speed and quality control, why we should sometimes want to store derivable messages *redundantly*. As we are not discussing design problems for the moment, we shall just establish that the data base beside the schema has another subsystem, which we shall call the *data base nucleus*, or just the nucleus, and which comprises all explicitly stored messages in the data base, be they redundant or not.

The schema and the nucleus subsystems together constitute the *memory* function of the data base. However, just as a highly receptive but uncritical and talkative human being may cause his environment a lot of trouble, a data base consisting of nothing but a perfect memory would be vulnerable, unreliable, and sometimes even dangerous. Some kind of *filter* thus seems to be a necessary third component of the data base system, even from a strictly infological point of view.

Our view of the principal subsystem structure of the infological data base is summarized in Fig. 5.3.

DEFINITION 2: Formally we may define the infological data base as a triple data base,

$$DB = <S, N, F>$$

where S is a schema, N is a nucleus, and F is a filter. Together S and N determine the set M of messages that are contained in the data base, the *information contents* of the data base.

We shall devote the rest of this section to investigating the three basic components of the infological data base somewhat more thoroughly.

THE DATA BASE SCHEMA. The data base schema is equivalent to a statement of the infological model underlying the data base. The schema has two distinguishable subfunctions, which we may call the *semantic mission* and the *deductive mission*, respectively. We have already given an example of the deductive function above. In this capacity the schema

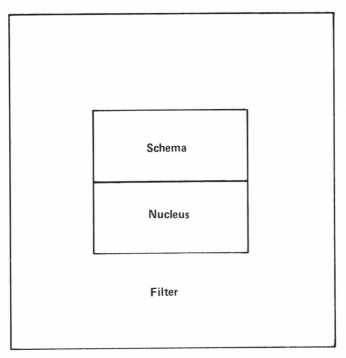

Fig. 5.3

"amplifies" the information explicitly stored in the nucleus N to become the total information contents M of the data base.

The deductive function of the data base schema is tied to the set of *derivation rules*, that is, message-generation rules, which determine how messages in the data base generate other messages. Formal definitions stating how the value of one attribute may be calculated from the values of other attributes are typical examples of derivation rules belonging to the deductive function of a data base schema. More sophisticated data bases may contain message-generation rules of probabilistic nature involving references to statistical distributions. An advanced data base might even be able to induce such probabilistic statements automatically from its own information contents. Naturally, such data bases could be particularly helpful in disciplines in which data are abundant, although powerful theory is lacking.

Formal definitions and even weaker correlations between attributes may be very useful for other than deduction purposes. For instance, the filter function may use them to protect the data base and its users against false messages. They may also guide the data base administrator in his continuous search for more efficient datalogical structurings of the data base. An advanced data base might itself suggest that a file structure, in which the strongly correlated attributes A_1 and A_2 are both stored explicitly, should be replaced with a structure consisting of (a) a derivation rule and (b) one or two files containing all instances of attribute A_1 and the "exceptional" instances of attribute A_2, that is, those instances that are not compatible with the derivation rule.

The *laws of logic and statistical inference* are obvious derivation-rule candidates. However, it would not be practical to require from any data base that it should have the full amount of deductive power that logical and statistical laws permit. They have to be combined with rules that limit the number of derivation-rule applications to be tried in different practical situations. Such limitations will, of course, restrict the deductive power of the data base, but on the other hand they will reduce the bad effects of erroneous input to the data base. If the data base has perfect deduction capabilities, the admission of a message, however farfetched it may be, that contradicts another message already contained in the data base would completely destroy the data base as a source of information, as any message would then be derivable. Thus there has to be an appropriate *balance* between the *deductive power* of the schema and the *purifying power* of the filter.

The *semantic function* of the data base schema consists in conveying the true meaning of the messages contained in the data base to the user. This is certainly a nontrivial task in which the names chosen for attributes as well as informal definitions and descriptions play important roles.

In order to get a comprehensive understanding of the semantic mission in its entirety, we must remember that there are many different persons involved in the creation, maintenance, and use of the information potential of a data base. Almost certainly all these persons have nonidentical frames of reference. The frame of reference of not even one person is invariant over time.

We face here a problem area that has caused great discomfort for many people who have seriously thought about the future of data bases.*

---

* For instance, C.W. Churchman (1968, 1971) has taken up the problem. He suggests an interesting "dialectical" technique, according to which the data base does not simply provide straight answers to seemingly simple questions. Instead the data base would try to generate "deadly enemy proposals" based on a picture of the world, a "Weltanschauung," which is contrary to that underlying the user's question. Thus the decision makers would at least become self-conscious about their implicit assumptions.

For many kinds of data bases the problems do not seem to be insurmountable in practice, however, provided they are attacked with imaginativeness and with appropriate, timely attention during the data base design process. The idea of semantic mission within the schema subsystem of the data base should be of some help in these efforts. A simple example of what could be done, when the problem area is consciously considered, is given by the ARKDABA system† in Sweden. Whenever during his conversation with the data base the user becomes uncertain about the particulars of the infological model underlying the ARKDABA system, he may immediately call the system's attention to this by pressing a button, and the schema function of the data base then promptly supplies him with the appropriate metainformation (see The Infological Data Base Concept in Section 5.2), for example, the informal definition of the variable "net income." Similar action is automatically taken by the system when the user inadvertently reveals that he does not have a sufficient understanding of the infological (or other) assumptions on which the system is based; then a tutorial subsystem is invoked.*

THE NUCLEUS. The nucleus of a data base is a set of messages sufficient to generate, in combination with the schema, the information contents of the data base. If no message can be removed from the nucleus without changing the information contents of the data base, we say that the nucleus is infologically minimal, or nonredundant. As has been said before, there may be datalogical as well as infological reasons for allowing the nucleus to be redundant.

Whereas the general idea of the nucleus as a kernel or subset of messages, from which the other messages of the data base are derived, seems clearly conceivable even from an infological point of view, we cannot always give a strictly infological justification for or against considering *a particular* message as part of the nucleus. Several distinct sets of messages may, independently of each other, fulfill the infological condition (as stated above) for being a nonredundant nucleus, and any set containing one of these sets as a proper subset would be a feasible

---

† A data base for interactive, real-time production of statistics on individuals and households being designed at present at the National Central Bureau of Statistics in Sweden.

* It seems natural to credit the filter function of the data base system with the latter kind of action (see below), as it aims at protecting the user from being misled by the data base.

redundant nucleus. Selecting one of these redundant or nonredundant nucleus candidates as *the* nucleus of the data base is ultimately a design decision in which datalogical efficiency considerations inevitably come in. Thus we could say that the exact demarcation of the nucleus of a data base is a datalogical problem that has to be solved under certain infological constraints. More concretely it is the problem of deciding which of the messages should be stored in files, and which of them should be made retrievable from file-stored messages by means of programs.

In principle, the data base nucleus may contain any kind of messages. In practice, however, many data base nuclei will be infologically equivalent to a set of complete elementary messages, although for datalogical reasons some of them will be represented by consolidated file entries.

Any message in a data base nucleus may be true, false, or meaningless. It is the task of the filter to keep the false and meaningless messages out of the data base. However, most data bases will contain such messages, first, because no filter function can be expected to be perfect, and second, and more interestingly, because it would sometimes be an enormous waste of information to throw away messages, even though we know them to be false. "The infological distance" between a false message and a true one may be relatively short, as in cases of slight measuring errors, for instance. For many practical purposes such false messages can be as useful as true ones. When the information supply function fails to deliver isolated messages—for example, because a respondent has filled in his questionnaire incompletely or not at all—it may even be justified to *impute* ("guess intelligently") the missing message on the bases of available, relevant information. It has been said about this technique that the only thing we know for certain about the imputed messages is that they are false. Yet it may be a useful technique, for instance, in connection with statistical data bases,* where isolated deficiencies usually "vanish" in the aggregation process. However, whenever false messages are admitted into the data base, it is of the utmost importance to keep the quality of the outgoing messages under control. This, again, is a filter subfunction.

THE FILTER. The filter function of the infological data base should protect the data base and its users against false messages and messages

---

* A *statistical data base* is a data base whose output messages are *aggregated* from a lot of messages concerning individual objects (for example, table cells).

that are not meaningful according to the specifications and definitions embedded in the data base schema.

The actions of the data base filter may take several guises. For instance, it could make the data base refuse input messages that are not meaningful within the particular infological model underlying the data base. Similarly, the filter could monitor the output messages, assembled by the data base, for oddities. Not only could the filter act on the in- and out-going transactions. Whenever the data base system is idle—that is, when it does not interact with its environment—it could, through its filter function, try to "purify" itself by carrying out different kinds of consistency checks, thus utilizing the redundancy that may exist in the base, as pointed out earlier.

Besides performing quality control of actions, the data base filter could also do such things as prevent disclosure of confidential information to unauthorized interactors. In this capacity the filter may in effect make the same physical data base appear infologically different to different users.

A data base with a *selective filter*, as described in the previous paragraph, may be regarded as a special case of a *multischema data base*, that is, a data base with several schemas, equivalent to several infological models, which make the same physical data appear as different infological data bases.

Among the multiple schemas of multischema data bases there has to be one schema that is more fundamental than the others, namely, the schema that is assumed when the data base assimilates information from its environment (for example, the general impossibility of observing without categories in which to observe, that is, without a model of the observed).

Data Base Dynamics

Typically the information contents of a data base are ever changing. In Section 5.3 we shall investigate more systematically how different kinds of interactions may affect the data base when it is seen as "the organism" in a "stimulus–organism–response" model. Here we shall only make a few general remarks about the dynamic aspect of the infological data base.

In Definition 2 we defined the infological data base formally as a <schema, nucleus, filter> triple. Thus by changing the schema, the nucleus, or the filter, we also change the data base. Naturally the typical, most frequent way of changing the data base will be to add or delete a particular message, that is, to *change the nucleus* of the data base. In so doing we immediately change the information contents of the base except in certain redundancy situations. By *changing the schema* we may or may not change the information contents of the data base at once. For instance, the substitution of one definition for another will probably directly affect the set of messages contained in the base, whereas the introduction of a new attribute will not have any effect on the information contents of the data base until messages involving references to the new attribute arrive. A *filter change*, finally, will typically have indirect, mediate effects only. However, an alteration of the filter's selectivity toward confidential messages, for example, may immediately and drastically change the effective data base from a particular user's point of view.

Figure 5.4 provides an alternative starting point for the discussion of data base dynamics. It shows two different ways of classifying the set of all messages, M_Ω. According to classification A, M_Ω consists of three subsets,

A_1: The set of *false messages*
A_2: The set of *meaningless messages*
A_3: The set of *true messages*

According to the other classification, B, M_Ω consists of the subsets,

B_1: The set of *unknown messages*, that is, messages that neither are at present in the information contents of the data base under consideration nor have been so at any earlier point of time
B_2: The set of *known messages*, that is, messages that are at present contained in the data base
B_3: The set of *forgotten messages*, that is, messages that are not at present in the data base but have been so at some earlier point of time

The set B_2 of known messages may be further subdivided into

B_{21}: The set of *stored messages*, that is, messages that are contained in the data base nucleus
B_{22}: The set of *virtual messages*, that is, messages that are contained in the data base without being stored in the nucleus (see Basic Subsystems of the Infological Base in Section 5.2).

The subsets B_{21} and B_{22} are exclusive. We may also define B_{23} as follows:

B_{23}: The set of *derivable messages*, that is, messages that are derivable from other messages in the data base by means of the derivation rules in the data base schema

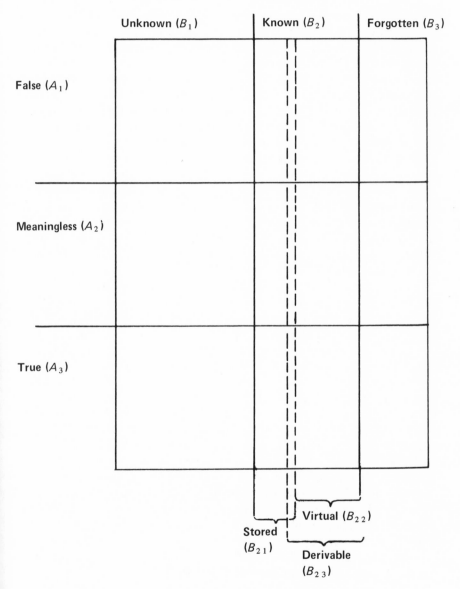

Fig. 5.4   A cross classification of the set of all messages M_Ω

Note that B_{22} is a subset of B_{23}. The data base (nucleus) is nonredundant if and only if $B_{22} = B_{23}$. If $B_{22} = B_{23} = \phi$, the data base has no deductive power, in which case the schema has only got a semantic submission.

It is obvious that classification B is tied to the particular data base under consideration. Classification A is not data base independent either, however. We can see this if we analyze what happens if we change the data base schema, that is, if we modify the particular infological model underlying the data base. First, such a change may imply a modification of the set M_Ω of all messages. For example, the introduction of a new attribute or a new object relation will expand M_Ω. A modification of the schema may also change the meaningfulness of a particular message in M_Ω. Suppose, for instance, that "person" is an object type and "weight" is an attribute that has been defined to be relevant to "persons" only. Then it is meaningless to talk of the weight of an object that is not a "person." However, if we modify the infological model and the schema so that "weight" becomes relevant to another object group as well, say "car," then messages informing about the weight of cars suddenly become meaningful; our modification of the data base schema caused a transition of messages from subset A_2 to subsets A_1 and A_3.

For data bases that are based on identical infological models, and thus have identical schemas, the M_Ω sets are identical, and so are the subsets according to classification A, because (a) the common schema uniquely determines a common subset A_2 of meaningless messages, and (b) if we assume that there is *one* objective reality, the same meaningful message has to belong either to the subset A_1 of false messages in both data bases or to the subset A_3 of true messages in both bases. However, the classification B need not coincide for two data bases, even if they are based on the same infological model and have a common schema, because one of the bases may already know (or has already forgotten) a lot of messages that the other data base has not yet learnt (or forgotten). The remark leads us to the subject of classification B. Obviously, the assimilation by the data base of an unknown message implies a $B_1 \rightarrow B_2$ transition. If the message was already known by the data base, the addition transaction might lead to nothing or to a transition from B_{22} to $B_{21} \cap B_{23}$; in the latter case the message is redundantly stored although it is derivable. Similarly, a deletion transaction might lead to one of the transitions $B_2 \rightarrow B_3$, or $B_{21} \cap B_{23} \rightarrow B_{22}$.

The information contents $M(t)$ of a data base $DB(t)$ at a particular point of time t can easily be identified as the subset B_2 of known messages.

From Fig. 5.4 we find immediately that

$$M(t) = B_2 = (A_1 \cap B_2) \cup (A_2 \cap B_2) \cup (A_3 \cap B_2)$$

The mission of the data base filter may be expressed as (a) keeping down the number of messages in $(A_1 \cap B_2)$: "consistency checking"; (b) keeping down the number of messages in $(A_2 \cap B_2)$: "syntax checking"; (c) preventing confidential messages in $(A_3 \cap B_2)$ from being disclosed to unauthorized users: "secrecy checking": and (d) preventing $(A_3 \cap B_2) \rightarrow (A_3 \cap B_3)$ transitions, unless they are desired by the data base owner: "security checking."

5.3   THE INTERACTION PROCESS

As was noted in the previous section the dynamic aspect of the data base is of utmost importance. The object system changes, and so do the contents of the data base. In fact the ability of the data base to deliver relevant, accurate, and timely information about states and changes of states in the real world is the principal reason for its existence. It is obvious that this ability presupposes an extensive exchange of information, an extensive *communication*, between the data base and its environment. In this section we shall delve a little deeper into the nature of the different kinds of interactions that take place between the main data base system and the surrounding systems with which the data base communicates more or less incessantly during its lifetime.

The design of the communication processes between the data base and its environment is a very important part of the total data base design task. However efficiently the data base system works internally, this will be of little value unless the data base and the interactors around it can efficiently exchange information and control.

In order to systematize the data base interaction problem area, we shall now discuss the use of two different classification schemes. The two classifications reflect two different aspects, both of which should be kept in mind at data base design time. The interaction classification to be discussed first is based on the subdivision of the data base environment into eight subsystems, which were shown in Fig. 5.2. This classification of data base interactions stresses the circumstance that there are several different categories of people who are to be able to communicate constructively with the data base. Different interactor categories may require access to the data base for quite different reasons. This, in combination with educational and other differences, could call for the design of different interaction procedures and languages for different interactor categories.

On the other hand the formal structure of two data base requests may be very similar, even though they emanate from two different subsystems of the data base environment. If we are able to identify structural similarities at an early design stage, we may be able to reduce considerably the total amount of design and construction work to be done. Lower development costs and less complex software will be immediate effects of such reductions. Indirectly, less complex software will lead to cheaper data base operation. As a tool for detection of structural similarities between different data base interactions, we next present a classification scheme that is based on the so-called S-O-R* model. The latter model has been used by psychologists in order to describe and explain human behavior. Here we use the model for description and analysis of the behavior of another "organism," the data base.

A Classification of Interactions Based on the Subsystem Structure of the Data Base Environment

In Fig. 5.2 we identified eight environment subsystems surrounding the infological data base. Five of these systems, or functions, were found to be heavily and directly engaged in data and information exchange with the main data base system as follows:

1. *The information supply function*, covering all processes, persons, equipment, and so on, engaged in observing particular phenomena in the object system, coding (classifying) the observations in terms of the particular infological model underlying the data base, representing the coded observations by data messages, and transforming and transmitting the data until they finally reach the data base

2. *The information consumption function*, covering all processes, persons, equipment, and so on, engaged in identifying, operatively, information needs in the decision processes for which the data base is meant, formulating the information requests in terms of the particular infological model underlying the data base, submitting the requests to the data base, receiving, interpreting, and analyzing the answers from the data base, and influencing

---

* S-O-R means stimulus–organism–response.

and making decisions concerning particular aspects of the object system

3. *The data base administration* function, embracing all planning, systemeering, programming, operation, and supervision activities in connection with the design, construction, and running of the data base

4. *The computer function,* covering the technological devices allocated to the data base, and the people, processes, and so on, engaged in managing and operating these devices

5. *Other data bases* than the one under consideration.

We shall say that each of these five environment subsystems defines an *interactor category*. In this section we shall focus our interest on the first three functions of those listed above. The corresponding interactor categories will be called *information suppliers, information consumers*, or users, and *data base administrators*.

As suggested earlier, each of the three interactor functions may be further subdivided. Accordingly there are subcategories of interactors under each of the three categories above. Many of these subcategories, like coders and programmers, may inherit names from closely related functions in predata base information processing. For other subcategories, corresponding to more or less new functions, there are no appropriate labels today. We shall feel free to introduce names for these functions and categories whenever needed. For example, it is important to be able to talk about two subcategories of data base administrators which we shall call *information structurers* and *data structurers*, respectively. The two functions are clearly distinguishable and care should be taken to avoid conceptual confusion.*

The tasks of the *information structurers* are related to the infological model underlying the data base, which means that they are related to the schema and filter functions of the data base. The information structurers should be concerned with the practicality and consistency of the operative infological model, and whenever desirable they should undertake changes like the specification of new object types, properties, attributes, object relations, definitions, and names. They could also be

---

* Particular care should be taken in the case of a small data base in which the two functions may be exercised by the same people. There are the same arguments for and against double assignments in data base administration as in any other kind of organizational activity.

responsible for the appropriate distribution of information about what information is accessible from the data base, for activating potential information consumers not yet heard of, and so on.

The *data structurers*, on the other hand, should be concerned with tasks related to the internal, datalogical structuring of the data base. Whenever the infological or technological environment changes, the data structurer should be prepared to do such things as altering the demarcation between the nucleus and the virtual part of the data base (see Section 5.2), restructuring the files, and redesigning the strategies for efficient processing of transactions.

In parallel with the three main interactor categories we could also talk about three major types of data base interactions, namely, *supplier interactions, consumer interactions*, and *administrator interactions*, each of which could be further subdivided, following the subclassification of the corresponding interactor categories. For example, we can distinguish between *information structuring* and *data structuring* interactions.

EXERCISE 1: Make a further subdivision of the main interaction classes suggested in the text above.

EXERCISE 2: To which interaction classes would you assign the following tasks:
1. Consolidation of two data base files into one?
2. Changing the secrecy status of the attribute "income" from "confidential" to "public"?
3. Retrieval of a list showing the names and present positions of those employees in the organization who have a certain education?
4. Retrieval of a list of attributes, the values of which have been requested less than 10 times during the last month?
5. Retrieval of a list showing the names and telephone numbers of those employees whose weekly time budget reports have not yet been received by the data base system?
6. Update of the income figure of a certain employee?
7. Introduction of a "new employee" record?
8. Introduction of a new attribute?
9. Changing the representation mode of an attribute from "decimal" to "binary"?
10. Changing the definition of the attribute "disposable income"?

EXERCISE 3: In "conventional," "nondata base oriented" information systems the so-called "application programmer" has an important role. In a data base oriented information system the functions of the "application programmer" are likely to be spread among several interactor categories. Give examples of different "application programmer" functions, and for each of them state the appropriate interaction class.

A Classification of Interactions Based on the S-O-R Model

In Fig. 5.1 we visualized the data base as a black box with input transactions coming in from the environment and with output transactions leaving the data base in the opposite direction. We noted that input and output transactions usually appear in pairs: An input transaction causes the appearance of an output transaction. If we call the data base an *organism*, an input transaction a *stimulus*, and the resulting output transaction a *response*, we recognize the basic parts of a so-called S-O-R model.

A stimulus S resulting in a response R may also transform the organism: $O \rightarrow O'$. The response R may in turn act as a stimulus on the environment and produce another input transaction S' and an environment transformation $E \rightarrow E'$. We shall call the septuple (a)

$$<S, O, O', R, E, E', S'>$$

a *closed interaction* and the quadruple (b)

$$<S, O, O', R>$$

an *open interaction*. The quadruple (c)

$$<R, E, E', S'>$$

will be called the *complementary open interaction* of (b) with respect to (a).

Sometimes a response may occur without being caused by an identifiable, preceding stimulus. This phenomenon is called *spontaneous behavior* and is sometimes claimed to be typical of living organisms.* According to this criterion a data base may very well be considered a living organism. For example, it may be impossible to trace a "time-to-reorganize" signal from the data base back to any particular input transaction. Similarly, we may imagine situations in which an input transaction does not cause any output, and in which an organism transformation may or may not take place. An automatically initiated and performed reorganization may exemplify organism transformation without either input or output.

---

* See for example, Carzo-Yanoyas (1967).

When we use the S-O-R model as a structuring tool for data base interactions, we keep hold of the circumstance that in a particular interactive situation;

(S): A *stimulus* from the environment may or may not occur
(O): The *organism*, that is, the data base, may or may not be transformed
(R): A *response* from the data base to the environment may or may not appear

As a situation characterized by a *null stimulus*, $S = \emptyset$, a *null transformation*, $0 \rightarrow 0$, and a *null response*, $R = \emptyset$, cannot very well be regarded as interactive, this leaves us with $2^3 - 1 = 7$ basic interaction types. This is a classification scheme that is meaningful for both open and closed interactions. It is not meaningful for complementary open interactions, though, because it refers only to the S, O, O', and R components, and not the E, E', and S' components of the closed interaction septuple $<S$, O, O', R, E, E', $S'>$.

The seven basic interaction types may be grouped into several structures, one of which is displayed in Fig. 5.5. The structure of Fig. 5.5 has two basic substructures, labeled *spontaneous behavior*, characterized by the null stimulus, and *triggered behavior*.

Spontaneous behavior may occur if we have designed the data base to take its own initiatives. Such design could be very practical for missions that have to be carried occasionally but that have low priority at any particular point of time. There are a lot of maintenance tasks that fit this description. For example, in connection with any data base system there has to be a manual or automatic function, which collects information about different aspects of data base performance and which now and then suggests more or less radical datalogical or infological restructurings of the data base. The restructuring may concern the nucleus, the schema, or the filter, or several of these subsystems. The spontaneous behavior may include the *data base modification* $(0 \rightarrow O')$, or it may leave the data base *invariant* (null transformation) and only result in an output transaction, which may recommend some environment subsystem (for instance, a particular subfunction of the data base administrator) to initiate some kind of triggered behavior (for instance, a partial redesign of the file system).

If we, despite what has been said, should try to identify a particular data base external originator of spontaneous behavior, the only candidate seems to be the *designer* of the data base system, whereas the

S – O – R	Interaction Type
$\phi - * - *$	Spontaneous behavior
$\phi - 1 - *$	modified data base
$\phi - \phi - *$	invariant data base
$1 - * - *$	Triggered behavior
$1 - 1 - *$	modified data base
	nucleus modification
	addition of message
	deletion of message
	substitution
	schema modification
	filter modification
$1 - \phi - *$	invariant data base
	query
	about the object system proper
	about the information
	modification failure

Fig. 5.5   A classification of interactions based on the S-O-R model. $\emptyset$ is the null stimulus (transformation, response), 1 is the other than null stimulus (transformation, response), and * is any kind of stimulus (transformation, response).

particular data base external originator of triggered behavior is, of course, the triggering stimulus from an *operative* process in an environment subsystem.

We distinguish between triggered behavior that modifies the data base and triggered behavior that leaves the data base invariant. Data base modifying behavior is initiated by a *modification transaction*. Different kinds of modifications are suggested by some of the subheadings in Fig. 5.2 and will be further discussed in the next subsection. The most typical interaction type to leave the data base invariant is the query, which is initiated by a *query transaction* and will be further discussed in the next subsection and in Section 5.4. However, interactions that aim at data base modification but are not successful—for instance, because the interactor is not authorized to carry out the desired modification—formally belong to the same interaction category as queries.

Major Data Base Transaction Types

It is by means of data base transactions that the exchange of data, information, and control between the data base and its environment takes place. Without data base transactions there would be no data base interaction. Formally a data base transaction has the structure

$$dbt = <\text{operator, parameter}>$$

where the *operator* is a stimulus that initiates a certain *kind of behavior*, or action, on part of the data base or the environment interactor, depending on the direction of the transaction, and the *parameter* modifies the behavior of the data base or interactor by providing the process, initiated by the operator, with certain input.

If the transaction is directed from the environment to the data base—that is, if it is an *input transaction*—the operator could, for instance, initiate the addition or the deletion of a message. The operator would then put the data base into addition or deletion "mode," whereas the actual piece of information to be added or deleted would be supplied by the parameter part of the transaction.

If the transaction is, instead, directed from the data base to an interactor—that is, if it is an *output transaction*—the operator could, for instance, put the interactor into receiving or replying mode, whereas the parameter would in those cases be the information to be received or the question to be replied to, respectively.

Naturally, the operator need not be represented by a specific string of characters or the like. Just as often the stimulus may be inseparable from the string of characters representing the parameter. For example, a query operator may be explicitly represented by a question mark (?), or implicitly represented by the grammatical structure of the message supplying the parametrical input to the query process.

It seems natural to say that data base transactions with identical operator parts belong to the same *transaction type*. It also seems natural to claim that there should be at least one transaction type for each interaction type. However, as we have seen, there are several ways of classifying interactions, and for each way the classification may be "deep" or "shallow." Ultimately it is a design problem of defining the set of transaction types (operators) for a particular data base system. The problem is structured by the classifications given in the first two subsections of Section 5.3. For instance, we may ask ourselves at goal-setting and design time what operators (if any) we should define for a particular environment subsystem, say, information supply and a particular row in Fig. 5.5, "query about the information".*

The number and scope of the operators we define for a specific task will also depend on whether we choose to achieve a certain total amount of *communication variety* by means of a few operators allowing a wide range of parametrical input or by means of a larger number of operators, each of them with more rigid requirements on the parametrical input.

MODIFICATION TRANSACTIONS. If we look back at Fig. 5.5, we find that there are several kinds of data base behavior that can be triggered by a modification transaction. First, the modification may concern either the nucleus, or the schema, or the filter function of the data base. We may also distinguish between additions, deletions, and substitutions of information. An *information addition* transaction has the structure

<ADD, message>

where ADD is an operator that puts the data base into "information reception mode," and "message" denotes the particular message to be received by the data base.

The message parameter of the information addition transaction may be of any kind and complexity. Let us assume, however, that it is equivalent to a set

$$M = [m_1, \ldots , m_n] \tag{1}$$

of n elementary messages. Then it should be observed that this does not necessarily mean that the transaction adds exactly n e messages to the information contents of the data base. On the one hand some of the e messages in M, say,

$$M_i = [m_1, \ldots , m_i] \tag{2}$$

may already be known to the data base as stored or derivable messages. On the other hand, other messages than those contained in either M or

$$B = \text{the information contents or the data base} \tag{3}$$

---

* This particular combination might, for instance, make the designer recognize that the data base system he is designing should embrace language, metainformation, and retrieval routines enabling a particular supplier category to ask questions about the information they should supply, for example, how a particular attribute is defined. Similar questions may, of course, be asked by several interactor categories, but probably each category will have its specific requirements as to the language.

may be derivable from MUB and thus truly added to the data base by the transaction. Let

$$\Delta B = \Delta B \ (B, \ M) \tag{4}$$

denote the set of e messages which, due to the transaction, are transitioned from the set of unknown messages to the set of known messages (see Fig. 5.4). ΔB contains as subsets both the set of messages in the transaction parameter that are really new to the data base,

$$M_{i+1,n} = M \setminus M_i \tag{5}$$

and the set of messages that are derivable from $M \cup B$ but not from B alone.

The cardinality of ΔB,

$$\#(\Delta B) \tag{6}$$

could be taken as a measure of the *quantity of information* added to the data base by the transaction. Note that $\#(\Delta B)$ may be less than, equal to, or greater than n. If

$$\#(\Delta B) = 0$$

the transaction adds no new knowledge at all to the data base.

The definition of information quantity suggested above implies among other things that the same transaction may add different amounts of information to different data bases. This seems perfectly reasonable, particularly if we define "information" as "new knowledge." What is "new knowledge" may certainly differ from one data base to another, be the data base "natural"—that is, a human mind—or "artificial." The argument also suggests that the stated definition of information quantity could be just as useful for communication between people as for communication with a data base. The magnitude of information conveyed by a certain message must be a function of the subjective frame of reference of the receiver as well as of the (objective) message itself.

An *information deletion* transaction has the structure

$<$DELETE, message$>$

where DELETE is an operator that initiates an abolition process within the data base "organism", and "message" denotes the particular message to be abolished from the data base.

We assume again that the message parameter is equivalent to a set $M = \{m_1, \ldots, m_n\}$ of n elementary messages. The deletion transaction may imply different kinds of actions depending on the status of each e message $m_i \ (i = 1, \ldots, n)$ within the information contents, B, of the data base (see Fig. 5.4).

1. If m_i is not known to the data base, $m_i \; \varepsilon \; B$, no action at all is needed. However, in this situation the deletion transaction from the interactor to the data base would probably be followed by a "warning transaction" from the data base to the interactor.

2. If m_i is a stored, nonderivable message, m_i should be canceled, which may cause both datalogical and infological problems. First, if m_i is redundantly stored in several files, it has to be removed from all the files where it occurs. Second, if m_i is canceled, all virtual messages in B that are not derivable from $(B \setminus \{m_i\})$ will be automatically canceled as well. If this was not the interactor's intention, the virtual messages concerned have to be stored explicitly before m_i is canceled. Third, by a deletion (as by an addition) the information and data contents of the data base are changed. This implies that a lot of metainformation, "information on information" and "information on data" has to be changed, too, if it is to remain correct.

3. The worst situation appears if m_i is a derivable message. Then either (a) we have to restructure the data base so that m_i becomes a stored, nonderivable message, which may be canceled as described under (2), or (b) the data base has to have the *exceptional storage feature*; that is, the nucleus of the data base has to have a part in which messages are stored, which in cases of contradiction should have priority over the rest of the information contents of the data base; thus the *exceptional messages* should nullify their negations, even if the latter should happen to be derivable from other stored messages by means of the "ordinary"* set of derivation rules of the data base schema.

If we let $\Delta B = \Delta B \,(B, M)$ denote the set of e messages that, due to the deletion transaction, are transitioned from the set of known messages to the set of forgotten messages, we may again take $\#(\Delta B)$ as a quantitative measure of the change in the information contents of the data base caused by the transaction. This time the change is negative, of course. In connection with deletions, $\#(\Delta B)$ will usually be greater than n; it will be less than n only if at least one e message in M is not known to the data base of case (1) above.

An *information substitution* transaction has the structure

<SUBSTITUTE, message 1, message 2>

where SUBSTITUTE is an operator, and "message 1" denotes the message to be replaced with "message 2."

Formally, a substitution is nothing but a deletion immediately followed by an addition. In practice, however, the two messages, the deleted message and the added one, are always related to each other in some characteristic way. For instance "message 1" may be a message that has been *erroneously* added to the data base, and "message 2" may be the correct message, which should have been added in the first place.

Another typical example of information substitution is the *traditional update* situation in which a message like

$<$object i, $<$attribute A, value $j>$, time $t_j>$

is replaced with

$<$object i, $<$attribute A, value $k>$, time $t_k>$

where $t_j < t_k$ is similar to "current time." Such transactions are very frequent in connection with *situational data bases*, which aim at reflecting the "current situation" in the object system and nothing more. Even in *historical data bases*, in which the history of the object system is also reflected, update transactions may be common, however, if only a *partial history* of the object system is saved. It is then natural to define the partial history in terms like "the latest n time versions of message type . . . ," and then the addition of time version x becomes tied to the deletion of time version $x - n$.

QUERY TRANSACTIONS. According to Fig. 5.5 the query type of interaction is a kind of triggered behavior that leaves the data base invariant. The triggering stimulus is contained in a *query transaction*,

$<$operator, parameter$>$

which normally results in a nontrivial *reply transaction* from the data base to the interactor.

There are several kinds of query transactions. First, we may distinguish between queries about the object system proper and queries about the data base contained information about the object system proper (see Section 5.2). However, if the metadata bases containing the metainformation are designed according to the same infological principles as the data base proper—and there is no reason why they should not be—there is no structural difference between the two kinds of queries.

If we are looking for structural differences between different kinds of queries, we may instead distinguish between (a) yes/no queries, (b) retrieval queries, and (c) process queries.

What is typical of *yes/no queries* is that the parameter part of such a transaction will always be a *complete message, m*. If m is contained in the data base, the obvious reply to the query is "yes"; and if a message, which logically contradicts m, is contained in the data base, the latter will certainly reply "no" to the query. If neither m nor its contradiction is contained in the data base, some kind of qualified "I don't know" response should be expected; what exactly will happen in such a situation is dependent on our infological design of the data base schema. A sophisticated data base might give an answer in terms of probabilities, for instance.

In *retrieval queries* the parameter will be an *incomplete message*, *m*, that is, a message in which at least one of the terms is ambiguous or completely missing. The reply is expected to contain those messages that *satisfy m*. Naturally, the "I don't know" problem mentioned above is present in connection with retrieval queries, too, and once again the action taken by the data base in such situations will depend on our infological design of the data base schema.

In process queries the operator or the parameter part* will contain a *processing request*, meaning that not only should a specified set of messages be retrieved, they should also be processed in a certain way before presentation. For instance, the processing request could imply aggregation and statistical analysis.

5.4 DIFFERENT KINDS OF RETRIEVAL QUERIES

If a data base system is to reply to a yes/no query, it has to retrieve a particular message or its contradiction. If the request to be processed is instead a process query, the first task of the data base system is to retrieve a number of messages that are to be processed further. If the data base transaction belongs to the "information substitution" or "information deletion" category, the data base system has to retrieve the message that is to be replaced or deleted. Even if the transaction is of "information-addition" type, the data base may have to perform a retrieval operation in order to check if the message to be added, or possibly its contradiction, is already contained in the base. Furthermore, the processing of a data base transaction, which primarily concerns information about the object system proper, will inevitably generate a lot of secondary transactions concerning the information contents of so-called metadata bases (see the Infological Data Base Concept in Section 5.2) within the main data base. Many of the secondary transactions will be of retrieval type.

Thus most transactions from an interactor to a data base will among other things imply processing that is equivalent to the processing of one

---

* As was stated above we often have a choice between specifying a few, very flexible operators or a larger number of operators with more rigid requirements upon the parametrical input.

or more retrieval queries. That is why we consider the study of retrieval queries to be of particularly great importance. In order to perform the study in a systematical way we shall use the theory of $\alpha\beta$ queries and $\alpha\beta\gamma$ queries.* These query patterns are believed to cover the bulk of retrieval queries in today's and tomorrow's data base systems.

$\alpha\beta$ Queries

Many retrieval queries conform to the pattern

1. For all objects having the property P^α, retrieve the values of the attributes $A_1^\beta, \ldots, A_m^\beta$, at the times $t_1^\beta, \ldots, t_m^\beta$, respectively.

This query pattern will be called the $\alpha\beta$-query pattern. Formally, an $\alpha\beta$ query may be described as a set of m incomplete e messages

2. $<P^\alpha, <A_i^\beta, ?>, t_i^\beta>$ $i = 1, \ldots, m$

where P^α is an ambiguous object reference, which means that it refers to a property that may very well be had by several objects. For example, in the $\alpha\beta$ query

3. List name, department, and salary of all employees.

the ambiguous object reference P^α is "to be an employee (now)."

In general P^α need not be a simple, atomic property reference like "to be an employee." Instead P^α may be a very complex reference expression involving a lot of references to $<$attribute, value$>$ pairs, object relations, times, and so on. For example, in the $\alpha\beta$ query

4. What are the addresses of the textile-manufacturing enterprises with more than 15 employees and producing articles containing the poison with the industrial name POI?

the P^α property is seen to be

5. $P^\alpha =$ textile-manufacturing enterprise with more than 15 employees and producing articles containing the poison POI.

---

* This theory is developed by Sundgren (1973, Chapters 5 and 6).

This property is generated from the atomic properties,

6. P_1^α = to be textile-manufacturing
P_2^α = to be an enterprise
P_3^α = to be an article
P_4^α = to be a poison

and the complex, <attribute, value> properties,

7. P_5^α = number of employees > 15
p_6^α = industrial name = POI

which involve the attributes,

8. A_1^α = number of employees
A_2^α = industrial name

respectively. Among the entities generating P^α are also the object relations.

9. R_1^α = produce
R_2^α = contain

and the tacitly understood time,

10. t^α = now

Thus in general

11. $P^\alpha = g(P_i^\alpha, A_j^\alpha, R_k^\alpha, t_m^\alpha)$

where P_i^α represents atomical local properties, A_j^α represents attributes, R_k^α represents object relations, and t_m^α represents times. The represented entities are called, respectively, the α properties, the α attributes, the α relations, and the α times of the $\alpha\beta$ query (1).

Note that the difference between α attributes and β attributes is not inherent in the attributes. Instead the classification of attributes into α attributes and β attributes is a functional, context-dependent classification. One and the same attribute may be an α attribute in one query and a β attribute in another.

EXERCISE 1: Compare the queries:
    12. List name, address, occupation, and telephone number of
        all single males aged 25 and earning more than $10,000.
    13. List income, age, and registration number of all dentists
        whose names begin with a C.

In query (12) the α attributes are marital status, sex, age, and
income, and the β attributes are name, address, occupation, and
telephone number. In query (13) the α attributes are occupation and
name, and the β attributes are income, age, and registration number.
Thus income and age are α attributes in (12) but β attributes in (13),
whereas occupation and name are β attributes in (12) but α attributes in
(13).

All times, both α and β times, involved in (12) and (13) were tacitly
assumed to be identical and equal to current time, or now. In general, a
lot of different α and β times may, of course, occur in a retrieval query
conforming to the $\alpha\beta$-query pattern.

Both at data base design time and at data base operation time a
need for graphical communication and documentation techniques will
often arise. Figure 5.6 shows for the example (4) how $\alpha\beta$ queries (1) may
be analyzed and illustrated graphically. The squares in the figure
represent sets of objects (object targets) which are demarcated by the
properties symbolized by the lines entering the squares from different
directions. Vertical lines entering the squares denote relation-dependent
properties, that is, properties that are generated from object relations. A
horizontal line entering an object-target square from the right denotes a
property, which is also common to all the objects in the target set, but
which is not relation dependent. A horizontal line entering an object-
target square from the left denotes a property asked for by the query, a
requested value of a particular attribute. The triangles in the figure
denote properties. By means of generation rules, represented in the figure
by circles with operator symbols in them, the triangle properties may be
combined into derived properties, which in turn may generate other
derived properties.

With only a little training it should be possible for all who are
interested in the design of a data base as well as for all who will directly
interact with the data base at operation time to understand and even to
draw for themselves diagrams like Fig. 5.6. We can also see that different
sets of α and β times in the query to be represented will not cause any
problems if this technique is used. As a matter of fact we may in many
practical situations make the infological structure of a query still easier

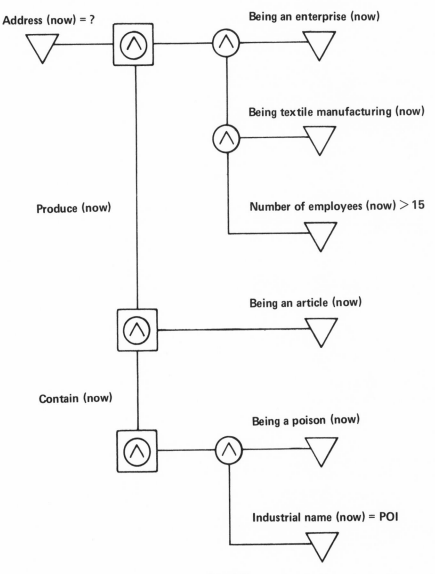

Fig. 5.6

to survey by adopting a few simplifying conventions. These conventions are (a) the default time reference "now" is left out; (b) atomical properties* are represented directly in the squares rather than by means of separate triangles linked to the squares by straight lines; and (c) logical conjunction is regarded as the default property generation rule, and the corresponding circles are left out. Applying these conventions to Fig. 5.6, we get Fig. 5.7, which is obviously much "cleaner."

In many practical situations graphical communication is not economically feasible. We then have to consider the problem of representing infological structures verbally instead of graphically. One alternative is shown in Table 5.1, which is essentially a "verbal reflection" of Figs. 5.6 and 5.7. Note, however, that we have to introduce the auxiliary symbols A, B, and C.

Table 5.1

OBJECT GROUP	PROPERTIES
A	Enterprise
	Textile-manufactures
	Number of employees > 15
	Address = ?
B	Article
C	Poison
	Industrial name = POI

OBJECT RELATION	DOMAINS
Produce	A, B
Contain	B, C

EXERCISE 2: Give the graphical representation of the $\alpha\beta$ queries (3), (12), and (13).

EXERCISE 3: Analyze the query

14. Retrieve civic registration number, age, and family income for all married couples where the husband's father is a fisherman and the wife's mother was born in France.

---

* Atomical properties are those that do not have the $<$attribute,value$>$ structure.

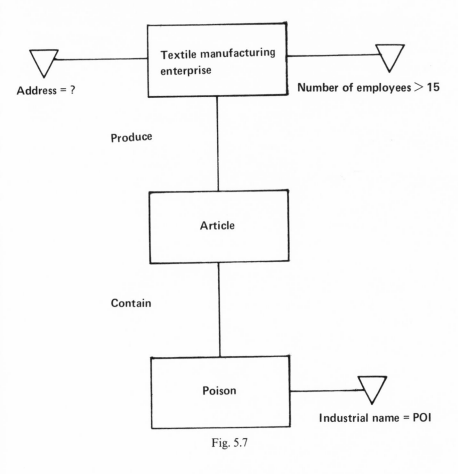

Fig. 5.7

This query does not immediately conform to the pattern (1).
Try to generalize the formulation (1) so that queries like
(14) may also be regarded as $\alpha\beta$ queries.
Hint: For all object *tuples* .... .

EXERCISE 4: Try to represent (14) graphically.
Hint: Use the symbol to represent the set of married couples.

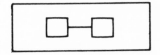

$\alpha\beta\gamma$ Queries

An $\alpha\beta$ query requests the retrieval of a single e message or an unstructured conjunction of e messages. More general retrieval requests will possess one or more of the following characteristics:

1. The query requests the retrieval of a structured conjunction of e messages, for example, a list of e messages sorted by one or more arguments.
2. The query requests the fabrication of aggregate messages from sets of e messages. For example, the request "display the average salary figure in company X" implies aggregation of a set of e messages, containing one salary e message per employee in company X, into one single aggregate message.
3. The query requests the retrieval of a structured conjunction of aggregate e messages, for example, a table of averages sorted by one or more arguments.

Many retrieval queries possessing at least one of the characteristics (1) - (3) conform to the $\alpha\beta\gamma$ pattern, which is to be discussed in this section.*

Let us start our study of $\alpha\beta\gamma$ queries with two simple examples:

1. List the names and telephone numbers of all employees *by department*.
2. Compute *average* income 1971 *for different social classes* in Stockholm.

We have italicized the part of the queries that distinguishes them from the $\alpha\beta$ queries discussed at the beginning of this section.

Suppose there are three departments, D1, D2, and D3. Then query (1) consists of three subqueries that conform to the $\alpha\beta$ pattern:

1.1 List the names and telephone numbers of all employees in department D1.
1.2 List the names and telephone numbers of all employees in department D2.

---

* An exhaustive study of $\alpha\beta\gamma$ queries requires the conceptual framework of the so-called box theory, which has been developed by Sundgren (1973, Chapter 6). However, it is beyound the scope of this text to discuss that theory. Here we shall only try to give a general understanding of the infological structure underlying $\alpha\beta\gamma$ queries.

    1.3 List the names and telephone numbers of all employees in department D3.

EXERCISE 5: Identify the α parts and β parts of (1.1)—(1.3) and visualize the queries graphically with the technique presented in the beginning of this section.

Having solved the exercise the reader may easily confirm that the α parts of the subqueries of (1) conform to the pattern

3. $P_1^\alpha = P_0^\alpha \wedge (V^\gamma = a_1)$

        $\vdots$

$P_n^\alpha = P_0^\alpha \wedge (V^\gamma = a_n)$

In (1) the common α property P_0^α is "to be an employee," and the attribute V^γ, which is also common to the α parts of all subqueries, is "department name"; V^γ is called the γ attribute of the $\alpha\beta\gamma$ query.

    In general an $\alpha\beta\gamma$ query may contain an arbitrary number of γ attributes, say, k: $V_1^\gamma, \ldots, V_k^\gamma$. Each of the γ attributes may take an arbitrary number of values. We shall let n_i denote the number of values taken by V_i^γ $(i = 1, \ldots, k)$.

EXAMPLE 1: In the request

4. Compute the average length of life for human beings by nationality and sex.

P_0^γ is "to be a human being," V_1^γ is "nationality," V_2^γ is "sex," $k = 2$, n_1 is the number of nationalities, and $n_2 = 2$.

EXERCISE 6: Assume that there are three nationalities: "African," "Asian," and "European"; and two sexes: "male" and "female." Find for query (4) the system of equations corresponding to (3). How many rows does the system contain?

EXERCISE 7: Find the system of equations (3) for an arbitrary $\alpha\beta\gamma$ query, that is, an $\alpha\beta\gamma$ query with k γ variables, $V_1^\gamma, \ldots, V_k^\gamma$. How many rows does this system contain? Interpret the meaning of an arbitrary row in the system.

Three characteristics of a general $\alpha\beta\gamma$ query were stated in the beginning of this section. The characteristics were labeled(a), (b), and (c).

So far we have only discussed characteristic (a). However, in (2) and (4) we have already encountered examples of $\alpha\beta\gamma$ queries possessing the characteristics (b) and (c). Let us repeat query (2).

    5. Compute *average* income 1971 for different social classes in Stockholm.

Assuming that there are three social classes, C_1, C_2, and C_3, this query requests the output of three messages, looking something like

    5.1   Average income in Stockholm 1971 was $\$a_1$, for social class C_1.

    5.2   Average income in Stockholm 1971 was $\$a_2$ for social class C_2.

    5.3   Average income in Stockholm 1971 was $\$a_3$ for social class C_3.

The object part of each of these messages is a *group* of objects. For example, the object part of (5.2) is the group of Stockholmers belonging to social class C_2. The β attribute of (5), and of the three subqueries corresponding to (5.1)–(5.3), is "average income." Now compare query (5) with the query,

    6. List income 1971 for all Stockholmers by social class.
This is an $\alpha\beta\gamma$ query that has the same structure as (5), but whereas (5) was seen to request the output of three messages, we realize that (6) demands the presentation of a set of messages that contains as many members as there are individuals living in Stockholm. However, (6) also says that these messages should be listed by social class. Thus the output messages will be sorted into three groups corresponding to the subqueries

    6.1 List income 1971 for all Stockholmers belonging to social class C_1.

    6.2 List income 1971 for all Stockholmers belonging to social class C_2.

    6.3 List income 1971 for all Stockholmers belonging to social class C_3.

These subqueries conform to exactly the same pattern as the subqueries of (1) above and may be analyzed in the same way. The α parts of (6.1)–(6.3) conform to pattern (3). The common α property P_0^α is "to be a

Stockholmer," and the common γ attribute V^β is "social class."

If we compare (5) and (6) we find the following relations between the two $\alpha\beta\gamma$-queries: (a) The object part of the single message (5*i*) is an object group, the group of Stockholmers belonging to social class C_i. Each object in this group occurs in the object part of exactly one of the reply messages corresponding to (6*i*). Conversely, each object occurring as the object part of a reply message corresponding to (6*i*) will be contained in the object group, which is the object part of the single message (5*i*). Thus the object part of (5*i*) is an *aggregation* of the object parts of (6*i*): $i = 1, 2, 3$. (b) The β attribute in (6) is V^β = income. The β attribute in (5) is $\overline{V^\beta}$ = average income. The value of V^β referred to in (5*i*) is a function of precisely those values of V^β that are requested by (6*i*), because the average income of a group of individuals is a function of the respective incomes of the individuals who make up the group. Thus the value of $\overline{V^\beta}$ in (5*i*) is *aggregated* from the values of V^β requested by (6*i*): $i = 1, 2, 3$.

More generally we may say that an *aggregate* $\alpha\beta\gamma$ query requesting information about *n* object groups, $O_1, \ldots, O_n$, *may always be be dissolved into n sets*, $S_1, \ldots, S_n$ of *structurally similar disaggregate* $\alpha\beta\gamma$ queries in such a way that (a) the object part of any message in S_i is contained in O_i, and any individual object in O_i is the object part of exactly one message in S_i: $i = 1, \ldots, n$; (b) the β information requested about O_i may be deduced from the messages in S_i: $i = 1, \ldots, n$.

If the data base nucleus (see Section 5.2) contains the disaggregate but not the aggregate messages corresponding to an aggregate $\alpha\beta\gamma$ query, the datalogical processing of the query has to be very similar to the infological analysis and synthesis indicated by (a) and (b) above. It is an important data base design decision to determine if the data base nucleus should contain the aggregate reply to an aggregate query, or if it should instead contain the disaggregate messages from which the aggregate reply may be deduced. Given that the data base should be able to reply to a certain set of queries, the latter method will normally save secondary storage capacity, because a lot of different aggregate messages will be derivable from a relatively low number of disaggregate messages.

EXAMPLE 2: Suppose that a country has 10 million inhabitants, and that we have defined 1000 administrative areas, 500 occupations, 100 income classes, 4 residential forms, and 2 sexes. Then an $\alpha\beta\gamma$ query like

    7. State average fortune by region, occupation, income class, residential form, and sex.

requests the computation of 1000*500*4*2 = 400 million aggregate messages. If explicitly stored in the data base nucleus, these aggregate messages would occupy much more secondary storage space than the 10 million disaggregate messages from which the aggregate messages may be desired.

EXERCISE 8: Give examples of situations in which it could be advantageous to store aggregate messages in the data base nucleus.

EXERCISE 9: Give examples of situations in which it could be advantageous to store redundantly both disaggregate messages and derivable aggregate messages.

EXERCISE 10: From a computer privacy point of view we can argue that it is safer to store only aggregate information about groups of individuals instead of storing disaggregate information about single individuals. Unfortunately, there are situations in which aggregate $\alpha\beta\gamma$ queries require logically (and not only for performance reasons) the retrievability of dissaggregate messages. An example of such a situation is the following aggregate $\alpha\beta\gamma$ query:

> 8. Compute how large proportions of different categories of employees in company X have increased their incomes by less than 20 percent since 1970.

Analyze this query and explain why it requires the retrievability of disaggregate messages about individual employees. What other protection measures could be undertaken in order to ensure privacy in such situations?

Hints: (a) Does anyone *outside* the data base need the presentation of the disaggregate messages from which the aggregate reply to the query (8) is desired? (b) Does the data base require the individual employees to be identified by name or by means of numbers that are known to somebody outside the data base?

EXERCISE 11: Identify and analyze the α, β, and γ parts of the following aggregate $\alpha\beta\gamma$ queries:

> 9. Compute the total income earned by (a) married male Swedes, (b) single male Swedes, (c) married female Swedes, and (d) single female Swedes, respectively.

10. Compute the total number of Swedes by marital status and sex.

11. Compute average income in Sweden for people belonging to different sexes and different groups of marital status.

How are (9), (10), and (11) logically related to each other?

CONCLUSIONS

We described the general data base structure as one containing a schema, a nucleus (the "main file"), and a filter. Data base transactions can be classified by their effects on any of these, in distinct combinations. The S-O-R model (stimulus–organism–response) sometimes used by psychologists in the study of human behavior was also found useful for the data base interactions.

The queries presented to a data base often have the general type of presenting two classes of attributes, the α attributes which are specified together with the associated values and the β attributes whose values are asked for. This structure is made the basis for much of the discussion of data base interactions.

Review Questions

1. It is not easy to find one single characteristic that is typical of all data bases, and that is one reason why we have refrained from stating a short, formal definition of the data base concept. Having read this chapter, what features would you require from a data base?

2. Many people seem to take it for granted that the files of a data base should be on direct-access storage, and that the data base system should be capable of handling all kinds of interactions within a few seconds. What do you think? Give examples of data base applications in which some of the files could very well be on serial storage, and in which the turn-around times for different kinds of interactions can range from seconds to hours, or even days or weeks.

3. The set of programs, or software, used for the realization of a data base oriented information system, is often called a "data base management system," DBMS. There are several DBMS available on the market today. Which do you know of, and what do you know about their schema nucleus, and filter characteristics?

4. We have presented two schemes for classification of data base interactions. Both of the schemes can be used as the modularization

basis of a modularized DBMS. Discuss this. Can the two modularization schemes be combined into one?

5. What are the advantages of a modularized DBMS (a) if you are about to design and construct your own DBMS? (b) if you are about to buy a DBMS from a computer manufacturer or a software house? and (c) at run time?

6. Most programming languages in use today, for example, COBOL, require an information request to contain three functional parts: (a) an *input description*, describing the input files; (b) an *output description*, describing the desired result of the request; and (c) a *process description*, describing how the input should be transformed into the output. What do you think will be the relative importance of these functional parts in future data base interaction languages.
   Hints: (a) What should the data base schema contain? (Information that is contained in the data base need not be repeated in the request submitted to the data base.) (b) What about the need for process descriptions if the desired result of a request is expressed by an $\alpha\beta$ query or an $\alpha\beta\gamma$ query?

7. A programming language that requires the processes to be explicitly specified is often called "procedural," or "constructive." The opposite is called "nonprocedural," "result oriented," or "descriptive." (a) In view of Question 6 above, what degree of procedurality, high or low, do you think will characterize future data base interaction languages? (b) "Natural–formal" and "reality oriented–computer oriented" are two other dimensions that can be used for classifying data base interaction languages. What development trends do you think can be expected in these dimensions? Discuss also the advantages and disadvantages of natural language as a means of communication.

8. Use the concepts introduced in this chapter in order to describe systematically the interaction between the data base of a seat reservation system and its environment. Assume that the customers have to apply to operators who are connected to the data base via display terminals. Who are the end users of this data base system? The data base system may be demarcated from its environment so as to include or exclude the display terminal operators. What difference does it make whether you choose one demarcation or the other? Which demarcation is most natural from the point of view of the end user?

CHAPTER 6

DESIGN OF THE FILES AND PROCESSES OF A DATA BASE SYSTEM

In this book we use the term "systemeering"* to denote the analytical and creative task of designing data bases and other systems. In the previous chapter we treated the infological aspect of the data base systemeering task. From the infological point of view, a data base was found to be equivalent to a black box reservoir of information, capable of communication with an environment that contains "information suppliers," "information consumers," and other interactor categories. We also identified three basic subsystems, or functions, of the infological data base: the nucleus, the schema, and the filter.

---

* See footnote, page 205.

6.1 DATALOGICAL DATA BASE SYSTEMEERING

The infological approach to the data base should help the system-eers to concentrate their initial efforts on the design problems that are of interest to the ultimate users of the data base. Those are the design problems that concern *what* the data base should be capable of doing, more than *how* it should be done. Ultimately, however, a data base has to be a system of data, stored on physical media, and data transforming processes executed by computers or other processors. Thus the data base systemeer has to combine the infological view of the data base with datalogical, computer-oriented considerations. He has to consider how he can best utilize available storage and processor resources in order to realize the desired infological functions of the data base.

It is important that infological, user-oriented systemeering and datalogical, computer-oriented systemeering are not looked on as two independent tasks. Instead the datalogical design of a data base should be regarded as a natural extension of the infological design. In the absence of an adequate conceptual framework, however, it has turned out to be very difficult for user-oriented systemeers and computer specialists to communicate with each other in a constructive way. We hope that the conceptual tools presented in earlier chapters of this book will help to bridge the communication gap. In this chapter we shall show how the tools may be used to attack some important datalogical subproblems of the total data base systemeering task.

Resources and Processes

Like many other systems a data base may be regarded as a set of related resources and processes.

In general, a *resource* may be any kind of asset, physical or abstract, monetary or intangible, and so on. People, disk storage, health, computer programs, knowledge, leisure, CPU time, and energy could serve as examples of resources from different kinds of systems.

A *process* is an abstract entity producing change by transforming a set of resources, the input resources, into another set of resources, the output resources, and by initiating, suspending, activating, and termi-nating other processes.

The relationship between a process and a resource may be of several kinds. For example, a process may (a) use a resource exclusively for a certain period of time and then release it, (b) share a resource with other processes, (c) return a resource in its original state, (d) return a resource in a different state, (e) create a resource, or (f) destroy a resource. Figure 6.1 visualizes the process and resource structure of an arbitrary system.

In Chapter 5 we discussed the interaction between the environment and the data base in terms of a black box S-O-R model. We said that an input transaction stimulus S somehow caused or resulted in an output transaction response R and a transformation of the data base "organism" $O \rightarrow O'$. We need the process concept to explain *how* the result comes about. The input transaction, seen as a stimulus*, initiates or activates a data base process, which in turn activates other processes, and so on. Any data base process is initiated either by a stimulus from the data base environment, that is, from an external process, or by a stimulus produced by another data base process. After its initiation, the data base process exists as an alternately active and passive (suspended) process until it is terminated by itself or by another internal or external process. After that, the process instance does not exist any longer. It can never be activated again.

Data base processes use, release, create, and destroy resources, which are either *internal* resources, belonging to the data base system, or *external* resources, belonging to the data base environment. Among the created resources may be an output message, and among the destroyed resources may be a piece of paper upon which the message is written. The total transformation of the data base organism caused by an input transaction consists of all changes of states, creations, and destructions of internal resources that take place during the data base interaction which is initiated by the input transaction.

Naturally, for different purposes we may use different degrees of resolution in order to explain the behavior of a data base system. Both the processes and the resources may be described with different degrees of detail. On the one hand a certain interaction may be analyzed in terms of a process with just a few subprocesses, or steps, using a few main resources. On the other hand the execution of each instruction of the programs governing the processing of the interaction may be regarded as a separate subprocess, each bit of storage may be regarded as a separate resource, and so on. The *internal* resources of a data base system are *data* forming either (a) *programs*, defining patterns of behavior for sets of data base processes, or (b) *other data structures*, like files, index tables, and so-called control blocks.

Besides the data resources, which are internal to the data base

---

* The input transaction may often be seen both as a stimulus and as an external resource.

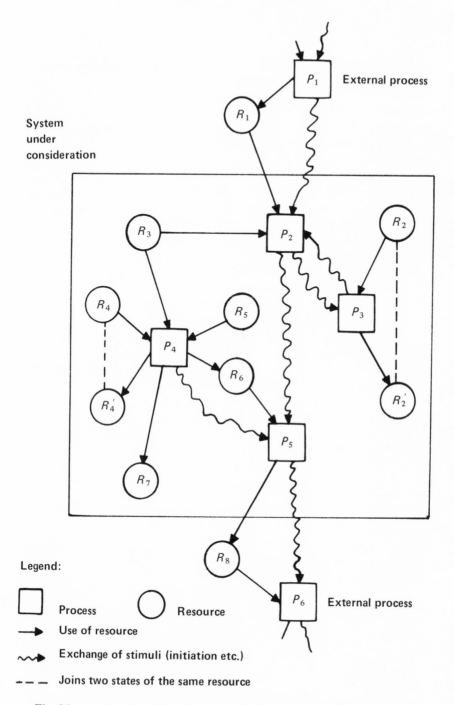

Fig. 6.1   A system viewed as a set of related resources and processes.

255

system, data base processes interact with *computer resources*, which belong to the computer subsystem of the data base environment (see Section 5.2) and are thus *external* to the data base system. Primary and secondary storage, processors, data transmission channels, and input/output devices are typical examples of computer resources. However, manual resources may also be part of the computer subsystem of the data base environment.

Figure 6.2 shows a typical pattern of relationships between a data base process and a set of data base internal and data base external resources. A closer analysis would make it possible to classify the relationships into different categories. For example, some resources will either be completely blocked or not used at all by a particular process at a particular point of time. Other resources may be shared by several processes, each of which uses the resource to some degree less than 100 percent. There are also resources that may, in principle, be used by any number of data base processes at a time. So-called reentrant programs belong to the latter category of resources.

We may define a resource as more or less *elastic* (Codd, 1971) depending on how easy it is to replace the resource with some other resource. For example, main memory may be an elastic resource

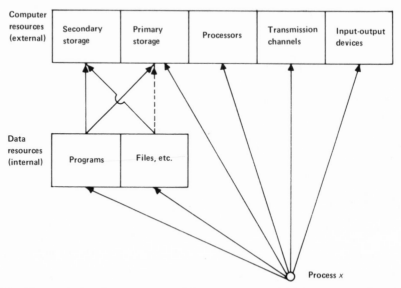

Fig. 6.2   A data base process and the resources to which it is related, directly and indirectly, at a particular point of time.

provided the operating system of the computer contains efficient algerithms for paging and swapping (Watson, 1970).

Data Base Subsystems

From the preceding sections we may conclude that the datalogical data base systemeering task essentially consists in planning for (a) the data structures to be used for the representation of the information contents of the data base, (b) the processes that are to communicate with each other and with the data base environment thereby possibly transforming the data resources of the data base, and (c) the programs that are to govern the behavior of the processes. Task (a) will be called *file design*, because most data base data will belong to a file of some kind, either a *proper file* or an *auxiliary file*. A proper file is one that contains data representing information about the object system proper. An auxiliary file is one that contains metadata, that is, data representations of metainformation (see Section 5.2). The tasks (b) and (c) are closely related to each other and both will be referred to as *process design*.

A data base is a typical example of an imperceivable system (Langefors, 1966). Such a system has to be partitioned into subsystems if it is to be designed. Thus we have to group the files and processes of a planned data base in such a way that files and processes brought together into the same subsystem are in some practical sense more related to each other than files and processes brought to different subsystems.

Figure 6.3 shows a partitioning of the set of all data base processes (and files) into eight subsystems. We shall briefly discuss the meaning and scope of each of these subsystems.

The subsystem labeled *proper files* is the datalogical counterpart of the infological "nucleus" subsystem (see Section 5.2). Besides the entries of the proper files it also contains the programs for accessing the files as well as auxiliary data, index tables, control blocks, and so on required by the access programs.

The *catalogues* subsystem contains data representing "information on information" (see Section 5.2) together with programs for processing this information. It contains the formal and informal definitions of attributes, object relations, and other infological entities, and it also contains programs corresponding to the more or less intricate deduction and induction rules of the infological model underlying the data base.

The *interaction* subsystem is the communication interface between the data base and its environment. Among other things it contains the compilers and interpreters of the data base interaction languages. It will translate the input transactions into the *internal dialect* (Nordbotten,

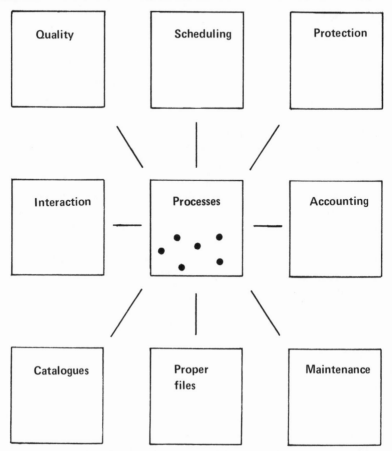

Fig. 6.3   A structuring of the set of all data base processes into eight data
base subsystems.

1967) of the data base, and, conversely, it will edit the output
transactions appropriately.

The *quality* and *protection* subsystems are the datalogical counterparts of the infological "filter" function (see Section 5.2). The importance of these subsystems will grow rapidly as the complexity of data
bases increases.

The quality control problems seem to have been more or less
neglected by the manufacturers of the data base software that is
available on the market today. In the protection area these systems are
usually equipped with a few features such as data protection through

password techniques, and certain logging and recovery functions. However, many problems remain to be solved, even on the theoretical level.

The *accounting* subsystem should collect statistics about different aspects of data base utilization and performance, not only to make it possible to distribute costs among different users of the data base, but also in order to supply the *maintenance* function or the data base administrator with adequate information for reorganization decisions.

The *scheduling* subsystem, finally, is responsible for the planning and coordination of the other processes. For instance, it should dynamically find efficient strategies for processing particular retrieval requests, and it should administrate the queues in front of hardware resources like disk drives and channels.

We cannot overemphasize the importance of the subsystem structure of a data base that is given in Fig. 6.3. Quality, scheduling, protection, interaction, accounting, catalogues, files, and maintenance are believed to form a feasible subsystem structure for many data base design projects on a particular stage of analysis. There are two qualifications to be made, however. First, the particular character of an individual data base may distort the proportions between the subsystems so as to make it more feasible even at an early stage of analysis to divide one of the subsystems into several functions. Second, the further breakdown of the structure of Fig. 6.3 almost certainly will not result in a perfect tree structure. Occasionally it will be found purposeful to isolate a function on one level that may serve several functions on the next higher level.

For each one of the eight subsystems in Fig. 6.3 the data base systemeer has to design *both* (a) files and other data structures *and* (b) processes and programs. However, it is obvious that some of the subsystems are dominated by data structuring problems, whereas the process design problems are more pronounced within other subsystems. The "proper files" subsystem represents one extreme and the "scheduling" subsystem the other. However, the access algorithms of the proper files will certainly have to be carefully designed, whereas the scheduling activities will no doubt require auxiliary files and other data structures of some sophistication. Thus when we talk about file structuring and process design in subsequent sections, it should be kept in mind that the methods and techniques presented are applicable not only to the proper files and the scheduling subsystems, respectively. Possibly after some reinterpretation the discussions and results will, to some degree, be relevant to all data base subsystems. We recall from Chapter 5 that a data base may be considered to contain several metadata bases, that is, data bases that inform about the information and the data contained in the data base itself, rather than about the object system proper.

6.2   FILE DESIGN

Formulation of the File Design Problem

Schematically the data base systemeer has to do the following in order to design the (proper) file system of the planned data base:

1. Define formally, in terms of e concepts, what information the data base should contain.
2. Define formally, what kinds of transactions (for example, what kinds of $\alpha\beta$ queries) will hit the data base at operation time. Also specify response-time requirements and expected frequencies during different time intervals for the transaction types that will occur.
3. Define the structure, capacity, and speed of available memories.
4. Define files corresponding to the e concepts and map these files into the available memories.

The tasks (1) and (2) are user-oriented, infological systemeering tasks, whereas (3) and (4) are computer-oriented, datalogical problems. In this chapter we assume that (1) and (2) have been solved. This does not mean that we assume that there exists perfect knowledge about the information contents of the data base and about the interactions that will take place at operation time. It only means that we have arrived at some systematized subjective judgment as to these parameters. Needless to say, the future end users of the data base should take active part in this formalized guesswork.The design task (4) may be further subdivided into the tasks,

4a. Establish an initial structure of elementary object files, property files, and relational files.*
4b. Transform the initial file structure by means of the intraentry, interentry, and interfile structuring operators that were defined and discussed in Chapter 4.
4c. Allocate (map) the transformed file structure to available memories.

The tasks (4a) and (4c) will be discussed in the following subsections. In Section 6.3 we shall treat the tasks (3) and (4c).

---

* These concepts were defined in Chapter 4.

Establishment of an Initial File Structure

The first file-structuring step consists in establishing a feasible initial file structure. This file structure need not fulfill all design goals, but it should be feasible in the sense that it seems reasonable to believe that a few applications of the file-structuring operators will lead to a satisfactory solution of the structuring problem; nor is it necessary or even desirable to define in detail the entry descriptions* and access algorithms* of the initial file structure, as these entries will change during the continued structuring work.

The file-establishment design step involves the demarcation between the data base nucleus and the rest of the data base information contents. We shall say that an *e* concept, which is made part of the data base nucleus, is *established as a real file*, and that a derivable *e* concept,[†] which is realized by means of schema algorithms, is *established as a virtual file*. It could sometimes be a wise decision to establish an *e* concept both as a real file and as a virtual file.

What, then, are the datalogical advantages and disadvantages of a virtual file compared to a real one? The main datalogical advantage achieved by algorithmizing a file is, of course the decrease of space needed to represent the messages of the data base. This decrease may be so substantial as to imply secondary effects such as a decrease in average access time within the data base as a whole. On the other hand the retrieval of a virtual entry will ordinarily consume more resources than the retrieval of a real file entry. There are two reasons for this. First, the retrieval of a virtual entry will usually imply the retrieval of several real entries, because the logical precedents of the algorithmized message may very well be spread over several files. Second, the breaking down of transactions concerning virtual entries into transactions concerning real entries and, conversely, the assembly of retrieved real entries into requested virtual entries will imply a lot of processing and, very likely, accesses to catalogues, tables, and other auxiliary data on secondary storage.

We said above that sometimes it might be well motivated to establish an *e* concept redundantly, both as a virtual file and as a real one. There are also good infological and datalogical reasons for duplicating real files in certain situations. One typical example is that it may lower the average response time for a certain mix of data base

---

* These concepts were defined in Chapter 4.

† The information analysis during the specification process resulting in the particular infological model underlying the data base should show which *e* concepts are derivable from others.

queries if we make the design decision that a particular *e* concept should be established both as an object *e* file and as a property *e* file. We should always remember, however, that each duplication will not only increase space demand, but will above all increase the problems of data base maintenance, including addition, deletion, and substitution transactions.

If there are to be several time versions of a particular *e* concept in the data base, we have to decide whether to establish one *e* file per time version, or one *e* file with separate *e* entries for different time versions, or one *e* file with one *e* entry per object. An important circumstance here is whether the data base is supposed to contain a complete history with respect to the *e* concept, or if, say, the 10 most recent time versions will do.

EXAMPLE 1: Suppose that a data base should contain a complete history with respect to the *e* concept <PERSON, INCOME>. This means that the data base should contain an ever-growing number of time versions of the particular message type. Then it is a design decision to choose among the following file-structuring alternatives:

1. One object file per time version of the message type—this choice implies an ever-growing number of files.
2. One object file for all time versions of the message type, and one file entry for all time versions of the message type for each relevant object, that is, one file entry per person. This choice implies a constant number of ever-growing entries, as long as the number of persons remains constant.
3. One object file for all time versions of the message type and one file entry per time version and person. This choice implies an ever-growing number of constant-length entries.

Alternative (3) requires the entry points of the file to contain a time component. Otherwise the entry points would not be unique entry identifications as required by the definition in Chapter 4.

If we decide to establish a particular *e* concept as a real file, the next design decision is to choose one of the three basic file types defined in Chapter 4. Thus we shall establish the *e* concept as an object *e* file, a property *e* file, or a relational *e* file. This is a choice that cannot be made for only one *e* concept at a time, because the *e* concepts of an infological model are related to each other, and these relations have to be efficiently reflected in the file structure to be designed. On the other hand we cannot make the choice for *all e* concepts simultaneously, because the set of all *e* concepts of an infological model will usually be an imperceivable system, and such systems have to be partitioned into perceivable subsystems in order to be designable. Perceivable subsystems of the set of all *e* concepts will be called *e-concept complexes* and the corresponding subsystems of the total file structure will be called *file complexes*.

How should these subsystems, or complexes, be demarcated? Here again we are guided by general systemeering principles: There should be relatively *many* relationships *within* each complex, or subsystem, and relatively *few* relationships *between* different complexes. The next question is what kind of relationship it is, the number of which should be minimized between complexes. It seems that two *e* concepts are related in a relevant way from the designer's point of view as soon as it is logically necessary for both of them to be involved in the processing of the same data base transaction. Thus it becomes an important design task to find and document these relationships in a way that will enable the designer in the next step to establish perceivable complexes of *e* files for further design activities. One possible technique will be described here.

In order to be able to carry out the analysis described above we must have some idea of the pattern of transactions that will hit the data base. We must be able to state formally to what extent different *e* concepts are related to each other in the sense that they are involved in the processing of the same transaction. In this task we may utilize our findings in Chapter 5. In Section 5.4 we established the $\alpha\beta$-query pattern:

1. For all objects having the property P^α, retrieve the values of the attributes $A_1^\beta, \ldots, A_m^\beta$ at the times $t_1^\beta, \ldots, t_m^\beta$, respectively.

We recall that the property P^α may be generated from a set of so-called α attributes, α times, and α relations. We also recall that we claimed pattern (1) to be fairly general, and not only for retrieval queries. Other transaction types will often result in retrieval requests, too.

According to pattern (1) a retrieval query consists of two parts, an α part and a β part, involving α-e concepts and β-e concepts, respectively. Given a query and the specification of an infological model, it should not be difficult for the designer to identify these *e* concepts and the corresponding *e* files. It is his task to investigate systematically all imaginable transactions and to document these findings in a form that is useful to the continued analysis. One possible technique is indicated by Fig. 6.4.

Figure 6.4 shows a matrix, spanned by an α axis and a β axis and

Fig. 6.4 $\alpha\beta$ matrix.

	F_1	F_2	F_3	F_4	F_5	F_6	F_7	F_8	F_9	F_{10}	F_{11}	F_{12}	F_{13}	F_{14}	F_{15}
F_1		7		11	8										
F_2				11	16				2	2					
F_3		14			16										
F_4															
F_5															
F_6		5					2						1		
F_7		6		19	9								2		
F_8				5	2				15	22					
F_9															
F_{10}		3							7						
F_{11}													9		9
F_{12}					7								5		20
F_{13}		2			1										
F_{14}				1									15		11
F_{15}													8		

having one row and one column for each e concept. A figure in a particular matrix entry, say, $<F_i, F_j>$, indicates that there will occur transactions involving F_i in the α part and F_j in the β part. The value of the figure is a weight indicating how frequent or important (from response-time point of view, for example) the transactions are in which the particular file combination occurs. Naturally, in practical design situations the figures in the matrix will usually be highly subjective estimates, but formalized informed judgment is often the best the designer can hope for.

After rearrangement of rows and columns, an $\alpha\beta$ matrix could look like the one in Fig. 6.4 in which it is not too difficult to find a feasible subsystem structure of the kind we are looking for, that is, a structure of file complexes with many intracomplex relationships and few inter-

complex relationships.* In Fig. 6.4 there seem to be three complexes of e concepts, C_1 comprising F_1–F_7, C_2 comprising F_8–F_{10}, and C_3 comprising F_{11}–F_{15}, which are "in a natural way" demarcated by the expected transaction pattern as reflected by the weights in the matrix.

Thus we have found the $\alpha\beta$ matrix to be a tool by means of which an imperceivable system of e concepts may be partioned into a set of perceivable complexes. However, the $\alpha\beta$ matrix may also be of great help in the next file-design step. This step is the one in which we determine for each e concept within a complex whether it should be established as an object file, a property file, or a relational file. We shall use the complex C_1 in Fig. 6.4 as an example, and to simplify the task we shall only consider the choice between object files and property files.

The complex C_1 consists of seven e concepts, F_1–F_7. Of these, F_4 and F_5 are seen to be expected to occur only in the α parts of the $\alpha\beta$ queries that will hit the data base; F_1, F_3, and F_6 are expected to occur only in the β parts; F_7 will typically occur in the β part, but on some rare occasions it will be an α-e concept; and F_2 will most often be an α-e concept, but almost as often it will occur in the β part of the expected $\alpha\beta$ queries. Now let us analyze what this implies for our choice of file types.

The function of the α part of an $\alpha\beta$ query is to demarcate a set of objects that have a stated property, P^α, in common. The objects in the demarcated set are the objects about which the query requests further information. Thus the input to the processing of the α part is a particular property, P^α, and the output should be a set of object references, referring to the object that has the property P^α. This processing can be done most easily if all e concepts involved in P^α are implemented as property files, because we recall that the entries of such files contain references to precisely those objects that have a particular property in common.

Suppose that the processing of the α part of the $\alpha\beta$ query has given us explicit references to the objects that have the property P^α. Then the processing of the β part should result in the retrieval of the values of the β attributes for these objects. This processing could be easily done if the β-e concepts are implemented as object files.

Thus e concepts that often occur as α parts in $\alpha\beta$ queries are strong property e-file candidates, whereas object e-file establishment is to be preferred for β-e concepts. For complex C_1 in our example this means that F_4 and F_5 should be established as property files, and F_1, F_3, F_6, and F_7 as object files. For F_2 redundant establishment as both an object file and a property file should be considered.

---

* There are statistical methods for solving this problem, given the matrix.

Our simple example has shown that infological analysis of the expected transaction pattern is the key to the initial file structure. In general we shall have to analyze $\alpha\beta\gamma$ queries as well as $\alpha\beta$ queries, and we shall have to break down other transaction types into their retrieval query constituents. It goes beyond the scope of this book to give examples of such analyses, but it should be pointed out that tools like the $\alpha\beta$ matrix are of great help in the more general analyses, too. The reader should recall that an $\alpha\beta\gamma$ query is always equivalent to a (structured) set of $\alpha\beta$ queries in which the γ attributes occur in the α parts. Thus the example of the $\alpha\beta$ analysis above is fundamental to all file design, even if the transactions are expected to have a more complex structure than is indicated by the $\alpha\beta$ pattern.

After the initial file structure has been established, the designer should use the file-structuring operators defined in Chapter 4 in order to arrive at a final file structure that conforms more efficiently to the storage and access structure of available memories. This will be discussed further in the next section. Often the final file structure will be a set of so-called *directory–file complexes*. A directory–file complex is a complex of object and property files in which all object files have been consolidated into one file, the *main file* of the complex, and in which the property files have been combined into one or more *directory files*; these together make up the *directory* of the complex. An example of directory–file-complex design will be analyzed later in this section.

EXERCISE 1: Discuss what kinds of files (object files or property files) should be chosen for the *e* concepts in (a) complex C_2, and (b) complex C_3, according to Fig. 6.4.

EXERCISE 2: The chain arrangement imposes a much stronger sequential character on the set of its segments than does the bundle arrangement. This statement is true when the segments are stored in distinct access blocks but not when they are in the same block. Explain why.

EXERCISE 3: The arrangement of a file entry as a bundle of chains allows a natural adaptation of the entry structure to the access block structure of the file storage unit used. Discuss how to apply this fact.

EXERCISE 4: It may appear as if the set of three basic structurings —contiguous, bundle, and chain—would only admit of tree structures. Show that more general structures can be built by the three basic ones.

EXERCISE 5: Discuss the potential advantage that the contiguous arrangement may sometimes have over the other forms.

File Structure Transformations

The initial file structure accomplished by the data base systemeer is a set of virtual and real *e* files in which the real *e* files are grouped into file complexes as described in the previous section, and in which each real *e* file has been specified as an object *e* file, a property *e* file, or a relational *e* file. By defining the initial file structure, the systemeer has structured the file-structuring task itself. He has partitioned the "grand file-structuring problem" into a number of relatively independent, manageable subproblems. We shall now discuss how to go on with the design of the demarcated file complexes.

Initially each file in a file complex is an *elementary* file with an internal structure that is given by *the data base normal format* (see Chapter 4). It is not likely that this initial, "normal" structure is the structure that best fits the available memory structure and that will result in an optimal trade-off between such design criteria as response speed, memory utilization, and ease of maintenance. At least the systemeer should try to find a more efficient file structure. How should he do this systematically?

There is no available theory today that can lead the systemeer directly to an optimal file structure for a particular data base. The best thing the designer can do at the present state of the art is to investigate and compare different feasible file structures in a systematic way. Then the systemeer needs a method that generates feasible alternatives, structures to be investigated and compared.

One method for generating file-structure alternatives is to apply, tentatively, different combinations of the file-structuring operators, defined in Chapter 4, to the initial "normal" file structure. This process can be iterated until we end up with a file structure that is sufficiently efficient, even if we might not be able to prove that it represents a perfectly optimal trade-off between different design criteria.

Let us recall the file-structuring operators from Chapter 4 in order to see what each one of them can do for an improved overall efficiency of the file structure. First, we remember that there are three main categories of operators, namely, (a) intraentry structuring operators, (b) interentry, intrafile structuring operators, and (c) interfile structuring operators. We shall discuss each of the three main types of file structure transformations separately.

INTRAENTRY STRUCTURING. There are four intraentry structuring operators to be discussed: entry compression, reordering of terms, entry chopping, and ordering of segments.

Entry Compression. There are several variations of the entry-compression operation. The purpose, which is always the same, is to reduce the volume of data to be stored and transmitted. There is another characteristic, which is typical of most forms of information and data compression. This characteristic may be expressed as a general rule: Compression of one entity usually has to be balanced by increased sophistication with another. For instance, communication between people may be much more laconic if they have a common, extensive frame of reference. The more elaborate the frame, the less elaborate the framed has to be. In the case of entry compression the framed is the entry itself, whereas the frame is the entry description and, to some extent, the algorithm which uses the entry description in order to interpret the contents of the entry.

One variation of entry compression, *compression by suppression*, attracts interest in situations in which "data missing," "attribute not relevant," and similar conditions are frequently appearing within the entries of a file. For any term that should occur with some value in all entries of a file, we can define one of the possible values as a "default value," which may be suppressed instead of being explicitly represented in the entries to which it pertains. If this form of entry compression is at all worthwhile, it will probably be most advantageous if the most frequent term value is chosen to be suppressed. After compression by suppression, the entries of the file will inevitably be of variable length. This leads to a more complicated entry administration which is well known to all practitioners and also follows from the general rule stated above. The entry description has to be expanded, and the access mechanism may be less efficient in finding and interpreting entries.

Another variation of the compression operation, *compression by extraction*, is applicable when the entries of a file contain a term that is predetermined to have the same value throughout the file.

EXAMPLE 2: Consider the following file:

<PERSON, JOHN>,	<WEIGHT, 70>,	1971
<PERSON, CAROL>,	<WEIGHT, 50>,	1971
<PERSON, JIM>,	<WEIGHT, 88>,	1971
<PERSON, AL>,	<WEIGHT, 62>,	1971
<PERSON, EVE>,	<WEIGHT, 65>,	1971

From the entries of this file we may extract the first term, which has the constant value PERSON; the third term, (WEIGHT); and the fifth term, 1971.

The extraction operation implies obvious storage and transmission gains. The disadvantages of the operation are often unimportant. However, they are less striking than in the case of suppression, because extraction conserves the fixed format of the original entries, that is, if they are fixed format in the first place.

However, by extracting terms from the entries of a file we may destroy *self-describing* properties of the entry. An entry is self-describing to the extent that the entry description need not be consulted in order to interpret the entry. Self-describing entries may be very useful under specific circumstances. Consider, for instance, a file system consisting of numerous small files, serving an environment that submits queries, each of which requires fast response and access to many files. Having to access a lot of entry descriptions may then be time consuming as well as space consuming. There may not even be enough room in main memory for all relevant entry descriptions, with swapping as an efficiency degrading result.

Even if the original entries are not self-describing, extraction will cause the entry descriptions to grow. If the entries are stored on a cheap storage medium, whereas the cost of storing the entry descriptions is relatively high, compression by extraction may not be profitable even from a sheer space point of view even though the total number of stored bits is reduced.

Reordering of Terms. According to the file definition in Chapter 4, entries are tuples of terms, that is, the terms of an entry are considered to be ordered. In some situations, for example, if we are about to split the entries into segments, the initial ordering of terms may be inadequate. Then the reordering-of-terms operation has to be carried out.

Reordering the terms within one and the same entry segment will rarely have any important performance consequences. Two exceptions should be mentioned, however. First, if there is a term group structure and the group is sometimes processed as a unit, processing may be faster if the terms of the group are contiguously arranged. Second, if a few terms of a segment are often processed together—for example, because of the particular data requirements of the most frequent transaction types—it may be advantageous to allocate these terms to a contiguous secondary storage area, provided parts of storage blocks, and not only full storage blocks, may be read and transmitted by the access mechanism of the memory.*

---

* The distinction between storage blocks and access blocks will be discussed in Section 6.3 under the heading Memories.

Entry Chopping. The file-structuring operation that splits an entry into several segments is called *chopping*, or *segmentation*. By chopping the entries of a file into segments we prepare the file for two things: multiblock allocation and file overlapping. Multiblock allocation of an entry means the mapping of the segments of the entry into different storage blocks. Two files are overlapping, or have been overlapped with each other, if the entries of one file share data with the entries of the other. This in turn implies that the overlapping entries have segments that are mapped into the same storage block (see Fig. 6.5).

An unchopped entry contains only one segment, that is, one contiguous tuple of data terms. A chopped entry consists of several segments. One of the segments, the *initial segment*, contains the entry point of the entry. All other segments should be retrievable by a *segment collecting algorithm*, starting from the initial segment. The segment collecting algorithm is a *subalgorithm* of the access algorithm of the file. Very often the collecting algorithm makes use of *data pointers*, that is, auxiliary data terms, that are added to the segments when the entries are chopped, and that are intended to contain the address of the next segment. Other arrangements are also possible. The segment collecting algorithm may use the value of the entry point of the address of the initial segment to calculate the address of the next segment (see the discussion of synonym handling in Section 6.3). We may talk about *virtual pointers* in such cases.

ORDERING OF SEGMENTS. After an entry has been chopped into segments, there must exist a kind of minimum ordering between the segments, which ensures the retrievability of the collection of segments belonging to the entry. This ordering is implied by the segment collecting algorithm, and it conserves the entry as a logical entity.

In many cases, however, it may be efficient with regard to the goals of the design work to add more structure to the entries than is logically necessary. For instance, in order to ensure entry retrievability, *chaining* the segments will always be logically sufficient, but *bundling* the segments might considerably reduce the average number of accesses necessary to retrieve requested terms. These two basic methods of ordering the segments of an entry are visualized in Fig. 6.6.* Hybrid structures are easily conceivable and may be advantageous under special circumstances. For example, if the number of segments varies much

---

* See also Figs. 4.2 through 4.7 and Sections 4.2 and 4.3. Note that there is a third basic arrangement of segments, the contiguous arrangement. See, for instance, Fig 4.2.

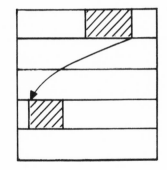

(a)

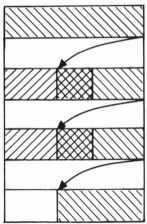

(b)

▨	File with two single-segment entries
▨	File with one entry consisting of four segments

Fig. 6.5   (a) Five storage blocks, two segments, one entry, and one file.
(b) Seven storage blocks, two files; one file with two single-segment
entries, the other with one entry consisting of four segments, two of
which overlap with the entries of the other file

between different entries of the same file, it may be inefficient to reserve pointer space for "the worst case" in all initial segments. A variable-length chain of fixed-span bundles (Fig. 6.7) may be more efficient and easier to administrate.

The advantages and disadvantages of different intraentry orderings are similar to those of the corresponding interentry ordering. The latter will be treated in the next section. It is difficult, however, to discover any gains obtainable from entering inverse pointers between entry segments

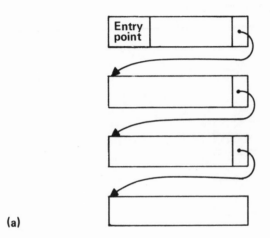

(a)

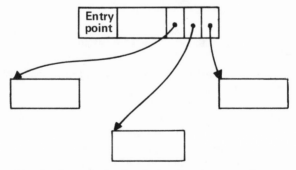

(b)

Fig. 6.6   Two basic methods of ordering the segments of an entry. (a) Chain
                  ordering of entry segments. (b) Bundle ordering of entry segments.

(a)

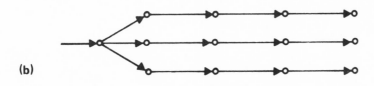

(b)

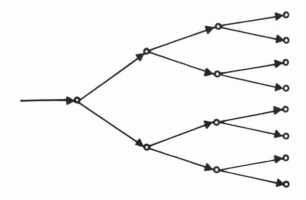

(c)

Fig. 6.7   Different structures formed by recursive use of the two basic structures: chains and bundles. (a) Chain of bundles. (b) Bundle of chains. (c) Bundle of bundles.

except when the segments may be entered without passing the initial segment, which may be possible if several files have been overlapped.

INTERENTRY STRUCTURING. There are two interentry, intrafile structuring operators to be discussed: ordering of entries and intrafile consolidation.

Ordering of Entries. According to the file definition in Chapter 4, the access algorithm of a file should be able to retrieve all entries of the file as the result of one request, which does not have to submit any entry-point values. Thus assuming that the access algorithm works deterministically, there has to be at least an implicit ordering* of the entries of a file. For example, the file may be explicitly or implicitly ordered as a *chain* or a *bundle* of entries. Many other structurings, built up from these elementary structures, are also possible (see Fig. 6.7).

The requirement that all entries of a file should be retrievable as the result of one request is not the only reason for ordering the entries. For instance, the search for a particular entry proceeds much faster if the entries are ordered into a tree according to the values of the entry point than if the whole file has to be scanned linearly until a match is found.

Ordering an object file might also be a way of representing object relations. Such ordering may often exist within, and also between, object files without explicit decisions by the designer. Suppose, for instance, that an object file entry contains the representation of a relational-type message. Then this entry points, by means of a name pointer, to another entry of the same or another file.

EXAMPLE 3: Consider the following object *e* file:

Entry Point	Other Terms
$---$ <PERSON, JIM> $---$ <PERSON, JOHN>	$---$ <PERSON, JOHN>, FATHER $---$ <PERSON, SAM>, FATHER

---

* By an *implicit ordering* of the entries of a file, we mean an ordering of which there are no visible signs in the entries. Implicit orderings are revealed by the way the access algorithm scans the file or by the way it retrieves single entries. *Explicit orderings* are materialized in the file entries by *name or address pointers.*

The entry $<$PERSON, JIM$>$ points to the entry $<$PERSON, JOHN$>$ in the same object *e* file by name. The name pointer has a double function. First, it tells the name of the father of the person identified by the entry point. As a matter of fact, the entry thus represents a property type name-of-father message, too. Second, the name pointer points, through the access algorithm of the file, to the entry that contains more information about the person's father than his name.

The ordering of an object file according to the values of an attribute (other than the entry point) could facilitate the search for objects having certain properties. A similar advantage could be attained by establishing a property file. The choice between the two alternatives may deserve careful consideration.

If we establish an explicit interentry ordering, we have to maintain that structure. Besides space consumption, this is the chief potential problem connected with file ordering. Strangely, however, it may be advantageous to use more pointers to help administrate the existing ones. For example, inverse pointers may be very helpful when an entry is to be deleted from an explicitly ordered file.

Intrafile Consolidation. There are two cases of intrafile entry consideration worth mentioning. First, suppose we have established a *quasifile*, that is, a file in which several entries have the same entry-point value. Then it is wise to transform the quasifile into a *proper file* by entry consolidation.

EXAMPLE 4: Consider the *e* concept $<$ENTERPRISE, INDUSTRY$>$, in which the attribute INDUSTRY is multiple valued, as one enterprise may belong to several industries. Before consolidation we may have the following quasifile:

ENTERPRISE	INDUSTRY
A	STEEL
B	TEXTILE
C	FOOD
D	PULP
A	MANUF
C	DISTRIB
D	PAPER
D	TIMBER

After entry consolidation within the file we obtain a proper file with variable-length e entries as follows:

A	STEEL	MANUF	
B	TEXTILE		
C	FOOD	DISTRIB	
D	PULP	PAPER	TIMBER

Second, suppose we have an $<$object, time$>$ pair entry-point file, that is, a file in which there may be several entries concerning the same object and the same attribute (or object relation), separated only by the time component of their entry point. If we consolidate the entries of such a file *per* object *over* time, we obtain c entries, which may be identified by single-object identifications.

INTERFILE STRUCTURING. There are two interfile structuring operators to be discussed: file consolidation and file overlapping.

File Consolidation. The interfile consolidation operator is defined differently for the three basic kinds of files.

Two *object files*, F_1 and F_2, are consolidated into a new file F_3 in the following way.

1. Matching* entries, ϵ_1 and ϵ_2, of the two files give birth to a c centry, ϵ_3, of the consolidated file F_3. The term tuple of ϵ_3 is built up by the term tuple of ϵ_1 followed by the term tuple of ϵ_2, from which terms identical with ϵ_1 terms have been eliminated, however (ϵ_1 and ϵ_2 have at least the entry point term or term group in common).

2. Nonmatching entries are transferred to the new file after "entry expansion" (see example below).

3. F_1 and F_2 are cancelled from the file system and F_3 is established. The entry descriptions and access algorithms of F_1 and F_2 are replaced by a new entry description and access algorithm belonging to F_3.

EXAMPLE 5: Consider the following object files:
$$F_1 = <\underline{PERSON}, INCOME, AGE, 1970>$$
and

---

* Two entries are *matching* if and only if their entry points are identical.

$F_2 = <\underline{\text{PERSON}}, \text{AGE}, \text{IQ}, 1970>$

$F_1 =$

PERSON	INCOME	AGE
JIM	50	30
JOHN	62	57
BETTY	35	40
DAN	20	19
MARY	45	55

$F_2 =$

PERSON	AGE	IQ
DAN	19	115
BETTY	40	95
SARAH	5	105
JIM	30	100
MARY	55	145

After consolidation we obtain

$F_3 = \text{consolidation} (F_1, F_2) <\underline{\text{PERSON}}, \text{INCOME}, \text{AGE}, \text{IQ}, 1970>$

$F_3 =$

PERSON	INCOME	AGE	IQ
JIM	50	30	100
JOHN	62	57	?
BETTY	35	40	95
DAN	20	19	115
MARY	45	55	145
SARAH	?	5	105

The JOHN and SARAH entries are nonmatching entries of F_1 and F_2, respectively. They have been *expanded* in F_3. The question marks resulting from the expansions call for further investigation. Do they represent missing but relevant values, or are the attributes not relevant to all objects in the new object domain (equal to the union of the old ones)?

Pseudo consolidation (by entry bundling) is implied as soon as two object files have identical entry points—for example, two person files, each with civic registration numbers as entry points.

Two *relational files* may be consolidated by application of the *natural join* relation operator.* The consolidated file will then contain the original files as *projections*.

EXAMPLE 6: Consider the following relational files:

R_1 = PRODUCE =

ENTERPRISE	ARTICLE
A	1
A	2
B	3
C	2
C	4

R_2 = CONSUME =

ENTERPRISE	ARTICLE
C	1
C	2
D	3
E	1
E	4

R_3 = consolidated (R_1, R_2) =

ENTERPRISE	ARTICLE	ENTERPRISE
A	1	C
A	1	E
A	2	C
B	3	D
C	2	C
C	4	E

---

* Codd (1970) has developed an extensive set of operators for manipulating general relations. Some of them, like "the natural join," seem to be very useful even with our slightly different approach to data base design and file structuring.

Two *property files* P_i and P_j may be consolidated into a new property file P_k in the following way. Suppose P_i and P_j contain entries corresponding to the properties $p_{i1}, \ldots, p_{im}$ and $p_{j1}, \ldots, p_{jn}$, respectively. We may form $r = m \times n$ conjunctive properties $p_{k1}, \ldots, p_{kr}$, corresponding to the elements of the Cartesian product

$$\{p_{i1}, \ldots, p_{im}\} \times \{p_{j1}, \ldots, p_{jn}\}$$

p_k = consolidated (P_i, P_j) should contain one entry for each of the r conjunctive properties, which is had by any object referred to in P_i och P_j.

EXAMPLE 7: Consider the property files, P_i and P_j, corresponding to the e concepts $<$PERSON, SEX$>$ and $<$PERSON, MARITAL STATUS$>$

$P_i =$

SEX	PERSONS
MALE	X, Y, Z, U, W
FEMALE	A, B, C, D, E, F

$P_j =$

MARITAL STATUS	PERSONS
SINGLE	X, U, C
MARRIED	Y, Z, W, B, E, F
DIV/WID	A, D

After consolidation we obtain

$P_k =$

PROPERTY	PERSONS
MALE ∧ SINGLE	X, U
MALE ∧ MARRIED	Y, Z, W
FEMALE ∧ SINGLE	C
FEMALE ∧ MARRIED	B, E, F
FEMALE ∧ DIV/WID	A, D

The consolidation operators we have defined in this section for different kinds of files are rather dissimilar to each other. Perhaps we should keep them apart by naming them differently, for example, *joining of relational files* and (conjunctive) *combination of property files*. "Consolidation" would then be reserved for object files.

There are several reasons why it may often be advantageous to consolidate (join, combine) several files into one.

1. The consolidated file will occupy less secondary storage space than the original files did as a whole.*

2. Consolidation reduces the number of files, which may be essential if the file structure is to be allocated to conventional tape memories.

3. If the consolidated file occupies less secondary storage space, a serial scan of the consolidated file will cause less data transmission between secondary and primary storage than a serial matching of the original files. Less total buffer space will be needed, too.

4. Consolidation will reduce the number of accesses needed to process data base transactions that concern more than one of the original files. On the other hand if such transactions are rare, consolidation will be detrimental, because the transmitted data volumes as well as buffer space demand will increase without any gain as to the number of accesses.

FILE OVERLAPPING. We start our discussion of overlapping with a linguistic remark. The verb "overlap" is both transitive and intransitive. The phrase "overlapping files" is thus ambiguous, as it may denote both the *action* (structuring operation) of overlapping files with each other and the *state* that prevails among a set of files after they have been operated on by the overlap structuring operator. We intend to live with this ambiguity.

We overlap two files by overlapping entries of one file with entries of the other. Two entries, ϵ_1 and ϵ_2, are overlapping if they have some *common data*, that is, if one segment σ_1 of ϵ_1 and another segment σ_2 of ϵ_2 are to be mapped into overlapping positions of the same storage block. The situation is schematically illustrated in Fig. 6.8.

There are two reasons for overlapping files. The first is that of *space economy*. By overlapping one entry with another we reduce space consumption by the size of the common storage block positions. On the other hand, if chopping is a necessary condition for overlapping (which it often is if an object file is overlapped with a property file), the pointers between segments consume space (or other resources if virtual pointers are used). We must also remember that a chopped entry requires more accesses if it is to be retrieved than a contiguous entry does.

---

* This is a rule with exceptions. It is generally invalid for relational files.

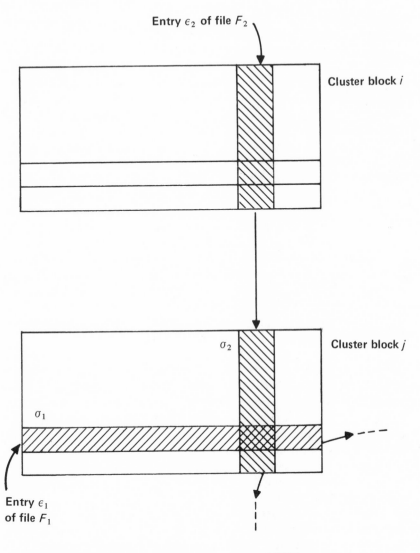

Entry ϵ_2 of file F_2

Cluster block i

σ_2

Cluster block j

σ_1

Entry ϵ_1
of file F_1

ϵ_1 and ϵ_2 overlapping since $\epsilon_1 \cap \epsilon_2 = \sigma_1 \cap \sigma_2 = $ ⬚ $\neq \phi$

Fig. 6.8   Overlapping files.

The other reason for overlapping files is that of *shorter response times* for certain transaction types. This is possible because the overlapping of files implies the creation of *new access paths* to the overlapping entries. Consider again the overlapping entries ϵ_1 and ϵ_2 of Fig. 6.8. Suppose that we have just retrieved segment σ_2 of entry ϵ_2 and that we then—for example, because of the inherent structure of the transaction being processed—wish to retrieve segment σ_1 of entry ϵ_1. If the two files had not been overlapped, we would have been forced to proceed along the "official" access path and use the access algorithm of file F_1. Now, as the files are overlapping, we know that segment σ_1 is in the same access block as σ_2, which is probably still in primary storage. We may thus save an access each time this particular transaction type occurs.

> EXAMPLE 8: Suppose F_1 is an object file containing names and addresses of people, and suppose that F_2 is a property file, the entries of which contain the identifications (civic registration numbers) of people have a particular occupation. The overlapping field XXX (see, Fig. 6.8) might then contain the identification of, say, a particular baker. It is then obvious that the overlapping file structure facilitates the processing of query transactions such as: "List the names and addresses of all bakers." More examples will be analyzed in Section 6.4.

What about the similarities and differences between file consolidation and file overlapping? The two structuring operations are similar in the sense that they both bring together, and integrate physically and logically, two or more files; but whereas consolidation means the death of the old files and the birth of a new, consolidated file, overlapping preserves the logical independence between the overlapping files: They keep their respective entry descriptions and access algorithms, although, as we have seen, advantage may be taken of both facilities—for example, both access algorithms.

There are also other differences between the two operators. The consolidation operator may only operate on files of the same kind, for example, two object files, two property files, or two relational files. As to the overlap operator, the following two argument combinations seem to be of greatest practical impact:

1. <object file, property file>
2. <relational file, object file>

EXAMPLE 9: Consider the following relational file $F_1 =$ TRADE 1970:

EXP COUNTRY	IMP COUNTRY	PRODUCT
SWEDEN	BRITAIN	PULP
JAPAN	GERMANY	WATCHES
JAPAN	USA	TV-SETS
YEMEN	SWEDEN	OIL
SWEDEN	USA	CARS
USA	SWEDEN	CARS
FINLAND	BRITAIN	PULP

Consider also an object file F_2, whose objects are defined as object tuples of the TRADE object relation, and whose attributes are VALUE and VOLUME. The objects of this file are so-called compound objects of transaction type, and we give them names according to the following pattern:

SBP = <SWEDEN, BRITAIN, PULP>

JGW = <JAPAN, GERMANY, WATCHES>

And so on. The file VALUE AND VOLUME OF TRADE 1970 may then look as follows:

OBJECT	VALUE	VOLUME
SBP	$ a	t tons
JGW	$ b	u units
JUT	$ c	v units
YSO	$ d	w m^3
SUC	$ e	x units
USC	$ f	y units
FBP	$ g	z tons

F_1 and F_2 may now be overlapped in an obvious way. As a matter of fact each entry of F_1 will be completely overlapped by an entry of F_2. Note that no chopping has to be done before overlapping in this case.

EXAMPLE 10: Consider the following object file F_3 = MONETARY UNITS 1970:

COUNTRY	MONETARY UNIT
SWEDEN	KRONA
JAPAN	YEN
YEMEN	RIAL
USA	DOLLAR
FINLAND	MARK

If we want to overlap F_3 with F_1 of the previous example, we get into trouble. The desired result might be the following:

EXPORT COUNTRY	IMPORT COUNTRY	PRODUCT	MONETARY UNIT OF EXP COUNTRY
SWEDEN	BRITAIN	PULP	KRONA
JAPAN	GERMANY	WATCHES	YEN
JAPAN	USA	TV-SETS	YEN
YEMEN	SWEDEN	OIL	RIAL
SWEDEN	USA	CARS	KRONA
USA	SWEDEN	CARS	DOLLAR
FINLAND	BRITAIN	PULP	MARK

Here F_1 is still intact, but F_3 has degenerated into a quasifile, as the entry-point uniqueness condition no longer holds for that file. The entries <JAPAN, YEN> and <SWEDEN, KRONA> have been duplicated. As has been pointed out earlier there are severe disadvantages connected with quasifiles. Any decision to establish such a file should be carefully considered.

An Analysis of a Directory–File Complex

A directory–file complex was defined earlier in this section as "a complex of object and property files in which all object files have been consolidated into one file, the *main file* of the complex, and in which the property files have been combined into one or more *directory files*, which together make up the *directory* of the complex." In many practical data base projects a critical design problem will be how to consolidate (combine) the property *e* files of the directories of different directory–file complexes. Should the systemeer choose a high or a low "degree of consolidation" for the property files of a directory? Should he redundantly represent the same *e* concept within several, differently structured directory files? These are very tricky problems and often cannot be satisfactorily solved except by means of intuitive decisions or "rules of thumb." Instead the systemeer should try to evaluate different alternatives systematically. In this section we shall illustrate how such an evaluation may be performed.

As our object of illustrative design analysis we have chosen a directory–file complex with the following characteristics.

1. The main file of the directory–file complex is an object file into which a number of object β-e files have been consolidated. It is not necessary for our analysis to know the exact number of consolidated e files. We assume that the file contains information about 10^6 objects.

2. The directory of the directory–file complex contains six property e files representing the e concepts

$$<O, A_1^{\alpha}>, \ldots, <O, A_6^{\alpha}>$$

where O is the same object group as the main file object group. We assume that each of the attributes $A_1^{\alpha}, \ldots, A_6^{\alpha}$ can take 10 different mutually exclusive values. We also assume that each of the α attributes occurs redundantly among the β attributes, that is, that the value of an α attribute for a particular object may be found both in the directory and in the main file.

3. In order to be able to evaluate different structurings of the directory, we also need to assume something about the factual distribution of the values of the attributes $A_1^{\alpha}, \ldots, A_6^{\alpha}$ among the objects in O. We simply assume that the distribution is perfectly uniform for each of the attributes, and that the attributes are perfectly uncorrelated. Nothing prevents a designer from making more realistic assumptions, but in an illustration the resulting, more complicated calculations would obscure interesting conclusions.

Note that so far we have only made "infological assumptions," that is, assumptions that are parameters in the particular infological model underlying the data base and that are thus as intelligible to infologically oriented users and decision makers as to datalogically oriented file designers. This will certainly make it easier for the designer when he needs intelligent guesses, or still better estimates of parameters that turn out to be crucial for the design decisions.

In addition to the assumptions about certain *file* parameters, the designer will also need to make assumptions about certain characteristics of the *transactions*, which will concern the particular file complex to be designed. As far as possible these assumptions, too, should be made in terms of characteristics that are infologically meaningful. For the analysis in this section, we make the following, infologically oriented assumption. .

4. The bulk of the transactions that will hit the file complex will conform to the general $\alpha\beta$-retrieval query pattern defined in Chapter 5 as follows: For all objects having the property P^α, retrieve the values of the attributes A_1^β, ... , A_m^β at the times t_1^β, ... , t_m^β, respectively.

For this example we assume that the requested values of the β attributes are all contained in the object main file of the directory–file complex (see assumption above). We further assume that P^α is the conjunction of from one to six different <attribute, value> belonging to the α attributes,

$$P^\alpha = \Lambda <A_i, v_{ij}> \qquad v_{ij} \epsilon A_i$$
$$i\epsilon\{1, \dots ,6\}$$
$$j\epsilon\{1, \dots ,10\}$$

The different property conjunctions are assumed to occur with equal probabilities.

Even with the rather strict assumptions stated in (1) through (4) above, there are numerous design alternatives for the particular directory–file complex under consideration. We shall analyze and compare nine different structurings of the directory, which are all feasible but which show highly varying performance characteristics. For each of the nine structures we have computed the following performance figures, which are clearly related to space and time efficiency goals:

5. Storage overhead = (Directory size)/(Number of objects) $\approx$ (number of directory files) $\times$ 6 decimal positions.*

6. The total expected number of directory and main file accesses per object requested by a retrieval query will contain 1, 2, 3, 4, 5, or 6 (selection) attributes.

REMARK REGARDING (5). It follows from assumption (2) above—the definition of property file—and the definition of the consolidation structuring operator for property files, that each directory file, elementary or consolidated, will contain one and only one reference to each of the 10^6 objects in O. The space needed to represent each of these object references is equivalent to ^{10}log 10^6 pos = 6 pos. Thus formula (5) actually gives a measure of the space needed to represent the references to each of the objects in O. Because of the assumptions (1) through (3) above, it is justified to assume that the space needed for entry points,

---

* We shall write "pos" instead of "decimal position(s)" during the rest of this
    section. For a proof of the approximate formula, see the remark below.

pointers, unused parts of storage blocks, and so on, will be small in comparison with this figure. With other assumptions these needs may have to be more carefully estimated.

By calling the quantity (5) "storage overhead" we indicate that the whole directory part of the directory–file complex is redundant because of assumption (2) according to which each A_i^α occurs redundantly among the A_j^β. For example, if quantity (5) is 12 pos, and each entry of the main file has a size of 100 pos, the relative storage overhead will be $12/100 = 12$ percent. This figure represents the space cost paid for the achievement of better retrieval performance.

REMARK REGARDING (6). In the calculations below we count one access per entry segment which has to be retrieved during the processing of a query. We do not allow for the extra accesses the access algorithm will often need in order to retrieve a particular entry; nor does our crude measure reflect, for example, the fact that the accessing of an initial segment of an entry will probably take longer than the accessing of subsequent segments. In order for our calculations to be at all realistic we must assume that all the files, including the main file, will be allocated to direct-access storage. If, in a realistic situation, we must also consider the alternative of allocating the main file to serial storage, the method of calculation presented here will have to be refined.

Let us now turn our attention to the quantitative and comparative evaluation of nine different directory–file structurings, all of which are feasible with respect to the data base environment as far as the latter was defined in (4) above.

STRUCTURE 1: One consolidated object type main file and six elementary property type directory files. The main file has one-segment entries. There is one directory file for each of the six α attributes.* Each entry of the directory files contains references to the objects for which a particular α attribute takes a particular value, $A_i^\alpha = v_{ij}$. According to assumptions (2) and (3) each directory–file entry will contain $10^6/10 = 10^5$ object references. With 100 references per segment,[†] each entry will consist of $10^5/100 = 1000$ segments.

---

* In the existing literature dealing with file organization issues such files are often called "inverted files" or "inverted list files." See, for example, Lefkowitz, 1969.

[†] We shall use the same segment size, 100 object references per segment ~6000 pos segment, for eight of the nine structurings to be investigated in this example. Naturally this is a design decision that requires argumentation in a real case.

In Table 6.1 we show the partial results leading in the last two columns to the values of the performance characteristics defined in (5) and (6) above. The calculations are commented on in the remarks following the table.

For two and three selection attributes two and three property file entries, respectively, have to be matched against each ether. It is assumed that this matching process may be carried out by the central processor in primary storage. In order for this to be possible, it is probably necessary with this structure, in which there are one thousand 100-object segments per entry, to keep the object references sorted in the directory–file entries. Thus the reordering-of-terms structuring operator has to be applied.

For four, five, and six selection attributes, four, five, and six property file entries, respectively, may be matched analogously, but it is more efficient in terms of accesses to match only three property file entries and then access the main file for the remaining 1000 objects.

In the calculations, the results of which are shown in the Table 6.1, we have assumed that the scheduling subsystem of the data base system will be capable of choosing dynamically one processing strategy when a query against the complex contains one, two, or three selection attributes, and another strategy when the number of selection attributes in the query is four, five, or six.

> STRUCTURE 2: One consolidated object type main file and $\binom{6}{2} = 15$ two-dimensional combined property type directory files.* The main file has one-segment entries. Each entry of the directory files contains references to objects for which a particular pair of α attributes takes a particular pair of values
>
> $$(A_i^\alpha = v_{ij}) \wedge (A_k^\alpha = v_{kr})$$
>
> There is one directory file for each of the possible $\binom{6}{2} = 15$ combinations of two α attributes. With 100 object references per segment, each directory–file entry will consist of $10^6/10^2/10^2 = 100$ segments.
>
> One processing strategy has been assumed for queries containing one to four attributes, and another for queries containing five or six attributes (see structure 1).

---

* A k-dimensional combined property file is a property file resulting from the consolidation, or combination, of k elementary property files.

STRUCTURE 3: One consolidated object type main file and $6/2 = 3$ two-dimensional combined property type directory files. The main file has one-segment entries. Each entry of the directory files contains references to objects for which a particular pair of α attributes takes a particular pair of values

$$(A_i^\alpha = v_{ij}) \wedge (A_k^\alpha = v_{kr})$$

There is one directory file for each of the three attribute pairs $<A_1,$

Table 6.1 Performance Calculations for Structure 1

Number of Attributes in Query	Number of Objects Satisfying Query	Number of Directory Accesses	Number of Main File Accesses	Total Number of Accesses per Requested Object	Storage Overhead (pos/ object)
1	100,000	1,000	100,000	1.01	36
2	10,000	2,000	10,000	1.2	36
3	1,000	3,000	1,000	4	36
4	100	3,000	1,000	40	36
5	10	3,000	1,000	400	36
6	1	3,000	1,000	4,000	36

Table 6.2 Performance Calculations for Structure 2

Number of Attributes in Query	Number of Objects Satisfying Query	Number of Directory Accesses	Number of Main File Accesses	Total Number of Accesses per Requested Object	Storage Overhead (pos/ object)
1	100,000	1,000	100,000	1.01	90
2	10,000	100	10,000	1.01	90
3	1,000	200	1,000	1.2	90
4	100	200	100	3	90
5	10	200	100	30	90
6	1	200	100	300	90

$A_2>$, $<A_3, A_4>$, and $<A_5, A_6>$. With 100 object references per segment, each directory–file entry will consist of $10^6/10^2/10^2 = 100$ segments.

The weighting procedure indicated in the footnotes of Table 6.3 might need some explaining. Thus let us have a closer look at queries involving two selection attributes (row 2 in the table). There are $\binom{6}{2} = 15$ different combinations of two attributes out of six. Only 3 of these 15 combinations, namely, $\{A_1, A_2\}$, $\{A_3, A_4\}$, and $\{A_5, A_6\}$, have both their member attributes within one and the same combined property file. Queries corresponding to these attribute combinations constitute 3/15 = 20 percent of all queries involving two selection attributes, and they require one access to each of the 100 segments of the uniquely determined property file entry. The other 80 percent of this kind of query necessitates the matching of ten 100-segment entries from two of the three property files against one another, which amounts to $2 \times 10 \times 100 = 2000$ accesses. This explains footnote (a); the other footnotes are similarly understood. As for the change of processing strategy when the query contains four to six attributes, see structures 1 and 2.

STRUCTURE 4: One consolidated object type main file and $\binom{6}{3} = 20$ three-dimensional combined property type directory files. The main file has one-segment entries. Each entry of the directory files contains references to objects for which a particular triple of α attributes takes a particular triple of values. There is one directory file for each of the possible $\binom{6}{3} = 20$ combinations of three α attributes. With 100 object references per segment, each directory file entry will consist of $10^6/10^3/10^2 = 10$ segments.

STRUCTURE 5: One consolidated object type main file and $6/3 = 2$ three-dimensional combined property type directory files. The main file has one-segment entries. Each entry of the directory files contains references to objects for which a particular triple of α attributes takes a particular triple of values. There is one directory file for each of the two attribute triples $<A_1, A_2, A_3>$ and $<A_4, A_5, A_6>$. With 100 object references per segment, each directory–file entry will consist of $10^6/10^3/10^2 = 10$ segments.

The footnotes of Table 6.5 are analogously explained as in connection with structure 3.

STRUCTURE 6: One consolidated object type main file and $\binom{6}{4} = 15$ four-dimensional combined property type directory files. The main file has one-segment entries. Each entry of the directory files contains references to objects for which a particular quadruple of α attributes takes a particular quadruple of values. There is one directory file for each of the possible $\binom{6}{4} = 15$ combinations of four α attributes. With 100 object references per segment, each directory–file entry will consist of $10^6/10^4/10^2 = 1$ segment.

Table 6.3 Performance Calculations for Structure 3

Number of Attributes in Query	Number of Objects Satisfying Query	Expected Number of Directory Accesses	Expected Number of Main File Accesses	Total Number of Expected Accesses per Requested Object	Storage Overhead (pos/object)
1	100,000	1,000	100,000	1.01	18
2	10,000	1,620[a]	10,000	1.162	18
3	1,000	1,860[b]	1,000	2.86	18
4	100	920[c]	820[d]	17.4	18
5	10	200	100	30	18
6	1	200	100	300	18

[a] $0.2 \times 100 + 0.8 \times 2,000$
[b] $0.4 \times 3,000 + 0.6 \times 1,100.$
[c] $0.2 \times 200 + 0.8 \times 1,100.$
[d] $0.2 \times 100 + 0.8 \times 1,000.$

Table 6.4 Performance Calculations for Structure 4

Number of Attributes in Query	Number of Objects Satisfying Query	Number of Directory Accesses	Number of Main File Accesses	Total Number of Accesses per Requested Object	Storage Overhead (pos/object)
1	100,000	1,000	100,000	1.01	120
2	10,000	100	10,000	1.01	120
3	1,000	10	1,000	1.01	120
4	100	20	100	1.2	120
5	10	20	10	3	120
6	1	20	1	21	120

With 100 object references per segment (cluster block) no more than four dimensions (attributes) per combined property file will pay with the assumptions of the example. For instance, five dimensions would leave 90 percent of the directory space unutilized, as only 10 ($= 10^6/10^5$) objects would have each property combination.

Table 6.5 Performance Calculations for Structure 5

Number of Attributes in Query	Number of Objects Satisfying Query	Expected Number of Directory Accesses	Expected Number of Main File Accesses	Total Number of Expected Accesses per Requested Object	Storage Overhead (pos/ object)
1	100,000	1,000	100,000	1.01	12
2	10,000	1,240[a]	10,000	1.124	12
3	1,000	991[b]	1,000	1,991	12
4	100	124[c]	460[d]	5.84	12
5	10	110	10	12	12
6	1	20	1	21	12

[a] $0.4 \times 100 + 0.6 \times 2,000$.
[b] $0.1 \times 10 + 0.9 \times 1,100$.
[c] $0.4 \times 10 + 0.6 \times 200$.
[d] $0.4 \times 1,000 + 0.6 \times 100$.

Table 6.6 Performance Calculations for Structure 6

Number of Attributes in Query	Number of Objects Satisfying Query	Number of Directory Accesses	Number of Main File Accesses	Total Number of Accesses per Requested Object	Storage Overhead (pos/ object)
1	100,000	1,000	100,000	1.01	90
2	10,000	100	10,000	1.01	90
3	1,000	10	1,000	1.01	90
4	100	1	100	1.01	90
5	10	2	10	1.2	90
6	1	2	1	3	90

STRUCTURE 7: One consolidated object type main file and 3 four-dimensional combined property type directory files. The main file has one-segment entries. Each entry of the directory files contains references to objects for which a particular quadruple of α attributes takes a particular quadruple of values. There is one directory file for each of the three attribute quadruples $<A_1, A_2, A_3, A_4>$, $<A_5, A_6, A_1, A_2>$, and $<A_3, A_4, A_5, A_6>$. With 100 object references per segment, each directory–file entry will consist of $10^6/10^4/10^2 = 1$ segment.

For an explanation of the footnote calculations, compare with structure 3.

STRUCTURE 8: One consolidated object type main file and $\binom{6}{4} = 15$ directory files of four-dimensional combined property type, each of which is overlapped with an object file containing the remaining $6 - 4 = 2$ attributes. The main file has one-segment entries. Each entry of the property type directory files contains references to objects for which a particular quadruple of α attributes takes a particular quadruple of values. At the same time each property file entry is overlapped with a number of object file entries, each of which contains the values of the remaining two α attributes for one of the objects in the property file entry. The situation is visualized in Fig. 6.9. There is one property file for each of the possible $\binom{6}{4} = 15$

Table 6.7 Performance Calculations for Structure 7

Number of Attributes in Query	Number of Objects Satisfying Query	Expected Number of Directory Accesses	Expected Number of Main File Accesses	Total Expected Number of Accesses per Requested Object	Storage Overhead (pos/ object)
1	100,000	1,000	100,000	1.01	18
2	10,000	100	10,000	1.01	18
3	1,000	86[a]	1,000	1.086	18
4	100	16.2[b]	100	1.162	18
5	10	11	10	2.1	18
6	1	2	1	3	18

[a] $0.4 \times 200 + 0.6 \times 10$.
[b] $0.2 \times 1 + 0.8 \times 20$.

combinations of four α attributes and one object file for each of the possible $\binom{6}{2} = 15$ combinations of two α attributes. With 100 object references per property file entry segment, each directory–file entry will consist of $10^6/10^4/10^2 = 1$ segment.

For this kind of structure storage overhead per object is calculated as

[(number of property type directory files)
$\times$ ^{10}log (number of objects)
$+$ (number of object type directory files)
$\times$ (number of attributes per object type directory file)
$\times$ ^{10}log (number of values per attribute)] pos
$= [\binom{6}{4} \times \,^{10}\text{log } 10^6 + \binom{6}{2} \times 2 \times \,^{10}\text{log } 10]$ pos
$= 120$ pos

STRUCTURE 9: One consolidated object type main file and $\binom{6}{3} = 20$ directory files of three-dimensional combined property type, each of which is overlapped with an object file containing the remaining $6 - 3 = 3$ α attributes. The main file has one-segment entries. Each entry of the property type directory files contains references to objects for which a particular triple of α attributes takes a particular

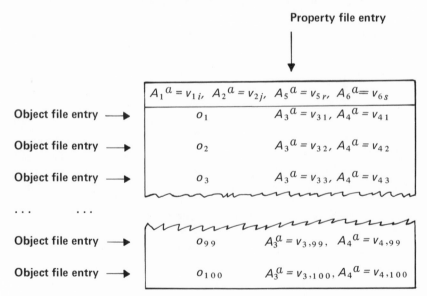

Fig. 6.9   One entry in a combined property file, containing the attributes A_1^α, A_2^α, A_5^α, and A_6^α, overlapped with 100 entries in a consolidated object file containing the attributes A_3^α and A_4^α.

Table 6.8 Performance Calculations for Structure 8

Number of Attributes in Query	Number of Objects Satisfying Query	Number of Directory Accesses	Number of Main File Accesses	Total Number of Accesses per Requested Object	Storage Overhead (pos/ object)
1	100,000	1,000	100,000	1.01	120
2	10,000	100	10,000	1.01	120
3	1,000	10	1,000	1.01	120
4	100	1	100	1.01	120
5	10	1	10	1.1	120
6	1	1	1	2	120

triple of values. At the same time each property file entry is overlapped with a number of object file entries each of which contains the values of the remaining three α attributes for one of the objects in the property file entry. There is one property file and one object file for each of the possible $\binom{6}{3}$ combinations of three α attributes. With 1000 object references per property file entry segment, each directory file entry will consist of $10^6/10^3/10^3 = 1$ segment.*

COMPARISON OF THE NINE STRUCTURES. The performance characteristics of the nine investigated structures may be condensed into Table 6.10.

The evaluation criteria we use in this example are storage overhead and response time. Even with as few as two decision criteria, it is not possible to select one of the nine suggested structures as definitely superior to the others. For this to be possible a formalized or intuitive trade-off rule has to be introduced. However, according to the well-known Pareto principle, we may at once rule out a few structures, which are definitely inferior, or dominated, regardless of the trade-off decision.

For example, structure 1 is dominated by structure 3, structure 5, and structure 7. This is remarkable, because structure 1 is no less than the frequently used inverted list approach (Lefkowitz, 1969). It is also remarkable that structure 1 requires as much as structures 2 and 3, and twice the amount of storage overhead required by the respective Pareto

---

* Note that we are using a different segment size for this structure.

superior structures. Structure 2 is dominated by structure 6 and structure 7. The latter requires, by the way, only one fifth of the overhead storage required by structure 2. Structure 3 is dominated by structure 5 and structure 7. Structure 4 is dominated by structure 6 and structure 8.

By assuming very little about the time–storage preferences not yet decided on, we may also rule out structure 6, structure 8, and structure 9, which are only slightly "faster" than structure 7, but which require considerably more space than the latter. Note, however, that the

Table 6.9 Performance Calculations for Structure 9

Number of Attributes in Query	Number of Objects Satisfying Query	Number of Directory Accesses	Number of Main File Accesses	Total Number of Accesses per Requested Object	Storage Overhead (pos/ object)
1	100,000	100	100,000	1.001	180[a]
2	10,000	10	10,000	1.001	180
3	1,000	1	1,000	1.001	180
4	100	1	100	1.01	180
5	10	1	10	1.1	180
6	1	1	1	2	180

Table 6.10 Condensed Performance Calculations

Structure	Storage Overhead (pos/ object)	Total Number of Accesses per Requested Object When Number of Attributes in Query Equals:					
		1	2	3	4	5	6
1	36	1.01	1.2	4	40	400	4,000
2	90	1.01	1.01	1.2	3	30	300
3	18	1.01	1.162	2.86	17.4	30	300
4	120	1.01	1.01	1.01	1.2	3	21
5	12	1.01	1.124	1.991	5.84	12	21
6	90	1.01	1.01	1.01	1.01	1.2	3
7	18	1.01	1.01	1.086	1.162	2.1	3
8	120	1.01	1.01	1.01	1.01	1.1	2
9	180	1.001	1.001	1.001	1.01	1.1	2

situation would be completely different if only frequencies were asked for by the queries, so that the main file never needed to be accessed; one should then be deducted from every access cell of the comparison table, and structure 9 is then seen to be up to 10 times as "fast" as, for instance, structure 8. We are thus left with a reduced comparison Table 6.11 containing only structure 5 and structure 7.

Table 6.11 Reduced Comparison Calculations

Structure	Storage Overhead (pos/ object)	Total Number of Accesses per Requested Object When Number of Attributes in QueryEquals:					
		1	2	3	4	5	6
5	12	1.01	1.124	1.991	5.84	12	21
7	18	1.01	1.01	1.086	1.162	2.1	3

Structure 7 is seen to require 50 percent more overhead space than structure 5, whereas the latter is significantly "slower" than the former for more complex queries.

CONCLUSIONS. One conclusion from the calculations in this section is that it should not be too difficult to construct an algorithm that (a) generates feasible alternatives to specified directory–file-complex design problems and (b) orders the feasible alternatives according to different design criteria.

The assumptions we made are unrealistic in detail but not in principle. Of course, we have chosen "nice figures" like integer powers of 10 for most of the parameters, but that is only a matter of calculation simplicity. Also, we may not have good enough estimates of the entities involved to make it worthwhile to use more precise figures than integer powers of integers such as 10 or 2.

In a realistic design situation we should hardly make the assumption stated in (3) that the factual distributions of the values of the attributes A_1^α, $\ldots$, A_6^α among the objects in O are perfectly uniform and uncorrelated. With more realistic, random distributions it might be impossible to calculate the expected performance characteristics analytically, but then we could resort to simulation. Under such assumptions we shall certainly have to allow for highly variable directory entry sizes in the file structures we suggest.

In assumption (4) we stated among other things that the bulk of transactions against the directory–file complex would be retrieval transactions. If instead update were the most important transaction type, this would naturally change our evaluation of different structuring alternatives. A general discussion of the retrieval–update trade-offs may be found in an article by Mullin (1971).

6.3   FILE ALLOCATION AND FILE ACCESS

The Role of the Memories During Different File Design Steps

Naturally the systemeer cannot completely disregard the storage and access structure of available memories during any file-structuring step. This is obvious because it is the limitations of economically feasible memories that make it necessary to do file structuring. From a strictly infological point of view any file representation of the e concepts of the data base is as good as any other.

However, the systemeer should try to make as few assumptions as possible during early file design steps concerning the memories to be used. Besides making things easier for the designer, such a strategy will make the resulting file design more general and less vulnerable to environmental change. During the file-structuring steps described in earlier sections of this chapter, it should seldom be necessary to make a stronger assumption concerning the memories than that a particular file has to be allocated to a memory of direct-access type. Naturally, when we do not assume detailed knowledge about memory performance characteristics and file → storage mapping functions, we cannot make detailed calculations of the expected performance characteristics of the file structure that will result from a particular file design decision. However, there are so many other sources of uncertainty that such precise calculations might be misleading. Very rough assumptions concerning memory performance characteristics will usually be quite satisfactory during early design stages. Thus detailed design decisions concerning memories and file allocation and accessing algorithms should be postponed to the final file design step. This step, the file allocation design step, will be the topic of this section.

Memories

In order for the data base designer to be able to pay *adequate* attention to computer hardware—neither too much nor too little—he has to be equipped with adequate concepts for describing different hardware facilities in a way that is relevant to his central problems. We shall try in this section to develop a basic set of such concepts, and we start by giving a definition of "data" (see also Chapter 1).

DEFINITION 1: If a person intentionally arranges one piece of reality to represent another, we shall call the former arrangement *data*, and we shall say that the arranged piece of reality is a *medium* that is used for *storing* the data.

In connection with EDP the medium may be a magnetizable surface, for instance. A *memory*, then, is defined in the following way:

DEFINITION 2: A *memory* is a structured medium, an ordered set of *storage positions*, $\langle p_1, \ldots, p_n \rangle$, where each p_i can be in at least two different *states*. The individual storage positions of a memory may be temporarily or permanently grouped into larger *storage structures*, called (storage) *blocks, tracks, cylinders*, and so on.

The blocks of a magnetic tape are a good example of a *temporary* storage structure. On the other hand the tracks and cylinders of a disk memory are obviously *permanent*.

From these definitions it follows that a memory, or any substructure of it down to an individual storage position, may be used for storing data, that is, for representing a piece (part of) of reality. The data that are actually stored in the memory (storage position, ...) at a particular point of time t will be called the *data contents* of the memory (storage position, ...) at t. If a memory (storage position, ...) is *not* used for storing data at a particular point of time u we shall say that the memory (storage position, ...) has the *null data contents* ϕ at u.

Stored data are not of much use if they cannot be accessed and processed. That is why we define the concept of an *accessible memory*.

DEFINITION 3: An *accessible memory* is a quadruple $\langle x, y, z, u \rangle$, where x is a *memory* and y is an *access mechanism* capable of presenting the data contents of any named storage position* of the memory to a *processor* z to which the memory is tied by means of a *channel* u. The *access time* needed to present a particular storage position p is a function of (a) the *distance* $\delta(p, p')$ between the demanded storage position p and the most recently demanded storage position p' within the same memory, and (b) the number of storage positions belonging to the same *access block* as p; that is, the number of storage positions that has to be transmitted from the

---

* A storage position may always be named by its ordinal number in the memory structure. See Definition 2 of memory above.

memory via the channel to the processor in the same *access operation*.

If the size of the access block were always equal to one, (b) would not have to be considered. However, for the memories available on the market today the sizes of the access blocks are usually larger than one. The hardware and operating systems now used are usually designed so as to make access blocks and storage blocks coincide. However, it is often possible by means of low-level programming* to demonstrate and make use of the fact that access blocks and storage blocks are different concepts, and that an access block may be both smaller and larger than a storage block.

The *distance function* δ defined above, is an important concept for classifying memories into different categories, such as "serial" and "direct" and subcategories of these. Rough classifications of this kind should be essential to human, possibly computer-aided, designers as well as to automatic maintenance and redesign functions of advanced data base systems.

It is customary (Langefors, 1961; Martin, 1967) to break down the total access time into components such as positioning time, rotational delay, and transmission time.

Such a breakdown is *meaningful* if and only if the resource utilization pattern is different during different phases of an access operation. This is often the case. For instance, the channel will certainly be occupied during transmission time, but during rotation or positioning time, or during both, it may be free for users of another memory, which is tied to the same channel. Besides being meaningful, the breakdown is *practical* at a certain design stage if and only if it will substantially affect the design decisions at that particular stage. This will certainly not be the case, for instance, if there is only a low probability that the environment will "simultaneously" produce two transactions, the processing of which will engage the same channel but different memories. In general, of course, it is very difficult to tell how much attention the data base designer should pay to positive and negative overlapping, or multiprogramming, effects. Naturally he has to consider the resource drain due to other applications than the data base system, if there are any. As to the data base application itself, it may be perfectly legitimate at early design stages to regard the computer essentially as a single-programming system, or if there are relevant statistics available, to multiply throughput

---

* For instance, IBM uses the terms "channel programming" and "chained scheduling" in this context.

and response time figures by certain rough percentages. The important thing is not to assume multiprogramming *benefits* without allowing for its *costs*. If the dynamics of a data base environment are very little under the control of data base designers and administrators and if the environment produces a lot of more or less simultaneous transactions requiring response within a few seconds, simulation techniques may be a great help in the design work.

File→Storage Mappings and the Intermediary Cluster Concept

In Section 6.2 we saw how elementary object, property, and relational files may be combined into more complex file structures. These file structures should then be mapped, or allocated, into accessible memories, which may be fairly complex structures of storage positions, blocks, tracks, cylinders, and so on. The allocation of a file structure to a memory may thus be a very complex mapping. Suppose now that we want to change the mapping. The reason for this may be that the file structure has to be changed because of the interaction between the data base and its environment. Alternatively, the reason may be that the storage structure is changed as the result of a modification of the hardware configuration, or because of new demands from other applications competing for the computer resources used by the data base system. However, changing the file → storage mapping may be very inefficient and may even generate serious errors unless it has been carefully planned for at the time of data base design. There is a remedy that is used, to some extent, in modern operating systems and that seems to be of such general importance as to motivate a position among the basic concepts discussed in this book. This remedy will be labeled here as "cluster" and is related to such concepts as "area" used by the CODASYL Data Base Task Group and "data set" used by IBM.

DEFINITION 4*: A *cluster* is a triple $<x, y, z>$ where
1. x is an ordered set of *cluster blocks*, each of which is a set of *cluster positions*, and is identified by its ordinal number within the cluster.
2. y is a *cluster description* describing how to rearrange the cluster positions of the cluster blocks into file entries and file-entry segments.[†]

---

* As is further discussed below, each cluster block may contain entries and entry segments belonging to different files.

† Recall the general file definition from Chapter 4.

3. z is an *access algorithm*, which, given a natural number i, delivers the cluster block identified by i for further processing.*

When a cluster block has been retrieved, the file entry retrieval process will (a) use the cluster description in order to select the cluster positions of the block that are contained in the requested entry (segment); (b) repeat (a) until all requested segments have been retrieved; and (c) use the file entry description in order to rearrange the retrieved entry or entry segments into "data base normal format."

The main idea behind the cluster concept is to split the complex file → storage mapping into simpler file → cluster and cluster → storage submappings, thereby making it possible to separate administration of storage from administration of files. Even in the future, storage administration will probably, to a large degree, be the responsibility of the operating system of the computer, particularly if the computer system has to be shared by several applications of which the data base system is only one. File administration, on the other hand, will be the responsibility of the data base system alone.

Figure 6.10 visualizes that both submappings, file → cluster and cluster → storage, may in general be "many to many." Thus, for example, different entries of the same file and even different segments of the same entry may in principle be allocated not only to different blocks within the same cluster, but even to different clusters. On the other hand entries and entry chopping segments from different files may very well be allocated to the same cluster block. Naturally there always have to be very good reasons for making design decisions resulting in complex mappings of the kind mentioned. For example, the systemeer has to have good reasons for applying the "file overlapping" operators because this file design operation will usually result in a complex file → cluster mapping.

The cluster → storage mapping may in principle be equally as complex as the file → cluster mapping. However, operating systems today do not allow particularly complex mappings between the set of cluster identifications[†] and the set of physical memory addresses, and it

---

* This further processing will be controlled by a file access algorithm. Thus a cluster block retrieval process will be a subprocess of a file entry retrieval process. See also the general file definition in Chapter 4.

† Cluster identification is equivalent to "relative block number within data set" in the IBM terminology.

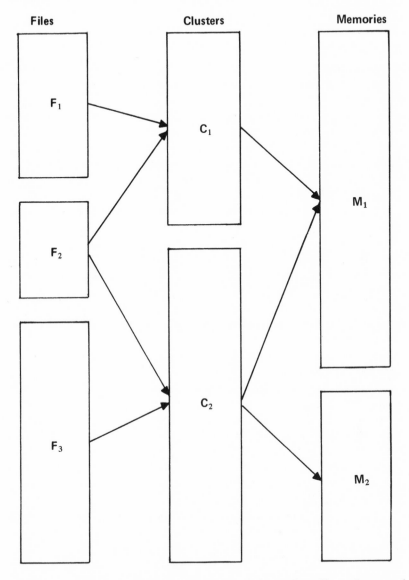

Fig. 6.10   The file → storage mapping and its submappings file → cluster and
            cluster → storage.

is hardly to be expected, or even to be desired, that this situation should be substantially changed in the future.

File Allocation

After the file establishment, intraentry, interentry, and interfile structuring operations have been applied and reapplied a number of times, we should have transformed the initial set of *e* concepts into a file structure that may easily and efficiently be allocated to a cluster structure that is compatible with the available storage structure. Although the earlier structuring operations will have put many constraints on the file → cluster mapping, there will usually be a few "degrees of freedom" left for this final file design step.

In order to be able to define a file → cluster allocation mapping we must have defined the file and the cluster. We assume here that we have defined the file in earlier structuring steps, so that we know approximately, for example, the number and size of the entries in the file. The cluster, on the other hand, will usually not be equally well defined when we start the first iteration of the file allocation design step. As was pointed out in the last section memory types that are common today possess both permanent and temporary structure. For example, the tracks and cylinders of conventional disk memories form a permanent structure, but each track may often be temporarily formatted into one or more storage blocks, at the designer's free choice.

Thus the formatting of a cluster into a set of cluster blocks is usually an important design decision. If we know approximately the size of the file entries, this design problem could be phrased as "How many file entries should be mapped to the same cluster block by the file allocation function?" This problem is also known as the "bucket-size" problem. It has to be solved under the constraints given by the permanent storage structure of the available memories. We may or may not assume that an access block is equal to a storage block.*

There is no general solution to the bucket-size problem. We shall just point to the factors that should be considered when this design decision is made. The principal advantages of a large bucket size are as follows:

---

* As was mentioned in the last section an access block may, in principle, be both smaller and larger than a storage block. However, it will usually require programming on the operating system level to make use of this theoretical possibility, if it is at all possible.

1. The available memory space is well utilized, because only a low percentage of the storage positions will be needed for block gaps.

2. When a hashing algorithm (discussed in the remainder of this section) will be used for allocating and retrieving the entries of the file, the expected number of memory accesses needed for the allocation or retrieval of an individual entry will be lower at larger bucket sizes if we assume a constant memory utilization rate (loading density or packing factor).

3. Relatively fast retrieval of *all* entries of the file because (a) the file will occupy relatively few storage positions, block gaps included; (b) the number of interrupts because of block gaps will be relatively low; and (c) in the case of a rotating memory, the number of "lost rotations"* will be relatively low because of the relatively low number of blocks occupied by the file.

The principal disadvantages of large bucket size are as follows:

1. The transmitted blocks will occupy a large amount of space in main memory.

2. The channel between secondary and primary storage will be busy for long periods at a time, which may cause serious delays in a multiprogramming environment.

3. Of the data transmitted between secondary and primary storage, only a relatively low percentage will actually be needed by the requesting process. Thus the effective transmission speed will be low.

When we have settled on both the file and the cluster characteristics, the remaining file design problem is the selection of a particular file → cluster mapping function. This problem will usually have to be solved under several constraints. For example, if we have ordered the entries of the file in one or more ways, it is usually assumed that the mapping function should as far as possible conserve one particular of these orderings. This means that entries that are consecutive according to the file ordering should be mapped to consecutive cluster locations, and, finally (by the operating system), to physically consecutive storage locations.

The file allocation problem is inseparable from the file-accessing problem. By logical necessity the file access algorithm has to be essentially the same as the file allocation algorithm. Thus the data base systemeer's design of the file → cluster mappings has important impli-

---

*It is a common experience that the time it takes for the access mechanism to pass the block gap is shorter than the time it takes for the processor to administrate the interrupt caused by the block gap. Thus one revolution will "be lost."

cations in several dimensions. The mappings finally determine such important parameters as storage utilization, response times, and maintenance work load. In the subsequent sections we shall discuss the different mapping methods that are available and their respective advantages and disadvantages.

Eight Different File Organization Types

A method for allocation and accessing of a file is often called a "file organization method." These methods may be grouped into $2^3 = 8$ different classes on the basis of the answers to the following three questions.

1. Does the file $\rightarrow$ cluster mapping function conserve the ordering of the file entries which is implied by the values of the entry identifiers? That is, will the "natural" ordering of the cluster blocks coincide with the "natural" ordering of the file entries in the sense that two consecutive file entries will always be mapped into the same or two consecutive cluster blocks?
2. Does the organization method imply the use of index tables or similar auxiliary data?
3. Is it possible to calculate the address of the cluster block into which an entry with a particular identification is mapped, without the aid of index tables or similar auxiliary data?

The eight possibilities are displayed in Fig. 6.11. Let us discuss each of them briefly.

METHOD 1: seq(addr)$\neq$seq(id), No Index, Noncalculatable Addresses. With method 1 organization there is no short cut to find a particular entry. Thus, on the average, half the file will have to be searched. This method is not always distinguished from method 5; they are both often called "physical sequential organization" (PSO).

METHOD 2: seq(addr)$\neq$seq(id), No Index, Calculatable Addresses. Method 2 is the "pseudo-direct organization" (PDO), which will be further discussed in subsequent sections. The PDO method possesses excellent performance characteristics. Storage requirements are modest; 70 to 80 percent of available memory may be loaded with file entries at file allocation time without significant risks of suddenly degrading response times with accompanying maintenance and reorganization problems. The "search factor," that is, the average number of accesses required to retrieve a particular file entry, will usually be slightly above 1, seldom more than 1.5. The PDO method is resistant to file dynamics;

it is elastic and can stand entry additions and deletion without dramatically degrading performance.

The problems with the PDO method arise from the fact that for most files, for most sets of entry identifiers, it is difficult to find a biunique mapping function. Usually address collisions will occur, that is, more than k entries will be mapped to the same cluster block, although there is only room for k entries per bucket. The overflow, or synonyms, will have to be taken care of by some complementary method, and the

Method Number	seq(addr)= seq(id)?	Index?	addr= f(id)?	Remarks
1	NO	NO	NO	PSO, version 1
2	NO	NO	YES	PDO
3	NO	YES	NO	Complete index (directory)
4	NO	YES	YES	Directory-file complex with name links
5	YES	NO	NO	PSO, version 2 interpolation binary search
6	YES	NO	YES	DO
7	YES	YES	NO	ISO, sparse index possible
8	YES	YES	YES	DO + directory files

Fig. 6.11   Eight different file organization schemes.

systemeer may not be trained to design such methods. We shall return to this problem in a later section.

METHOD 3: seq(addr)≠seq(id), Index, Noncalculatable Addresses. With method 3 there has to be a complete index, that is, an index that contains the cluster block address for every entry in the file (see method 7). In principle the index is a compressed copy of the proper file. There are as many <entry id, address> pairs in the index as there are entries in the proper file. Thus although we may have reduced the scale, we have not really solved the file allocation and accessing problem by introducing the index. We have only transformed the file organization problem into an index organization problem, which is by and large equivalent to the original problem, and which in turn has to be solved by means of one of the other seven methods discussed here.

Sometimes it may be possible to use an already existing proper file* as an index. This situation will occur in directory–file complexes. Consider, for example, a complex consisting of a property file

$$F^\alpha = <\text{PERSON,}\underline{\text{OCCUPATION}}>$$

and an object file

$$F^\beta = <\underline{\text{PERSON}}, \text{INCOME}>$$

Then, if each entry in F^α contains not only the names of persons with a particular occupation, but also the addresses of the corresponding entries in F^β, F^α will serve as an index to F^β. If F^α contains name links, but not address links, it could serve as an index to F^β only if there are other indexes or other access algorithms for F^β (see method 4); F^α alone will be an efficient access path to F^β to the same extent as F^β is involved in the β part of queries in which F^α is involved in the α part. For other kinds of transactions F^α will hardly be of any help in the accessing of F^β entries.

Like all index methods, method 3 will require at least two accesses in order to retrieve one particular file entry. The index will require a considerable amount of storage space, and it will also give rise to maintenance problems in connection with addition, deletion, and substitution transactions. Naturally, the secondary storage and the maintenance overhead will increase with the number of indexes per file.

---

* We recall that a proper file is a file that contains information about the object system proper. Normally an index will be an auxiliary file containing metadata only.

METHOD 4: seq(addr)$\neq$seq(id), One or More Indexes, Calculatable Addresses. Method 4 implies at least two access paths to the file: via index (directory), and via id-based address calculation. We may connect the former path to the latter by replacing the address links in the index(es) with name links that may be transformed into addresses by the address calculation algorithm. We gain important maintenance advantages by thus making the indexes (the directory files) independent of the main file. For example, we may reorganize the main file (by modifying parameters in the address calculation algorithm, or by changing the whole algorithm) without having to reorganize the indexes.

METHOD 5: seq(addr) = seq(id), No Index, Noncalculatable Addresses. A version of method 5 has been investigated by Ghosh and Senko (1969). They have studied how many accesses are needed to find a particular entry by *interpolation*, assuming (a) that successive subsequences of entries are allocated to successive memory buckets (for example, disk tracks), (b) that no extra access is needed to search *within* a particular bucket, and (c) that the identification a of the first entry and the identification b of the last entry of the file are known to the access algorithm together with the addresses of these entries. If c is the identification of an entry to be retrieved, the ratio $(c-a):(b-a)$ determines which bucket to access first.

Ghosh and Senko show that good values of the search factor are obtainable by the interpolation technique provided that (a) there are relatively many entries per bucket, (b) the entry identifiers are randomly distributed in the interval $<a,b>$,* and (c) the interval $<a,b>$ is relatively small. Interpolation is one access technique for a file that is organized according to method 5. The well-known *binary search* technique is another. The binary search access technique will result in a search factor of the magnitude $^2\log n$, where n is the number of entries in the file. With this technique the bucket size will not be of such great importance as with the interpolation technique.

METHOD 6: seq(addr) = seq(id), No Index, Calculatable Addresses. Unless the values of the entry identifiers of the file form some remarkably regular pattern, the conditions seq(addr) = seq(id) and calculatable addresses together imply the address calculation function to be an evergrowing function, that is,

---

* This can always be achieved by "preparing" the entry identifiers in a random number generator.

id$'>$id$''\rightarrow$addr(id$'$)$>$addr(id$''$)

If we do not make any assumptions about the distribution of the entry identifiers, there is no better function fulfilling this condition than the identity function

addr(id) = id

for all id. This method is the original pure version of *direct organization* (DO). For space economy reasons, direct organization cannot ordinarily be used for files with "natural" identifiers. For files the entry identifiers of which are created by the data base system itself, direct organization may be very efficient. It is the organization with the smallest search factor, $s = 1$.

METHOD 7: seq(addr) = seq(id), Index, Noncalculatable Addresses. Method 7 is often called *indexed-sequential organization* (ISO). In comparison with method 3, this method has an advantage, which is due to the ordering condition seq(addr) = seq(id). The ordering implies that the index need not be complete. It is customary to let the index contain address references only to the first or the last entry within each memory bucket in which the memory bucket may be a disk track, for example. Simultaneously, there may be still more sparse higher-level indexes for higher-level memory structures such as disk cylinders and whole disk units. On the other hand the ordering condition is also a source of complications. In summary the problems of indexed-sequential organization are as follows: (a) The ordering of entries has to be maintained. This implies more complex algorithms for addition and deletion of entries than if the file had not been ordered. (b) If the file is dynamic, that is, if it is frequently hit by addition and deletion transactions, there is a great risk of quickly degrading performance. This threat has to be met by an appropriate combination of the "space slacks" that are introduced all over the cluster structure to which the file is allocated, and the regular reorganizations of the whole file. (c) The index has to be properly maintained. Moreover, the index requires extra space and implies at least one extra access per retrieved entry.

METHOD 8: seq(addr) = seq(id), Index, Calculatable Addresses. Method 8 is organization 6 (DO) extended with one or more indexes (directory files). Like method 6 it may be useful for files the entry identifiers of which are consecutive, "artificial" numbers, created by the data base system itself.

PDO versus ISO

If we compare the PDO method and the ISO method for organization of a particular file, and if we use the design criteria (a) average number of accesses per retrieved entry (the search factor), (b) secondary storage requirements, and (c) ease of maintenance, we shall often find that the PDO method is superior with respect to all three of these criteria. The ISO method, however, has often been preferred in practical file design situations. On what grounds may such decisions have been made?

We think that there are several reasons why the ISO method is sometimes chosen in practical situations in which the PDO method would be theoretically better. Perhaps the most important reason is simply lack of adequate knowledge about the PDO method. As was pointed out in the previous section, the PDO method requires the designer to select (a) an address calculation algorithm, and (b) a method for handling the synonyms (collisions) that the addressing algorithm will almost inevitably generate. These design steps require some knowledge that is not too widely available today among data base systemeers. We shall try to improve the situation by devoting the next two sections to the two stated PDO problem areas.

To some extent the manufacturers of operating systems and other standard software have to be blamed for the theoretically nonoptimal choices that are currently made between the two methods. The standard software products often provide built-in solutions to the typical ISO problems (for example, the maintenance problems), whereas the addressing and synonym handling of PDO problems are often left entirely to the users of the products. Two common arguments in defense of the ISO method are the following: (a) Complete listings of the whole file are an often-requested output from the system, and in order to be useful these lists have to be sorted. (b) Update transactions against the file will occur in sorted batches, and the update process will run more efficiently if the transactions and the standing file are sorted on the same argument. According to both these arguments, the fact that ISO provides a "naturally" sorted file, whereas PDO does not, should be conclusive. However, let us take a somewhat closer look at the arguments.

First, argument (a) above reveals that the total information system, of which the data base is a part, is probably badly designed as a whole. What is the purpose of frequently produced extensive listings of the kind mentioned? Probably the sorted lists will be used in manual "look-up" operations, which could be much more efficiently performed without any listings if the operators are instead supplied with displays for direct interaction with the data base. Too many piles of paper have already been produced by computers.

As to argument (b), it is hardly likely that the natural ordering of the update transactions will arise spontaneously. Instead it is probably the result of a sorting process somewhere in the information system or its environment. Then, of course, we could instead sort the transactions on some other argument than the natural one. For example, we could sort the transactions on the argument that results from a transformation of the natural argument by means of a PDO addressing algorithm. With the transactions thus sorted the update process will run as efficiently with a PDO file as it would do with an ISO file when the transactions are naturally sorted.

How to Address a PDO File

The primary addressing problem with PDO files consists in finding an addressing function f that maps the members of the set of file entry identifiers

$$I = \{i_1, \ldots, i_n\} \tag{1}$$

to members in the set of available addresses

$$A = \{a_1, \ldots, a_p\} \tag{2}$$

It is a problem to find a good addressing function f, because I and A usually show quite different structural characteristics. On the one hand, A is usually equivalent to or may easily be transformed into a suite of consecutive natural numbers: 1,2,3, ... , p. On the other hand, the members of I are usually spread over an interval $<b,c>$, where the difference $(c - b)$ is much greater than n and p. (We assume that it is always possible to transform the entry identifiers into natural numbers in the first place.)

EXAMPLE 1: Swedish civic registration numbers have the structure

YYMMDD-XXX   (3)

YY   is a number, consisting of two figures, and indicating
          the year of birth of the person
MM   is a number in the set {01,02,03, ... ,12}, indicating
          the month of birth of the person

DD   is a number in the set $\{01,02,03, \ldots ,31\}$, indicating the day of birth of the person

XXX   is a number in the set $\{001,002,003, \ldots ,999\}$, which is used to distinguish persons, who were born on the same day, from each other

The numbers are spread over the interval

$$<000101001, 991231999 \tag{4}$$

which covers more than 100 times as many numbers as there are citizens in Sweden.

Ideally we should like the function f to be one to one, or biunique, so that at most one entry identification is mapped to each available address. Naturally, this can always be achieved if the address space A is sufficiently great. However, a good addressing function should not only generate few synonyms, it should also make efficient use of secondary storage; that is, we cannot allow p to be many times greater than n. In many situations we shall require the memory utilization rate, or the loading density factor

$$\mu = \frac{n}{p} \tag{5}$$

to be something like 70 to 80 percent.

We said that ideally f should generate no synonyms. The other extreme would be a function mapping all entry identifiers to one and the same address. In between these extremes we find *randomizing addressing functions*, that is, addressing functions that generate the same distribution of synonyms as would be generated by a perfectly randomizing mechanism. Such a mechanism would generate address a_j for entry i_k with the constant probability $1/p$ for all j and all k ($p_j = 1, \ldots ,p$; $k = 1, \ldots ,n$).

Why is it that we cannot choose a perfect randomizer as our addressing function? We cannot do this because only with the relative frequency $1/p$ will the perfect randomizer generate the same address for a particular entry at loading time and at retrieval time. Naturally we require the addressing mechanism *always* to generate the same address for a particular entry, otherwise we would not be able to retrieve what we have stored in the data base.

There are a lot of well-known algorithms with so-called *pseudo-*

randomizing properties, however. Such algorithms are usually used in random number generators for computerized lot drawings, simulations, and so on but they could just as well be used as addressing functions for PDO files. Given a starting value v_0, a pseudo randomizer will generate a sequence of apparently randomly distributed numbers, $v_1, v_2, v_3, \ldots$. The pseudo randomizer is not a perfect randomizer, because the starting value uniquely determines the sequence of random numbers; but this is just the property we want our addressing algorithm to have. If we use the entry identifiers in I as starting values, the pseudo randomizer will generate addresses that are apparently randomly distributed but are all the same uniquely determined by the entry identifiers.

From the existence of pseudo-randomizing algorithms it follows that a PDO file designer should never be satisfied until he has found an addressing function f that is at least as good as a random number generator. It is always possible to modify such a generator so that it can be used for addressing purposes.*

Pseudo-randomizing addressing algorithms have the advantage that their behavior can easily be investigated analytically. Let g_k denote the relative frequency of addresses to which exactly k entries are mapped by the addressing function $f(k = 0,1,2, \ldots)$. Using the Poisson approximation we may express the expected values of g_k for pseudo randomizers by means of the simple formula

$$E(g_k) = e^{-\mu} \cdot \mu^k / k! \qquad k = 0,1,2, \ldots \qquad (6)$$

In Fig. 6.12 we have tabulated some values of $E(g_k)$ for the loading densities $\mu = 0.7$ and $\mu = 0.9$. Thus, for example, if we have a storage utilization rate of 90 percent, we may expect 40.7 percent of the available addresses to be empty, 36.6 percent to be occupied by exactly one entry, 16.5 percent to be occupied by exactly two entries, and so on.

Although the performance of pseudo-randomizing addressing algorithms will usually be quite satisfactory (particularly in comparison with the performance of ISO), it should be kept in mind that they only represent what can *always* be achieved. Sometimes the designer may be able to find an algorithm that shows better performance than a pseudo randomizer. In order for this to be possible there must be some regularity among the entry identifiers that the designer can take advantage of.

A common type of regularity is exemplified in Fig. 6.13. We have

---

* One author has a lot of experience of the Tansworthe random number generator as addressing function for PDO files. This generator is very fast and yet possesses extremely good pseudo-randomizing properties. See Tansworthe (1965) and Whitlesey (1968).

k	$\mu = 0{,}7$	$\mu = 0{,}9$
0	49.7	40.7
1	34.8	36.6
2	12.2	16.5
3	2.8	4.9
4	0.5	1.1
5	0.1	0.2

Fig. 6.12   Percentages of $E(g)_k$ for the different values of k and $\mu = n/p$.

	$i \in I$	$\rightarrow$	$f(i) = i(\mathrm{mod}\, p)$
Suite 1	001		1
	002		2
	003		3
Suite 2	101		10
	102		11
Suite 3	201		6
	202		7
	203		8
	204		9
	205		10
Suite 4	301		2
	302		3
	303		4
	304		5

k	g_k (percent)
0	15.4
1	61.5
2	23.1
Σ	100.0

Fig. 6.13

315

there a set of $n = 14$ entry identifiers in the interval $<001,304>$. However, the entry identifiers are not at all randomly spread over this interval. Instead they form a regular pattern that could be described as follows. The set I may be divided into four subsets, each of which contains consecutive numbers only. Such subsets will be called *suites*. Moreover, the initial elements of the four suites, 001, 101, 201, 301, form another regularity. They form what we shall call a *pseudo suite* with the *period* $d = 100$.

For sets of entry identifiers that show one or both of these regularities the *division-remainder algorithm* may be a better addressing mechanism than a pseudo-randomizing function. When we use the division-remainder algorithm for addressing purposes, we divide all entry identifiers by a particular number p and use the respective remainders as addresses. Figure 6.13 shows how this algorithm works for a particular set of identifiers I and a particular $p(p = 13)$. The address space $A = \{0, \ldots, p - 1\}$ contains p different elements. In the example, 11 out of 13 potential addresses actually occur. For example, the entry identifier 202 is mapped to the address 202 (modulo 13) = 7.

The division-remainder algorithm has the following important characteristics: (a) A suite of r consecutive identifiers, $b, b + 1, b + 2, b + 3, \ldots, b + r - 1$, is always mapped into r consecutive addresses, $a, a + 1, a + 2, a + 3, \ldots, a + r - 1$. These addresses are all different provided that $r \leq p$. (b) A pseudo suite with the period d and containing r elements, $b, b + d, b + 2d, b + 3d, \ldots, b + (r - 1)*d$, is mapped into different addresses provided that $r \leq p$, and d and p are relatively prime, that is, they do not have any common divisor. If p is a prime number, the second condition is fulfilled for any value of d.

Because of the properties (a) and (b) above, the division-remainder algorithm with a carefully selected p will give a better, more uniform distribution of addresses than a pseudo-randomizing algorithm, provided that the set of entry identifiers contains such regularities as suites and pseudo suites. In Fig. 6.14 we have calculated the values of the earlier-defined function g_k, the relative frequency of addresses to which exactly k entry identifiers are mapped. Although the loading density $\mu = 14/13$ in Fig. 6.14 exceeds 100 percent, the values of g_k are better than expected for a pseudo-randomizing algorithm with much lower loading densities (see Fig. 6.12).

How to Handle the Synonym Problem for PDO Files

Unless the set of entry identifiers of a file shows a remarkably regular structure, it will be impossible to find an addressing function that simultaneously yields (a) different addresses for all entries, and (b) a high loading density. The more intensively we want to utilize secondary storage resources, the more often will it happen that the addressing algorithm generates collisions, or *synonyms*. Synonyms occur when different entries are mapped to the same address.

Memories are usually formatted into blocks, or buckets, of fixed size. Assuming that the entries are also of fixed size implies that there will be room for k entries per bucket, where k is a positive integer. If the addressing function maps more than k entries to the same bucket, the *overflowing* synonyms have to be taken care of by a complementary addressing algorithm, a so-called *synonym-handling algorithm*, or synonym handler. In this section we shall describe some different kinds of synonym handlers. We shall assume that $k = 1$, that is, that there is only room for one entry per memory bucket. However, the problems and the problem solutions are perfectly analogous for other values of k. Most synonym handlers described in the literature belong to one of the following classes:

1. Linear search (for secondary* addresses)
2. Random search based on the primary* address
3. Random search based on the entry identifiers
4. Pointer-linked chains of synonyms

Each of these four methods will be described below. (The account is based upon Thorburn, 1971.)

METHOD I. LINEAR SEARCH. Let $a_0(i)$ denote the primary address generated by the addressing algorithm for the entry i, and let $a_j(i)$, $j = 1, 2, 3, \ldots$, denote the secondary address generated by the synonym-handling algorithm if $a_{j-1}(i)$ turns out to be occupied. Then the linear-search method for synonym handling is defined by the formula

$$a_j(i) = a_0(i) + j \pmod{p} \tag{1}$$

where p is the number of addresses that are available for the file. Suppose that $p = 5000$ and that the primary address 4997 is generated for a particular entry. If this address is occupied, the linear-search method generates, in turn, the secondary addresses $4998, 4999, 0, 1, 2, 3, \ldots$, until a free address is found.

If the primary address generator is a pseudo randomizer and linear

---

* The addresses generated by the original addressing function are called *primary addresses*. Complementary addresses generated by the synonym handler are called *secondary addresses*.

search is used for generating secondary addresses, we may prove that the search factor s, that is, the expected number of accesses needed to retrieve an entry in the PDO file, is

$$s = \frac{2 - \mu}{2 - 2\mu} \tag{2}$$

where μ is the loading density.

METHOD II. RANDOM SEARCH BASED ON THE PRIMARY ADDRESS. According to method II the secondary addresses are generated by the synonym-handling algorithm from the primary address in much the same way as the primary address was itself generated by the addressing algorithm from the entry identifier. If both the primary address generator and the primary-address-based secondary address generator are pseudo randomizers, the search factor will be

$$s = -\frac{1}{\mu}(\log(1 - \mu) + S_0^\mu \frac{\log(1 - t)(t - 1 + e^{-t})}{t}dt)$$

$$= -\log(1 - \mu)/\mu + \sum_{n=2}^{\infty} a_n \mu^n \tag{3}$$

where

$$a_n = \frac{1}{n} \sum_{k=1}^{n-1} \frac{(-1)^k}{(k!(n - k))}$$

An example of a feasible synonym-handling algorithm belonging to this category is the one defined by the formulas

$$a_{2j}(i) \quad = a_0(i) - j^2 (\text{mod } p); \quad j = 0,1, \ldots , \frac{p - 1}{2}$$

$$a_{2j - 1}(i) = a_0(i) + j^2 (\text{mod } p); \quad j = 1,2, \ldots , \frac{p - 1}{2} \tag{4}$$

where p is assumed to be a prime number of the form $p = 4n + 3$. This algorithm is called *quadratic search*.

METHOD III. RANDOM SEARCH BASED ON THE ENTRY IDENTIFIERS. According to method III the secondary addresses are generated by an algorithm that, like the primary address generator, works on the entry identifiers. Thus the input to this kind of synonym handler will be an entry identifier, whereas according to method II the input would be the primary address of the entry. With random search based on the entry identifiers the search factor will be

$$-\log\frac{(1-\mu)}{\mu} \tag{5}$$

An example of this kind of algorithm is the *quadratic-quotient method* defined by the formulas,

$$
\begin{aligned}
a_{2j}(i) &= a_0(i) - k(i)*i^2 \ (\text{mod } p)\\
a_{2j-1}(i) &= a_0(i) + k(i)*i^2 \ (\text{mod } p)
\end{aligned}
\tag{6}
$$

where p is assumed to be a prime number of the form $p = 4n + 3$ and where $k(i) \neq 0 \ (\text{mod } p)$ and $a_0(i_1) = a_0(i_2)$ implies $k(i_1) \neq k(i_2)$.

METHOD IV. POINTER-LINKED CHAINS OF SYNONYMS. With method IV the secondary addresses are not calculated. Instead they are stored explicitly as pointers in such a way that the synonym entries form a pointer-linked chain starting at the primary address. Different chains, starting at different primary addresses, must not have any links in common. This can be achieved in two different ways.

1. The file is loaded in two steps. During the first step an entry is definitively stored if and only if a nonoccupied primary address is generated by the addressing algorithms. The overflowing synonyms are temporarily stored in a buffer area of some kind. During the second step the entries in the buffer are allocated to addresses that have not become occupied during the first step, and synonym chains are formed.
2. The file is loaded in one step. As soon as it has been established that a particular entry is an overflowing synonym, a nonoccupied address is found, and the entry is allocated to this address and linked to its predecessor in the chain of synonyms. However, if the primary address of an entry should be occupied by an overflowing synonym with another primary address, the latter entry is moved to another free bucket, the pointers of the synonym chain to which it belongs are properly adjusted, and the former entry is allocated to its primary address.

The first method can only be used when the whole file is loaded. When entries are added to an already existing file, the second method

has to be used. With a pseudo-randomizing primary address generator
and pointer-linked chains of synonyms the search factor will be

$$s = 1 + \frac{\mu}{2} \tag{7}$$

EXAMPLE 2: Figure 6.14 contains a very simple example which is
intended to show how the four investigated methods for synonym
handling work in practice. For this illustration we have used a small
file containing only 10 entries, which are assumed to be loaded as
indicated by the enumeration of the identifiers in I. The division-
remainder method with $p = 11$ is used for primary address generation:

$$\text{addr}(23) = 23(\text{mod } 11) = 1, \text{addr}(76) = 76(\text{mod } 11) = 10, \text{etc.}$$

COMPARISON OF THE FOUR METHODS. In Table 6.12 we have
tabulated the values of the search factor for the four methods for
different loading densities, μ. We can see that method IV (pointer-linked
chains of synonyms) shows the best search factor for all values of μ.
Random search based on entry identifiers (method III) is better than
random search based on primary addresses (method II). As to the search
factor, method I (linear search) is obviously the worst synonym-handling
strategy of the four methods that were investigated. We can also see that
the search-factor differences between the methods become more pronounced the more efficiently we utilize secondary storage, that is, with
growing values of μ. Methods I, II, and III degenerate completely when μ

Table 6.12

| Loading | Search Factor, s | | | |
Density, μ	Method I	Method II	Method III	Method IV
0.1	1.05	1.05	1.05	1.05
0.2	1.13	1.12	1.12	1.10
0.3	1.21	1.20	1.19	1.15
0.4	1.33	1.31	1.28	1.20
0.5	1.50	1.43	1.39	1.25
0.6	1.75	1.60	1.53	1.30
0.7	2.17	1.82	1.72	1.35
0.8	3.00	2.15	2.01	1.40
0.9	5.50	2.75	2.56	1.45
1.0	∞	∞	∞	1.50

$$I = \left\{ 23, 76, 80, 61, 56, 4, 11, 10, 8, 67 \right\}$$

Method I: Linear Search

Address	0	1	2	3	4	5	6	7	8	9	10	
	11	23	56	80	4	10	61	67	8		76	
Number of accesses	1	1	2	1	1	7	1	7	1		1	$\Sigma = 23$

Method II: Quadratic Search

Address	0	1	2	3	4	5	6	7	8	9	10	
	11	23	56	80	4	67	61		8	10	76	
Number of accesses	1	1	2	1	1	4	1		1	3	1	$\Sigma = 16$

Method III: Quadratic Quotient Method

$$k(i) = [i/p] + 1, p = 11$$

Address	0	1	3	4	5	6	7	8	9	10	
	11	23		80	4	67	61	56	8	10	76	
Number of accesses	1	1		1	1	3	1	2	1	3	1	$\Sigma = 15$

Method IV: Pointer-Linked Chain of Synonyms

Address	0	1	2	3	4	5	6	7	8	9	10	
	11	23 ↑2	56 ↑7	80	4	10	61	67	8		76 ↑5	
Number of accesses	1	1	2	1	1	2	1	3	1		1	

56	10	67	Temporary buffer

Fig. 6.14   Illustration of the four methods for handling overflowing synonyms in PDO files.

approaches 100 percent, whereas method IV is quite satisfactory even when the memory is full.

In order to understand the differences between different methods for handling the synonyms of a PDO file we shall analyze the following two questions. (a) How many queues of synonyms are formed? (b) To what extent will different queues interfere with each other?

Let us first consider (a). As to method IV (pointer-linked chains of synonyms), it is obvious that there is one single queue of synonyms "in front of" each primary address. For all entries with the same primary address this single queue will have to be searched serially at retrieval time. The same is actually true for method I and method II as well. When method III is used, however, there are as many queues as there are overflowing entries with the same primary address. This is so because when the generation of secondary addresses is based on the entry identifiers (and not on the primary address as in method II) different entries will give rise to different suites of secondary addresses even though they generate the same primary address.

If we disregard interference between different queues, it is obvious that retrieval will be faster if there are several queues per primary address than if there is only one common queue for all synonyms. Thus in this respect method III has an advantage over the other strategies. We also realize that it would be possible to invent other synonym-handling methods with other queue structures. For example, we could let the queues in front of a primary address form a bundle or tree pattern instead of one or more chains (see Chapter 4). Let us then consider (b). There are three typical degrees of interference between different synonym queues: Systematical interference, Random interference, and Systematical noninterference.

Method 1 (linear search) is an example of systematical interference. With this method the following situation will often occur at load time:

$a1$	$a2$	$a3$	$b1$	$b2$	$b3$	$b4$		

There are two queues of synonyms, a and b. The last synonym in a ($a3$) and the first synonym in b ($b1$) occupy consecutive addresses. Suppose now that another synonym, $a4$, is to be added to queue a. Then a and b will interfere with each other, and it is not a matter of a single accidental collision but of a series of collisions: $a4/b1$, $a4/b2$, $a4/b3$, $a4/b4$. Thus the interference between the queues is not merely random, but systematical. On the other hand with method IV, as it was defined above, interference between queues is systematically avoided (see 1 and 2 in the description of method IV). With methods II and III collisions between synonym queues will occur now and then, on a random, nonsystematical basis.

It is easy to realize that interference between synonym queues will slow down retrieval operations. As a matter of fact it is the systematical noninterference property of method IV that explains why this method shows better values of the search factor than the three other described methods. As method IV was found not to be best with regard to property (a) we may also conclude that there are synonym-handling strategies with better search factors than the search factors of any of the four methods that have been investigated here.

6.4 PROCESS DESIGN

Design of Programs, Process Instances, and Process Types

The term "process" is used with several distinct meanings in the data processing literature. In articles and books on operating systems, "process" usually denotes an individual entity, a *process instance*. On other occasions, such as in our Chapter 2, "process" is assumed to mean a class of similar process instances, a *process type*. It is usually obvious from the context which denotation is the intended one. However, in order to make a clear distinction between what we shall call "conventional systems" on the one hand and "data base systems" on the other, we need both the "process instance" concept and the concept of "process type" (or "routine"). Let us start by defining the relations between a process (instance), a routine (that is, a process type), and a program.

A *process* (instance) is an abstract entity, a theoretical construct, which we often find it practical to introduce as the bearer or the cause of an observed or a desired change, produced or to be produced by a system. In so doing the process uses, produces, and transforms both the internal and the external system resources. A process is born (initiated) at a particular point of time, and it dies (terminates) at another point of time.

During its lifetime, the behavior of a process (instance) is governed by a *program*, which is one of the resources used by the process. A program is a data structure representing a set of statements or instructions that are executable by a processor, for example, the central processor of a computer. A program is created by a process, and it may be destroyed by another process. During its existence, the same program may very well govern the behavior of several process (instances). Programs governing processes that do not modify the governing program may even govern several processes more or less simultaneously. A *routine* (or process type) is the set of all processes that have existed, are existing, or will exist, and that are governed by one and the same program and the same precedent *e* concepts (see Section 2.2). A routine is said to be *run* as often as one of its member processes is being executed. If an individual process (instance) p, belonging to the routine R, is initiated at t and terminated at $t + \Delta t$, we shall say that R is run at t, or more precisely, during the time interval $<t, t + \Delta t>$.

Routines, processes, and programs may be hierarchically built up by entities that are, themselves, routines, processes, and programs, respectively.

Let us now turn to the announced analysis of the differences between conventional systems and data base systems and the implications of these differences for the process design task.

We shall use the term "conventional system" for a computerized information processing system with the following characteristics. The system consists of a number of routines that become well defined at design time. Each routine is typically run at regular intervals, for example, once a month, once a week, or once a day. The length Δt of the time intervals $<t_1, t_1 + \Delta t>$, $<t_2 + \Delta t>$, and so on during which a routine is run is short in comparison with the time distance $t_2 - t_1$ between two successive runs of the same routine. Every time a particular routine is run, different time versions of the same standing files and temporary files (transaction files) are processed, and new time versions of the same standing files and output transaction files (report files) are produced.

Naturally, we can build a data base system around the standing files of a conventional system as defined above. However, if we devote a lot of scarce resources to the design and construction of a data base system, we will probably not be satisfied with a system that is only capable of interacting with its environment in the rigid way of a conventional system. In particular we probably would not be willing to determine *at design time* a well-defined set of routines to be run at regular intervals. Instead we would prefer different categories of interactors to be able to influence *at operation time* what kind of processing the data base system should be occupied with during a particular time interval. An information consumer, for example, should be able to initiate a particular kind of data base processing by means of a retrieval query transaction formulated in a result-oriented (nonprocedural) interaction language. Thus the temporary files of a data base system will often contain single transactions rather than batches of transactions of the same kind. Many transactions will appear at the convenience of different uncoordinated data base interactors in a way that is more or less out of the designer's control. The best the designer can do in such situations is to estimate the frequencies and time distributions of different transaction types.

The requirements on data base systems mentioned above have important implications both for the routine structure of a data base system and for the process design task. The routine structure of a data base system is typically more complex, more dynamic, and, above all, less explicit at design time than the routine structure of a conventional system. The data base systemeer may only be able to establish certain basic routines explicitly at design time. The set of basic routines would include, for example, (a) "routine skeletons," corresponding to the main transaction types that the data base system should be able to process, and (b) "dynamic design routines," which are responsible for the dynamic transformation of programs corresponding to the routine skeletons into complete programs by the time a particular data base transaction is actually being processed.

Thus the data base designer will not be able to design and schedule all data base routines (and indirectly all data base processes) at data base design time; nor will it be possible for the operations staff to make the missing planning and scheduling decisions at run time. Instead the data base designer has to design the data base system so as to make the system itself capable of planning and coordinating its own activities to a much greater extent than has been usual in conventional systems.

EXAMPLE 1: With the conventional philosophy the systemeers not only look for and document logical relations between *e* concepts, they also determine, permanently, what *e* concepts are to be contained in what files, and what files are to be used by what information processes. In a data base system the mapping of *e* concepts into files may have been changed between two executions of similar user requests as the result of automatically or manually initiated reorganization processes. This, in combination with the vast number of user transaction types that a data base system should be ready to process, makes it impossible to state an explicit file processing strategy beforehand for each imaginable situation. Planning processes, which are integrated parts of the data base system, have to make these decisions dynamically in accordance with certain basic rules that were formally stated and programmed when the data base was designed. The kinds of strategy choices concerning the processing of the standing files of the data base system that have to be made dynamically will be discussed in some detail in subsequent sections.

EXAMPLE 2: In a conventional system development situation the programmer may have the possibility and the responsibility of considering different subprocess structures for a certain information process. It may be his task to choose access methods, to determine ordering and possible overlaps of subprocesses, and so on. Similarly, the computer operations staff may have responsibility for the coordination of different batch executions so as to achieve reasonable throughput and turnaround times. The necessary conditions for such detailed preplanning are not present when data base requests are to be processed. Even if response-time requirements would permit the use of a professional programmer, it would hardly be possible for him to keep in mind the ever changing situation of the interior and the exterior of the data base system and to make feasible, not to speak of optimal, process structuring decisions. Thus a data base system has to include processes for this type of process planning as well as coordination activities.

EXAMPLE 3: Langefors and others have developed a *theory of process* grouping. In the development of conventional systems it is quite feasible to make process grouping decisions "manually" even though it has naturally been tempting and challenging to automatize this and other system design tasks. In a data base system many process grouping problems have to be solved dynamically and thus automatically.

The examples have shown that many different process design decisions, which have traditionally been the responsibility of systemeers, programmers, and operating staff, have to be made automatically, at processing time, in a data base system. This does not imply, for example, that the importance of programmers will decline in data base oriented information systems. It is obvious that the software for the dynamic planning processes themselves will require extremely advanced programming, as will all modules of a data base management system. Further, the data base administration function will continuously need skilled programming assistance. Finally, result-oriented languages will not eliminate the need for clever, problem-oriented algorithms. The application programmer will not have to worry about data management, however. He will have more powerful built-in functions at his disposal and might find it feasible to attack more complex applications than before.

Resource-Oriented and Transaction-Oriented Process Design

There are two basic categories of process design activities to be performed dynamically and automatically when a data base system is run on a computer. We shall call the two categories (a) "resource-oriented process design" and (b) "transaction-oriented process design." With some simplification we could state the general objectives of the two kinds of activities in the following way. The resource-oriented process design activities should see to it that the resources of the system are as efficiently utilized as possible under certain restrictions given by the transaction-oriented process design activities. Conversely, the transaction-oriented process design activities should see to it that each interaction between the data base system and its environment is as efficiently handled as possible under certain restrictions given by the resource-oriented process design activities. Still less precisely, we could state the two general objectives as (a) maximize throughput under certain response-time restrictions, and (b) minimize response time under certain throughput restrictions.

Even the vague goal formulations above suggest that there are many important trade-offs the designer of data base process design processes has to consider. There is the basic trade-off between a high utilization rate and a high service rate, which is well known from other kinds of systems. On a more detailed level trade-offs have to be made between the utilization rates of different resources as well as between the individual service rates with which different transactions from different interactors are processed. In this connection it is important that the designer or, still better, the system itself be able to identify the most scarce resources of the system as well as the variability in service demands that often exists. For example, all kinds of transactions from the data base environment do not require immediate response. It may be essential for good overall functioning of the data base system that the planning processes of the system be capable of identifying and postponing the processing of transactions that do not require response within the next couple of seconds, the next couple of hours, the next couple of days, and so on. Consider, for instance, a long-range planner. He may need a piece of information from the data base that requires extensive processing of many large files. It is quite possible that he will not be significantly delayed in his planning work if he has to wait a day or a week for the information he wants, provided he is certain that he will get a response within a day or a week, respectively, and that he will then get exactly the information he expects he will get. Such a situation has the following implications for the data base system. Immediately after the planner has submitted his request to the data base there has to be an intensive series of interactions between the data base and the interactor with questions and answers within seconds or possibly minutes. During this communication the information consumer should learn if the data base is at all capable of replying to the query, how long it will take, how much it will cost, and so on. He should also get some sample output showing how the ultimate answer will be presented,* and he should be able to modify the layout. The data base system should also see to it that the information consumer has a compatible conceptual frame of reference, so that he is aware of the meaning and the quality of the information output that he will ultimately get. Sometimes the data base itself may take the initiative and modify the initial query.†

The example of the long-range planner above should illustrate some aspects of transaction-oriented process design in data base systems. Other aspects will be treated in subsequent sections. Resource-oriented process design in data base systems has much in common with resource-oriented process design in conventional systems. Typically the dynamic, resource-oriented process design activities that take place in conventional systems are performed by the operating system of the computer, or by user-manufactured extensions to the operating system.‡ This is natural, because the resources are often demanded by several applications at the same time. As to the computer hardware resources, this may very well be true for data base systems, too. As has been pointed out earlier, the computer is formally a part of the data base environment and may be shared by the data base system and other applications, which may themselves be other data base systems.

In a conventional system the set of computer resources is more or less identical with the set of all resources that require dynamic, automatic administration. As was discussed earlier in Section 6.4 the situation is quite different in a data base system. For example, the standing files of a data base are examples of internal-system resources that are very central to the functioning of the data base system itself.

---

* If the data base is equipped with a "minibase" (see below) the information consumer could even get a rough idea of what the information contents of the ultimate answer will be. On the basis of the sample information he may, for example, decide that continued processing is not worthwhile.

† An example of this kind of "interactive modification of user requests" (IMUR) will be found in the end of Section 6.4.

‡ For example, the scheduling of the access requests to a particular disk storage device. These kinds of process design problems have for a long time attracted the attention of manufacturers and users of operating systems allowing multiprogramming.

They are also examples of resources that are often demanded during the same time interval by several different transactions. All together there are in data base systems internal resources that are natural objects of dynamic, automatic resource-oriented planning and coordination activities performed by the data base system itself and not by the operating system.

Transaction-Oriented Process Design Functions to Be Performed Dynamically by a Data Base System

It was explained earlier in section 6.4 why we cannot expect the process design for all imaginable data base transactions to be completed at the time of data base design. In order to get an overview of the transaction-oriented process design functions that have to be performed dynamically at the time of data base operation, we shall trace a particular data base transaction on its way through the data base system. We have chosen the processing of a retrieval query but this does not significantly lessen the generality of the analysis. The basic processing principles and process design problems of other transaction types* are, in effect, very similar to those of retrieval queries.

What happens first when the retrieval query hits the data base system is that it is recognized as a retrieval query. The interaction module† of the data base system will also select the appropriate compiler–interpreter, the compiler–interpreter of the interaction language in which the retrieval query has been formulated by the interactor. The external representation of the query will then be translated into some kind of normalized representation. Following Nordbotten (1967) we shall call this data base internal language the *internal dialect* of the data base system. Thus the external references to attributes, values, object groups, object relations, generation rules, and so on, will be translated into the vocabulary of the internal dialect, which will probably be much more laconic than the interaction language. Moreover, the grammatical structure of the transaction statements has to be analyzed and transformed into the grammatical structure of the internal dialect. This parsing process will be facilitated if the underlying structure of the interaction language is similar to that of some well-defined formal language such as first-order predicate calculus.

---

* Different kinds of data base transactions were systematically identified in Chapter 5.

† We shall refer in this section to the data base modules, or subsystems, suggested in Fig. 6.3.

The normalized statements corresponding to the retrieval query have to be analyzed further in order to eliminate references to entities that are not explicitly stored in the data base, but which are formally defined directly or indirectly in terms of stored entities. During this analysis the data base system has to consult the data base schema dynamically, at operation time, in much the same way as the systemeer of a conventional system has to consult the precedence matrices* at design time. We shall therefore call this dynamic data base process design task *dynamic precedence analysis.*[†]

After the dynamic precedence analysis the data base system knows what stored *e* concepts the retrieval query explicitly or implicitly refers to. The data base system also knows how these *e* concepts should be infologically processed in order to produce the desired result. However, each initial *e* concept may be stored in several files, and there may be several datalogical strategies corresponding to the same infological processing. The scheduling module of the data base system will have to consult the data base catalogs as well as the accumulated statistics in the accounting module in order to be able to make an executively optimal decision about which of the files to access and which of the strategies to choose.

In order to support the *modal* optimality of the dynamic choice of a file processing strategy, the data base system should collect and maintain as much information as possible about its own infological and datalogical characteristics. Obviously, it would not be *executively* optimal to design the data base system to do so. Even if "perfect" information about the data base were to be available at the time when a file processing strategy has to be chosen for our retrieval query, it might not be executively optimal for the scheduling process to make full use of it because of the implied resource consumption by the scheduling process itself.

An interesting alternative to the maintenance and utilization of elaborate data base statistics is the maintenance and utilization of *minibases*. A minibase is a miniature data base containing, for example, all available information about a random[‡] sample of the objects about which information is contained in the data base. In strategy choice

---

* The use of different kinds of precedence analyses and precedence matrixes in the design of conventional systems is treated in detail in Langefors (1966).

[†] The dynamic precedence analysis process includes such things as the breakdown of a complex $\alpha\beta\gamma$ query into $\alpha\beta$ queries. (See Chapter 5.)

[‡] In order to be random the sample should be selected by a criterion that is not related to any information contained in the data base.

processes the data base system often needs to know approximately how many objects have a particular combination of n properties $(n \geq 1)$.* If the number of properties is large, it will be feasible to store exact statistics about property combinations for low n:s only, often only for $n = 1$. With a minibase, however, no exact figures would be available; but on the other hand estimates could be calculated for arbitrary property combinations and arbitrary n:s, and this may be more valuable, particularly in cases in which not much is known at design time about the frequencies and response-time requirements of different query types.

Minibases also have other advantages. Sometimes the information available from a minibase could satisfy not only the needs of the process design processes but also the needs of the data base interacting information consumer. Thus under favorable circumstances an information consumer could get useful response to his retrieval request much faster and at a much lower cost from a data base with a minibase than from a data base that does not have this feature. Minibases could also be very helpful to the maintenance and reorganization functions of the data base system.

Let us assume now that the data base system has performed dynamic precedence analysis and chosen a file processing strategy† for the retrieval query that is under consideration in this section. This implies that the scheduling module of the data base system has now developed a plan, which tells what access requests to issue to what files, and in what order to initiate the respective file accessing processes. The schedule may be quite complex. Some file access requests may be independent of each other and may be processed in an arbitrary order or in parallel. Other file processes may be serially dependent, so that one has to be completed before the other may be initiated. Still other processes on the schedule may be parallelly dependent; that is, they have a common process precedent without being serially dependent. In Fig. 6.15, for example, processes A and C are independent of each other, D and K are serially dependent (with a precedence relationship of order 2), and E and J are parallelly dependent with the common precedent D.

---

*This information need may be almost as complex as the information need expressed by the original retrieval query, the efficient processing of which is the concern of the strategy choice process. Then it is important to note that very crude estimates may be quite satisfactory to the latter process, whereas the data base external information consumer is likely to need more precise information.

†Examples of retrieval situations and file processing strategies will be given later in this chapter.

The scheduling module must not only develop the file processing plan. It should also supervise the realization of the plan and be prepared to revise it dynamically.

It is the task of the files subsystem of the data base system actually to access the files. According to the file definition in Chapter 4, the access algorithms should take normalized entry requests as input and produce the requested entries edited in accordance with the data base normal format. The file access algorithms may in turn employ sub-algorithms such as segment collecting algorithms, hashing algorithms for

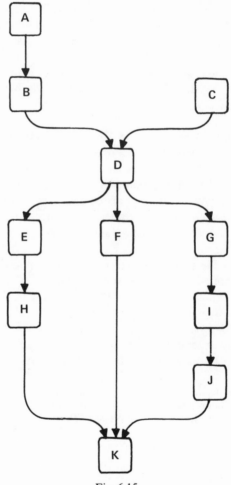

Fig. 6.15

the retrieval of synonyms, and cluster access algorithms (which may belong to the operating system). When a file access process is executed, it will initiate subprocesses corresponding to the subalgorithms.

The output from the individual file processes could be said to constitute subreplies corresponding to subqueries of the retrieval query originally received by the data base system. Infologically the synthesizing of the subreplies into a "grand reply" is the reverse process of the dynamic precedence analysis discussed earlier. Matching processes and processes corresponding to "standard operators"* are examples of probable subprocesses of the synthesis.

Finally, before the grand reply is presented to the data base interactor, it has to be translated from the internal dialect to the appropriate external format in accordance with the interactor's specifications.

This completes our analysis of the processing of a retrieval query transaction. It should be emphasized that we have only followed the main stream of the processing. For example, we have not treated the important subprocesses which are handled by the quality and protection filter functions of the data base systems. However, the processing of a request from one data base subsystem to another will often, in principle, be very similar to the processing of an external transaction from the data base environment to the data base. Many of the data base subsystems will themselves have subsystem structures similar to the subsystem structure of the whole data base; that is, they will have their own internal file systems, containing metainformation, their own interaction and scheduling modules, their own filter functions, and so on. Thus if we reinterpret the analysis in this section and apply it iteratively and recursively, it should be relevant to most transaction-oriented process design activities undertaken by the data base system or any of its subsystems.

The Processing of an $\alpha\beta$ Query

An $\alpha\beta$ query is defined as a retrieval query conforming to the following general pattern:

QUERY 1: For all objects having the property P^α, retrieve the values of the attributes $A_1^\beta, \ldots, A_m^\beta$ at the times $t_1^\beta, \ldots, t_m^\beta$, respectively.

---

* "Standard operators" are operators, or generation rules, that are once and for all defined to the data base system. Common examples are mathematical operators and statistical operators computing means, deviations, and correlations, performing regression analyses, and so on.

In the previous section we gave a general overview of the transaction-oriented process design tasks that a data base system has to solve dynamically. Among other things we mentioned that the data base system must be able to choose dynamically a feasible and efficient file processing strategy for any particular transaction that is being processed. In this section we shall try to concretize this task and the problems connected with it by means of examples. We adopt the following general assumptions as to the structure of the query to be processed and the file structure of the data base at processing time:

1. The Query 1 is an $\alpha\beta$ query where

$$P^\alpha = P_0^\alpha \wedge (A_1^\alpha = V_1^\alpha) \wedge \ldots \wedge (A_{n_\alpha}^\alpha = V_{n_\alpha}^\alpha)$$

and P_o^α is an object-type property like person, car, enterprise, customer, or pupil. All times involved in the α and β parts of the query are identical (t).

2. The files under consideration in the subsequent analysis are object files and property files representing time version t of different sets of e concepts $<O,A_i>$. The attributes involved in the files are classified as α attributes, β attributes, or x attributes, depending on whether they belong to the α part, the β part, or no part at all of the $\alpha\beta$ query that is being processed.*

3. For the files under consideration in the subsequent analysis we also assume that the objects referred to in the entry points of the object file entries and in the exit points of the property file entries have the property P_o^α in common.

With the assumptions adopted as to the type of transaction and the general structure and contents of the files, there are still many different process design situations that may occur depending on the particular combination of query and detailed file structure and file characteristics. We shall partition these situations into a few typical classes, and for each class we shall devote a section below to examples and discussion of the design considerations that have to be made dynamically by the planning and scheduling module of the data base system.

In order to show the typical features of each retrieval situation to be analyzed, we shall use a tool called the *relevance matrix*. It is defined for each combination of $\alpha\beta$ query and file system in the following way (see Fig. 6.16).

There is one row in the matrix for each α attribute and one for each

---

* Note that the α, β, x classification of attributes is only defined with respect to a particular query. The same attribute of the same file may be an α attribute with respect to one query and a β or an x attribute with respect to another.

F_1^o	F_2^o
S	D

F_1^p	F_2^p	F_3^p	F_4^p
D	D	D	D

	F_1^o	F_2^o		F_1^p	F_2^p	F_3^p	F_4^p
A_1^a	a			c^1	c^3		
A_2^a	a				c^1	c^2	
A_3^a	a	a		c^2			c^3
A_4^a	a				c^2	c^3	
A_5^a	a	a				c^1	c^2

	F_1^o	F_2^o		F_1^p	F_2^p	F_3^p	F_4^p
A_1^β	a	a					
A_2^β	a	a					

	F_1^o	F_2^o		F_1^p	F_2^p	F_3^p	F_4^p
A_1^x	i^1	i		i^4	i^4	i	i^4
A_2^x	a			c^3			c^1
A_3^x	a	a					
A_4^x	a						
A_5^x	a						
A_6^x	a						

Fig. 6.16   Relevance matrix for an $\alpha\beta$ query. S is serial access only; D is direct access; a is accessible attribute; i is accessible and object identifying attribute; c is component attribute of compound key. The meaning of the superscripts is explained in the text.

β attribute in the $\alpha\beta$ query. Then there is one column for each of the files in the file system which contains at least one of the e concepts corresponding to the α and β attributes. Finally, there is one row in the matrix for each x attribute—that is, each attribute that is contained in at least one of the column files but that is neither an α attribute nor a β attribute.

The cells of the relevance matrix may contain different symbols. Thus if cell

$$(j,k) = a$$

then file k contains attribute j. If cell

$$j,k = i$$

then attribute j is an object identifying attribute contained in file k; if the file is an object file, the attribute is the (primary) key of the file. If cell

$$j,k = c$$

then attribute j is a component attribute of the compound key of file k.*

Some of the symbols in the cells of the relevance matrix have integer superscripts. For example, the F_1^o column has superscript 1 for the i symbol in the A_1^x row. This implies that the entries of the object file F_1^o are ordered (sorted) by the values of the object identifying attribute A_1^x. The F_2^p column has superscript 1 for the c in the A_2^α row, 2 for the c in the A_4^α row, 3 for the c in the A_1^α row, and, finally, 4 for the i in the A_1^x row. This implies (a) that the entries of the property file F_2^p are ordered by the values of the key component attributes A_2^α, A_4^α, and A_1^α (in that very order), and (b) that finally the object references (the exits) are sorted (by the identifying attribute A_1^x) within each entry.

We may add extra rows and columns to the relevance matrix in order to indicate further characteristics of the files or the attributes, respectively. For example, in Fig. 6.16 there is one extra row where an S indicates that the entries of the file are only serially accessible and where

---

* Consolidation (combination) of property files was defined in Section 6.2. If n elementary property files, representing n e concepts of $\langle O, A_1 \rangle, \ldots, \langle O, A_n \rangle$, are combined into one compound property file with the (primary) key attribute $A_1 \times \ldots \times A_n$ formed by Cartesian multiplication, then $A_1 \times \ldots \times A_n$ is said to be a *compound key* with the *component attributes* $A_1, \ldots, A_n$.

a D indicates that the entries of the file are also directly accessible via the key attribute.*

The relevance matrix could be used as more than an illustration tool. When the data base system is about to process a particular query, it will have to assemble data corresponding to the contents of the relevance matrix for the particular $<$query, file system$>$ combination. It will have to do this in order to be able to choose dynamically a feasible and efficient file processing strategy.

The following analyses should not be confused with the analyses in Section 6.2 even though they represent in a sense two sides of the same coin. The decisions considered in Section 6.2 were design time decisions, that is, decisions to be made by the systemeer when the data base is being designed. The designer may make the decisions manually or assisted by a computer. The decisions considered in this section are operation time decisions which have to be made automatically by the data base system. At design time the designer is free to choose any structuring of the files he thinks will fit the transaction pattern (more or less unknown) that will hit the data base system at operation time. At operation time, on the other hand, the data base system has to accept the existing file structure and make the best of it when it processes a particular (well-defined) data base transaction. Naturally, a series of bad experiences from such situations could and should lead the data base system to recommend that the designer restructure the files, if it does not possess the capability and authority of reorganizing its files automatically, on its own initiative.

A BASIC RETRIEVAL SITUATION. We start our process design analysis of Query 1 from a "basic" retrieval situation (Fig. 6.17) with the following characteristics:

1. The compound attribute $A_1^\alpha \times \ldots \times A_{n_\alpha}^\alpha$ formed by all the α attributes of Query 1 is the key of a compound property file.
2. All the β attributes of Query 1 are contained in one object file.
3. The exit points (object identifications) of the combined property file are entry points of the object file.

---

* According to our definition of a file (see Chapter 4) each entry of a file is always *serially* accessible. If the file is coupled with an access algorithm that makes each entry accessible through a number of (auxiliary) accesses, which is small, both absolutely and in comparison with the number of accesses necessary for serial access, the file entries are said to be *directly* accessible as well. Then the file is called a *direct-access file*, whereas other files are *serial*.

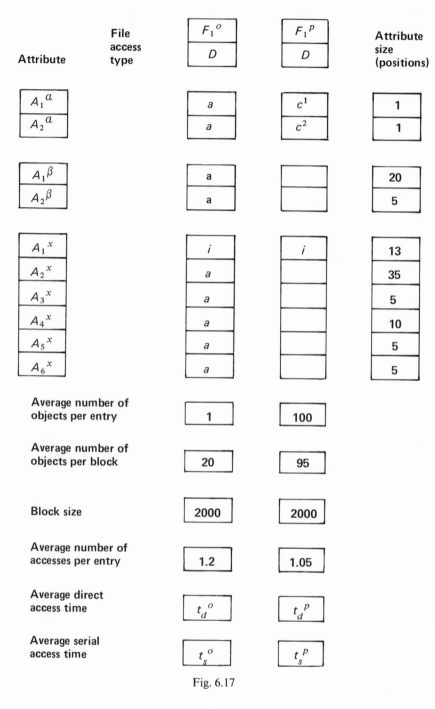

Fig. 6.17

4. The entry points of both files are directly accessible.

The obvious way of processing Query 1 under conditions (1) through (4) is *first* to access the appropriate entry of the compound property file, which will render the identifications of all objects having the α property, *and then* to access in turn the object file entries corresponding to these objects. The latter accesses will render the requested values of the β attributes.

If there are m objects having the α property the processing of Query 1 according to this strategy will probably require at least $(m + 1)$ secondary storage accesses—one for the compound property file entry and one for each of the m object file entries. The number could be less only if at any stage of the processing a demanded access block is already in primary storage; we may increase the probability of this occurring by sorting the object identifications resulting from the property file access(es) according to the object file sequence, if there is such a sequence.

For several reasons the actual number of secondary storage accesses will probably be greater than $(m + 1)$. For instance, (a) auxiliary accesses may be needed to determine, during query analysis, what files are to be accessed and then to "open" the files if they have not been opened already; (b) if the entry-point values of a file are more or less randomly scattered over a range of possible values, the accessing of an entry of the file will probably, on the average, require more than one access; and (c) the entries may have been chopped and all requested data may not be in the entry point segment; continuation segments may be in other access blocks than that of the initial segment.

Sometimes it may be advantageous to deviate from the obvious strategy of processing Query 1, even when all the "basic" conditions (1) through (4) are fulfilled. If the appropriate entry of the property file has been chopped and mapped into several access blocks, it may be worthwhile or even necessary to group the property file access process with the object file access process. We would then access one segment of the property file entry and then, possibly in parallel, access the corresponding object file entries and access the next property file entry segment.

A more dramatic change of strategy would be to replace the direct accessing of the directory–file pair* with a traditional serial search of the object file. This is logically possible provided that the object file contains not only the β attributes but also the α attributes. If a sufficiently large

---

* Note that the property file actually has the *function* of a directory to the object file.

fraction of the object file entries are to be accessed, serial search may be substantially faster than direct access; on the other hand, transmitted data volumes will probably increase, of course.

EXAMPLE 4: Let us compare the strategies

S_1:   directory–file search
S_2:   serial scan of the object file

in the situation illustrated by Fig. 6.17. According to S_1 we start by retrieving from the property file F_i^p the entry with the key

$$\langle A_1^\alpha, A_2^\alpha \rangle = \langle V_1^\alpha, V_2^\alpha \rangle$$

There are 10,000 objects referred to in the files. Suppose that a proportion p ($0 \leq p \leq 1$) of these have the property $(A_1^\alpha = V_1^\alpha) \wedge (A_2^\alpha = V_2^\alpha)$. Then there are 10,000$p$ object references in the retrieved entry, which, accordingly will occupy

$$q = \frac{10,000p}{(2000 - 2)/13} + 1 \approx (65p) + 1$$

blocks. The expected access time will be $1.05qt_d^p$ and the expected transport size 2000q positions. The next step would be the accessing of the 10,000p entries of the object file. The expected access time for this will be

$$1.2 \times 10,000p\, t_d^o = 12,000p\, t_d^o$$

and the expected transport size will be $2,000 \times 10,000p$ positions. Under strategy S_2, serial scan of the object file, access time will be

$$\frac{10,000}{20} \times t_s^o = 500t_s^o$$

and transport size will be 500×2000 positions. Let us summarize the results as follows:

Strategy	Access Time	Transport Size
S_1	$1.05qt_d^p + 12,000pt_d^o$	$2000q + 10^7 \times 2p$
S_2	$500t_s^o$	10^6

The first terms of the sums will certainly always be small compared to the second terms. This means, by the way, that it may well be worth considering a change of strategy from S_1 to S_2 even after the first step of S_1 has been carried out; actually carrying out this step could be the best way of estimating p, the value of which determines which of S_1 and S_2 is best.

If we assume $t_d^p = t_d^o = 40ms$ and $t_s^o = 4ms$, we get

Strategy	Access Time	Transport Size
S_1	$480p$	$10^7 \times 2p$
S_2	2	10^6

In this example we have not considered the possibility of reducing the total direct access time to the object file by sorting the object references into the physical order of the file entries.

OTHER THAN α ATTRIBUTES IN THE COMPOUND ATTRIBUTE KEY. In the basic retrieval situation defined in the previous section we assumed the key of the compound property file to be formed by all the α attributes of Query 1 and no others. Now suppose that there is a compound property file, whose key is formed by the α attributes $A_1^\alpha, \ldots,$ $A_{n_\alpha}^\alpha$ and some other attributes $A_1^x, \ldots, A_{n_x}^x$. Such a file may also be used in the first step of the processing of Query 1; the second step would still consist of accesses to the object file to look for the β values.

EXAMPLE 5: (See Fig. 6.18). Suppose we want the values of the β attribute INCOME for all objects having the value B on the α attribute REGION. There is a property file F_1 with the compound attribute key SEX $\times$ REGION and an object file F_2 containing the attribute INCOME.

R(SEX) = {M, F}, R(REGION) = {A, B, C}

and thus

R(SEX $\times$ REGION) = {$<$M, A$>$, $<$M, B$>$, $<$M, C$>$, $<$F, A$>$, $<$F, B$>$, $<$F, C$>$}

A feasible way of processing the request would consist of steps: (a) generate the entry points $<$M, B$>$ and $<$F, B$>$ using information about R(SEX); (b) access the two generated entries of F_1; this will yield a set of object references; (c) access the corresponding object entries of F_2 and fetch the INCOME values.

In general, if the compound property file key contains besides the α attributes n_x x attributes, the ranges of which contain $r_1^x, \ldots,$ $r_{n_x}^x$ values, respectively, the processing of the query according to the strategy lined out above will (d) generate accesses to

$$g = r_1^x x \ldots, \times r_{n_x}^x$$

different entries of the compound property file. If g is large in comparison with the total number of objects represented in the property file, many entries will be empty or nonexistent. Nevertheless it will usually cost at least one secondary storage access to learn that an entry is empty or nonexistent. On the other hand if g is small in comparison with the total number of objects represented in the property file, each generated entry will contain a lot of object references, maybe spread over several access blocks; we then have a situation very similar to that described in the previous section.

If g is not small, it may, in general, be advantageous to replace the step corresponding to (b) in the example above with a serial scan of the compound property file.

Attribute	File access type	$F_1{}^o$ D	$F_1{}^p$ D
α REGION			c^2
β INCOME		a	
x CIVIC REG NO		i	j^3
SEX		a	c^1
OCCUPATION		a	
NAME		a	
ADDRESS		a	
NATIONALITY		a	

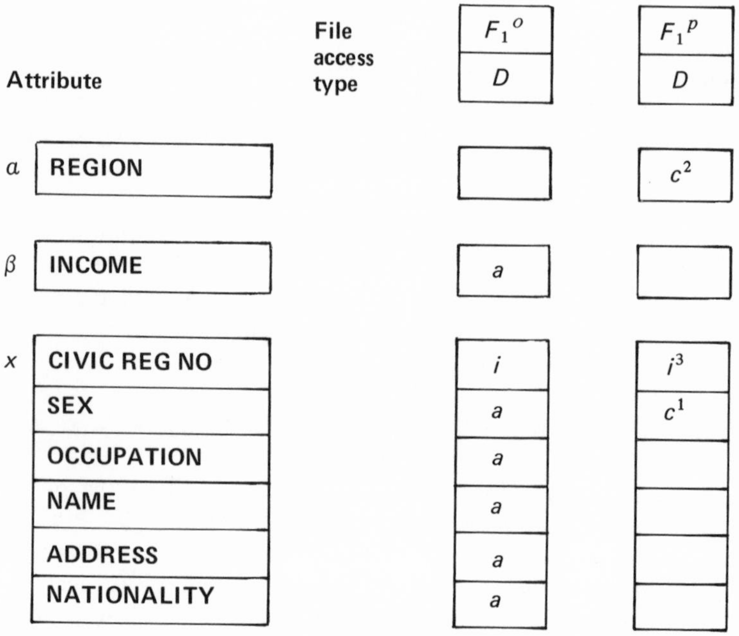

Fig. 6.18

EXAMPLE 6: Suppose there are 10,000 objects and $r_1^x = r_2^x = r_3^x = 10$ and suppose there are, on the average, 100 object references per property file access block. A serial scan of the property file will cost some 100 serial accesses, whereas direct access after entry generation is likely to cause more than $10^3 = 1000$ direct accesses.

There is an important exception to the rule that a large g will cause at least an equally large number of accesses. This exception occurs when the entries of the compound property file have been "physically" or "logically" *ordered* according to the values of the α and x attributes in such a way that the entries containing objects with the α property occur sequentially. Even if the hierarchical ordering should not be perfect with respect to the particular query, the number of accesses may be reduced.

EXAMPLE 7: Suppose a property file with the compound attribute key $\langle A_1^\alpha, A_2^\alpha, A_1^x, A_3^\alpha, A_2^x, A_3^x \rangle$ has been hierarchically ordered in the way indicated by the writing of the key.* Suppose that the range of each α attribute contains 10 values, and that the range of each x attribute contains 7 values. The processing of a query containing A_1^α, A_2^α, and A_3^α as the α attributes would then generate $7^3 = 343$ entries of the property file to be accessed. If, say, 300 of these entries were empty or nonexistent, many accesses would be in vain. However, the access work may be considerably reduced by taking the following seven entries as origins for serial searches:

e1: $\langle V_1^\alpha, V_2^\alpha, 1, V_3^\alpha, 1, 1 \rangle$
e2: $\langle V_1^\alpha, V_2^\alpha, 2, V_3^\alpha, 1, 1 \rangle$
e3: $\langle V_1^\alpha, V_2^\alpha, 3, V_3^\alpha, 1, 1 \rangle$
e4: $\langle V_1^\alpha, V_2^\alpha, 4, V_3^\alpha, 1, 1 \rangle$
e5: $\langle V_1^\alpha, V_2^\alpha, 5, V_3^\alpha, 1, 1 \rangle$
e6: $\langle V_1^\alpha, V_2^\alpha, 6, V_3^\alpha, 1, 1 \rangle$
e7: $\langle V_1^\alpha, V_2^\alpha, 7, V_3^\alpha, 1, 1 \rangle$

V_1^α, V_2^α, and V_3^α are the constant values of the α attributes of the query. The ranges of the attributes are supposed to be initial segments of the set of positive integers.

If empty entries are left out in the property file, the serial searches would actually start with the first nonempty successors of

---

* The values of A_1^α vary most seldom and the values of A_3^x most often when we scan the entries of the file according to the hierarchical sequence.

the entries stated above; only the (343–300) = 43 nonempty entries would be accessed. If the empty entries were *not* left out in the sequence, we would still have to access 343 different entries, but only 7 of these would be direct accesses, which are often more time consuming than serial accesses, and many subsequences of requested property file entries would be contained in the same access block.

With the types of secondary storage devices available today one ordering, at most, of the property file entries may be physically implemented at one time. By implementing more sequences, corresponding to different hierarchies of the attributes of a compound key, by means of data pointers we may make it occur more often than otherwise that the actual number of property file secondary storage accesses necessary to process a query will be less than g, as defined in (d) of Example 5. On the other hand, the data pointers cause space costs and maintenance efforts.

β ATTRIBUTES IN THE COMPOUND ATTRIBUTE KEY. If all β attributes as well as all α attributes of a Query 1 are contained in the key of a compound property file, there is no need to access any object file. By letting the β attributes vary independently of each other over their respective ranges, we obtain the entry-point values of the property file entries to be accessed.

EXAMPLE 7: (See Fig. 6.19). Suppose the value of the attribute SOCIAL CLASS is requested for all female inhabitants of region B, and suppose there is a property file with the compound attribute
   A = REGION × SOCIAL CLASS × SEX. R(REGION) = {A, B, C}, R(SOCIAL CLASS) = {1, 2, 3}
and
   R(SEX) = {M, F}
thus R(A) contains $3 \times 3 \times 2 = 18$ elements, and there are equally many entries in the compound property file. The processing of the query causes access to three of these entries, namely,
   e1:   <B, 1, F>
   e2:   <B, 2, F>
   e3:   <B, 3, F>

The processing strategy illustrated by the example is particularly advantageous if the result of the Query 1 is to be sorted according to the

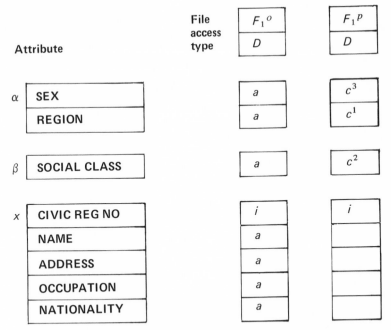

Fig. 6.19

values of the β attributes. This might be the case, for instance, if the query is a subquery of a table output request.

If, as well as the α and β attributes, the key of the compound property file contains one or more other attributes, x attributes, the process planning process has to make considerations similar to those accounted for in the previous section to determine, first, whether there is any hierarchical ordering of the entries of the compound property file, which may be used to reduce the actual number of accesses; and, second, whether a serial scan of the property file is to be preferred to the direct-access approach.

As a matter of fact these considerations are equally applicable when there are no x attributes, because the generation of entries by variation of the β attributes is perfectly analogous to the generation of entries by variation of x attributes as described in the previous section; compare the example given above.

SCATTERED α ATTRIBUTES. Consider a situation like that of Fig. 6.20. The α attributes of Query 1 are scattered over several property files, and none of them contains all α attributes. If we do not choose to scan the object file, we have to match entries of the property file in such a situation.

We shall look for the typical problems in connection with scattered attributes by studying the example of Fig. 6.20. To make the analysis a little more concrete there are a few numerical assumptions stated in the extra rows and column of the relevance matrix.

Let us examine four process design strategies, S_1, S_2, S_3, and S_4, which are all logically feasible. To describe the four strategies, we use an "almost-formal" shorthand notation.

Strategy S_1

1. match $(F_1^p(A_1^\alpha = V_1^\alpha, A_3^\alpha = V_3^\alpha), F_3^p(A_2^\alpha = V_2^\alpha, A_4^\alpha = V_4^\alpha, A_5^\alpha = V_5^\alpha)$
   giving $\{o_i\}$
2. access $(F_1^o, \{o_i\})$
   fetching (A_1^β, A_2^β)

Explanation. The entries of the property file F_1^p satisfying the condition $(A_1^\alpha = V_1^\alpha) \wedge (A_3^\alpha = V_3^\alpha)$ should be matched against the entry of the property file F_3^p with the key

$$\langle A_5^\alpha, A_2^\alpha, A_4^\alpha \rangle = \langle V_5^\alpha, V_2^\alpha, V_4^\alpha \rangle.$$

The objects resulting from this matching should be accessed from the object file F_1^o; these object file entries contain the requested β values.

Analysis. F_1^p contains $r = 10$ entries satisfying the condition $(A_1^\alpha = V_1^\alpha) \wedge (A_3^\alpha = V_3^\alpha)$. The object references of each entry are sorted; A_1^x is the object identifying attribute according to the relevance matrix. Each of the 10 entries is matched against the single entry of F_3^p with the particular $\langle A_5^\alpha, A_2^\alpha, A_4^\alpha \rangle$ key; these object references are sorted, too. According to the numerical assumptions of the example an expected number of

$$10 \times 3.0 + 1 \times 3.0 = 33$$

accesses have to be made to the property files in order to accomplish the matching. The expected transport size is

$$33 \times 4000 = 132000$$

decimal positions (pos). We make the additional assumption that

Attribute	File access type	F_1^o D	F_1^p D	F_2^p D	F_3^p D	F_4^p D	$^{10}\log r$
A_1^α		a	c^1	c^3			1
A_2^α		a		c^1	c^2		1
A_3^α		a	c^2			c^3	1
A_4^α		a		c^2	c^3		1
A_5^α		a			c^1	c^2	1
A_1^β		a					20
A_2^β		a					35
A_1^x		i	i^4	i^4	i^4	i^4	10
A_2^x		a	c^3			c^1	1
A_3^x		a					1
A_4^x		a					18
A_5^x		a					5
A_6^x		a					5
Average number of objects per entry		1	1000	1000	1000	1000	
Average number of objects per block		20	333	333	333	333	
Block size		2000	4000	4000	4000	4000	
Average number of accesses per entry		1.2	3.0	3.0	3.0	3.0	
Average direct access time		t_d^o	t_d^p	t_d^p	t_d^p	t_d^p	
Average serial access time		t_s^o	t_s^p	t_s^p	t_s^p	t_s^p	

r = number of attribute values

Total number of objects = 10^6

Fig. 6.20

$$\frac{10^6}{r^5} = 10$$

object references "survive" the matching process. Then on the average

$$10 \times 1.2 = 12$$

accesses will have to be made to the object file F_1^o, and

$$12 \times 2000 = 24000$$

decimal positions will have to be transported.

Strategy S_2

1. match $(F_2^p(A_1{}^\alpha = V_1{}^\alpha, A_2{}^\alpha = V_2{}^\alpha, A_4{}^\alpha = V_4{}^\alpha), F_4^p(A_3{}^\alpha = V_3{}^\alpha, A_5{}^\alpha = V_5{}^\alpha))$
   giving $\{o_i\}$

2. access $(F_1^o, \{o_i\})$
   fetching $(A_1{}^\beta, A_2{}^\beta)$

Explanation. The entries of the property file F_4^p satisfying the condition $(A_5{}^\alpha = V_5{}^\alpha) \wedge (A_3{}^\alpha = V_3{}^\alpha)$ should be matched against the entry of the property file F_2^p with the key

$$\langle A_2{}^\alpha, A_4{}^\alpha, A_1{}^\alpha \rangle = \langle V_2{}^\alpha, V_4{}^\alpha, V_1{}^\alpha \rangle.$$

The objects resulting from this matching should be accessed from the object file F_1^o; these object file entries contain the requested β values.

Analysis. The situation is perfectly analogous to that of strategy 1. The analysis and the calculations will be the same.

Strategy S_3

1. match $(F_2^p(A_1{}^\alpha = V_1{}^\alpha, A_2{}^\alpha = V_2{}^\alpha, A_4{}^\alpha = V_4{}^\alpha), F_3^p(A_2{}^\alpha = V_2{}^\alpha, A_4{}^\alpha = V_4{}^\alpha, A_5{}^\alpha = V_5{}^\alpha))$
   giving $\{o_i\}$
2. access $(F_1^o, \{o_i\})$
   testing $(A_3{}^\alpha = V_3{}^\alpha)$
   fetching $(A_1{}^\beta, A_2{}^\beta)$

Explanation. According to this strategy we match the entry of F_2^p with the key

$$\langle A_2{}^\alpha, A_4{}^\alpha, A_1{}^\alpha \rangle = \langle V_2{}^\alpha, V_4{}^\alpha, V_1{}^\alpha \rangle$$

against the entry of F_3^p with the key

$$\langle A_5{}^\alpha, A_2{}^\alpha, A_4{}^\alpha \rangle = \langle V_5{}^\alpha, V_2{}^\alpha, V_4{}^\alpha \rangle$$

By giving up the condition $(A_3{}^\alpha = V_3{}^\alpha)$ in the matching process we only have to match two entries against each other, but on the other hand more objects will "survive" the matching process; more precisely we make the additional assumption that

$$\frac{10^6}{r^A} = 100$$

objects will have to be accessed in the second phase. During the latter process we have to test the value of A_3 in the transmitted object file entries so that the requested β values are fetched in the appropriate cases only.

Analysis. According to the numerical assumptions of the example an expected number of

$$3.0 + 3.0 = 6$$

accesses have to be made to the property files in order to accomplish the matching. The expected transport size during this phase is

$$6 \times 4000 = 24{,}000$$

decimal positions. Then on the average

$$100 \times 1.2 = 120$$

accesses will have to be made to the object file $F_1{}^o$, and

$$120 \times 2000 = 240{,}000$$

decimal positions will have to be transported.

Strategy S_4

1. Scan $(F_1{}^o)$
   testing $(A_1{}^\alpha = V_1{}^\alpha, A_2{}^\alpha = V_2{}^\alpha, A_3{}^\alpha = V_3{}^\alpha, A_4{}^\alpha = V_4{}^\alpha, A_5{}^\alpha \doteq V_5{}^\alpha)$
   fetching $(A_1{}^\beta, A_2{}^\beta)$

Explanation. This is the serial-search strategy, which may sometimes be better than any directory–file search, for instance, because each serial access is usually faster than each direct access, which may outweigh the effect of a possibly greater *number* of accesses with the scanning strategy.

Analysis. According to the numerical assumptions of the example

$$\frac{10^6}{20} = 50\,000$$

accesses have to be made during the scanning of the object file F_1. The transport size will be

$$50\,000 \times 2\,000 = 10^8$$

decimal positions.

Summary

Strategy	Access Time	Transport Size
S_1	$33\,t_d^{\,p} + 12t_d^{\,o}$	156,000
S_2	$33\,t_d^{\,p} + 12t_d^{\,o}$	156,000
S_3	$6\,t_d^{\,p} + 120t_d^{\,o}$	264,000
S_4	$50,000\,t_s^{\,o}$	100,000,000

If we assign reasonable values to the parameters, we find that S_1 and S_2 are the best strategies in this example.

According to S_1 and S_2 we had to match *one* entry of one file against *several* entries of another file. With slightly different assumptions we might have had to match *many* entries of one file against *many* entries of another file. Then if we cannot keep all involved entries of at least one of the files in primary storage simultaneously, we have to *sort* the object references of each entry, if this has not been done before, *merge* the object references of different entries of the same property file, and *store* them as a *temporary file* on secondary storage before we can start the matching process as described above. The sorting and merging will require extra CPU time, which might not be important, and extra accesses when writing and reading the temporary files, which will probably have significance, although these small and temporary sets of data will, of course, be stored on much faster secondary storage devices than the permanent data base files.

OVERLAPPING RELEVANT FILES. Let us investigate a few typical examples of process design situations in which at least two of the relevant* files overlap each other.

---

* The relevant files of a query are the files of the columns of the relevance matrix of the query.

First consider the example of Fig. 6.21. We have there a relevant object file, containing among other things the β attributes, and this object file has been overlapped by three property files, each of which contains one of the α attributes of the query. More precisely, it is the object identifying values of the attribute A_1^x that the four files have in common. To show this we have affixed a subscript o to the i's in the A_1^x row.

In the first extra row below the kernel of the relevance matrix, the existing overlaps have been indicated. We distinguish between *overlapped* files, indicated by x, and *overlapping* files, indicated by a reference to the overlapped file. It is difficult to give a general, formal definition of this distinction, but we could say that of two overlapping files the overlapped one would be that which has been least affected to its inter- and intraentry structure by the overlap operation.

If we disregard for a moment the overlap relationships between the files, Fig. 6.21 shows a situation characterized by scattered α attributes. The typical strategy to use in such a situation would be to match property files against each other and access entries in the object file corresponding to objects surviving the matching process. According to the numerical assumptions of Fig. 6.21 this strategy would cause an expected number of

$$2000 + 1000 + 500 = 3500$$

direct accesses to the property files to be followed by, say,

$$\frac{10,000}{r_1^\alpha \times r_2^\alpha \times r_3^\alpha} = \frac{10,000}{5 \times 10 \times 20} = 10$$

direct accesses to the object file. Of course, it would be foolish not to recognize and take advantage of overlap relationships that do exist.* With the assumptions of the example it would obviously be a much better strategy (a) to access the appropriate entry of the relevant property file with the least average number of objects per entry, that is, F_3^p, and (b) to group this property file accessing process with a process during which the object file entries overlapped by the accessed property file

---

* Note that we discuss here which strategy to choose *at processing time*, when we have to accept the existing file structure. Quite another problem, to be considered *at file structuring time*, is whether any files should be overlapped with each other. If the files of the example had not been overlapped in the first place, there would certainly have been more than one object per block in the property files, and the matching would not have caused so many accesses.

entries are tested on their $A_1{}^\alpha$ and $A_2{}^\alpha$ values; in appropriate cases the β values are fetched. This strategy would cost only

$$\min(2000,\ 1000,\ 500) = 500$$

direct accesses to the $<F_3{}^p,\ F_1{}^o>$ file overlap pair.

With the latter strategy it does not make us any better off that the object references within each property file entry are sorted, which they are according to the assumptions of Fig. 6.21. With the former strategy, however, this assumption could be essential.

Next we consider the example of Fig. 6.22. In this figure it is the property file that has been overlapped by an object file. More concretely the situation could be as follows:

$$A_1{}^a = V_1{}^a,\ A_2{}^a = V_2{}^a$$

$$A_1{}^x\ (O_1),\ A_3{}^a\ (O_1)$$
$$A_1{}^x\ (O_2),\ A_3{}^a\ (O_2)$$
$$A_1{}^x\ (O_3),\ A_3{}^a\ (O_3)$$

$$A_1{}^x\ (O_n),\ A_3{}^a\ (O_n)$$

that is, an access block containing references to objects having the property

$$(A_1{}^\alpha = V_1{}^\alpha) \wedge (A_2{}^\alpha = V_2{}^\alpha)$$

also contains, beside each object reference $A_1{}^x\ (o_i)$, the value of the attribute $A_3{}^\alpha$ for each object having the property stated above.

If $F_2{}^o$ had not been overlapping $F_1{}^p$ as indicated by Fig. 6.22, we would have had to use a strategy consisting of the steps (a) access the entry $<V_1{}^\alpha,\ V_2{}^\alpha>$ of the property file $F_1{}^p$, and (b) for each object reference in the property file entry access the object file $F_1{}^o$, test $A_3{}^\alpha$ for $V_3{}^\alpha$, and fetch the β values in appropriate cases.

Recognizing the overlap we may, instead, use a strategy consisting of the steps (a) access the entry $<V_1{}^\alpha,\ V_2{}^\alpha>$ of the property file $F_1{}^p$ and test the overlapped $F_2{}^o$ entries for $A_3{}^\alpha = V_3{}^\alpha$; and (b) for each object reference surviving the $A_3{}^\alpha$ test, access the object file $F_1{}^o$ and fetch the β values. Under normal circumstances, the latter strategy will, of course, imply fewer accesses than the former.

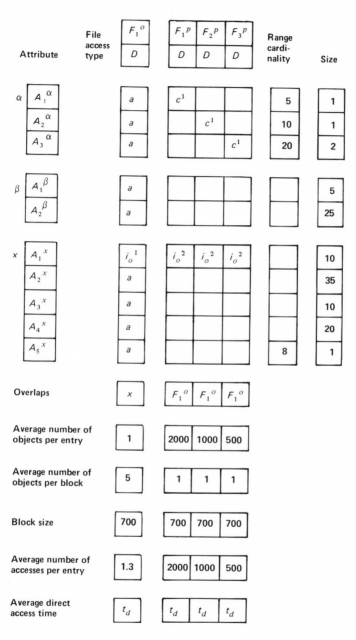

Total number of objects = 10 000

Fig. 6.21

353

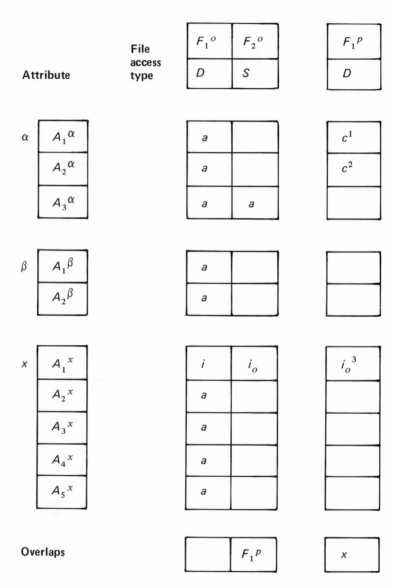

Fig. 6.22

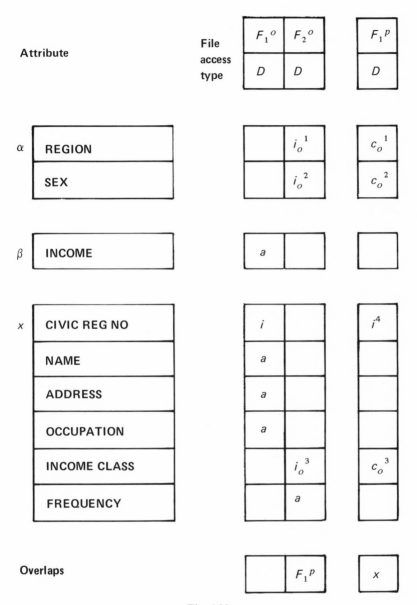

Fig. 6.23

As a third example of process design in connection with overlapping files we consider the situation represented by Fig. 6.23. We suppose that this situation has been caused by a query asking for

the *median income* of all *females* in *region C*

This query is not itself of type 1 but a straightforward analysis would generate the Query 1 type.

for all persons having the property (SEX = F)∧(REGION = C) re-trieve the values of the attribute INCOME

The retrieved INCOME values would then be sorted and the one in the middle would be delivered as the reply to the original query. Processing along these lines would involve the property file F_1^p and the object file F_1^o. It is well worth considering, however, how to make use of the object file F_2^o, which is overlapping F_1^p.

It is the key

REGION × SEX × INCOME CLASS

of the *compound object file* F_2^o which overlaps the key

REGION × SEX × INCOME CLASS

of the *compound property file* F_1^p. This means that the objects referred to in F_2^o are so-called compound or aggregate objects, each of which is defined as a set of objects having a particular, possibly compound, property in common. As well as the object identifying compound attribute stated above, F_2^o contains only the attribute FREQUENCY. The value of this attribute for a particular compound object is assumed to give the number of individual objects making up the compound objects, or, in other words, the number of persons having a particular

REGION × SEX × INCOME CLASS

combination.

An access block of the $<F_2^o, F_1^p>$ file overlap pair could have the following appearance

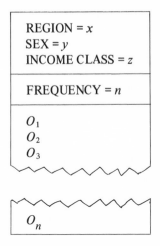

Taking the file structure, as given by the relevance matrix, into account, a feasible and efficient way of processing the original query would be (a) for each income class z_i $(i = 1, \ldots, r_z)$, access the entry $<C, F, z_i>$ of F_2^o and store the frequency value of the compound object in a primary storage table; (b) calculate cumulated frequencies according to the ordering that is assumed to exist among the income classes and find the middle income class z_{i_o}; (c) access the entry $<C, F, z_{i_o}>$ of F_1^p; and (d) access the object entries of F_1^o referred to in the property file entry and calculate the median value of the INCOME attribute among these objects.

We see that by using the compound object file in a few preliminary steps of processing we limit considerably the access and calculation work that has to be done in the last step.

This last example could also be used to illustrate a desirable data base function that we may call *interactive modification of user requests* (IMUR). When the processing of the median income query has passed step (b) above the IMUR function could present the partial result that

the requested median is within the income interval z_{i_o}

and ask the user if he is satisfied with this reply to his query. The IMUR function could also supply the user with information about how much it would cost in terms of hours and dollars to proceed through steps (c) and (d) in order to get a more precise answer.

CONCLUSIONS

When the systemeering of a planned data base has been driven to a sufficiently detailed level, the bulk of data base design problems may be sorted into two categories: file design problems and process design problems. In Chapter 6 we have tried to analyze these problem areas systematically with the conceptual tools presented in this book. We recognized some subproblems, which have already been thoroughly investigated in the literature, but we also discovered methodologically more or less white areas.

By means of the file-structuring operators discussed in this chapter and in Chapter 4 it should be possible to transform any set of e files, reflecting directly the e concepts of a particular infological model, into an almost arbitrary datalogical file structure. Formally defined file-structuring operators could be of great help in the systematization and documentation of "manually" performed file design. If file design and redesign is to be fully or partially automated, formally defined file-structuring operators, or equivalent tools, are indispensable.

For many data bases the file design task will in itself contain a difficult systemeering problem because of the large number of e files involved. We have studied how this problem may be tackled by means of a so-called $\alpha\beta$ matrix. Such a matrix is filled with rough estimates of the relative frequencies or "importances" of different kinds of $\alpha\beta$ queries, and on this basis the file system may be partitioned into more tractable subsystems, so-called $\alpha\beta$ complexes, or directory–file complexes. A quantitative analysis of the problem of designing a directory–file complex was given in Section 6.2.

In Section 6.4 we studied the planning, coordination, and scheduling of data base processes. We used the term "process design" for these kinds of activities. We found that there are characteristic differences between "conventional systems" and data base systems with respect to the process design problems. As to data base systems, many process design problems cannot be solved at design time before the system is put into operation. Instead they have to be solved automatically and dynamically at operation time by the data base system itself. Among other things a data base system has to perform precedence analysis and solve process grouping problems dynamically. These are tasks that are normally performed by (possibly computer assisted) systemeers, programmers, and operating staff in the development and running of a conventional data processing system.

The latter part of Chapter 6 was devoted to a study of transaction-oriented process design problems in connection with retrieval queries of the $\alpha\beta$ type. Some typical processing situations and strategies were identified and accompanied by examples of quantitative analyses. For illustrations we used a tool called "relevance matrix." It was argued that such matrices could turn out to be useful internal working tools for the data base systems themselves.

REVIEW QUESTIONS

1. If A is a person, or an organization, who wants a data base in order to satisfy certain information needs, and B is a person who wants a house to live in, then A and B have a lot in common. Discuss this. Compare in particular the tasks and (methodological) tools of the architect with those of the data base systemeer.
2. Systemeering is a task that is both recursive and iterative. Explain this statement. Is it still true if we substitute "programming" for "systemeering"? Why, or why not?
3. Discuss the advantages and possible dangers with formal system-eering tools such as formally defined file-structuring operators and the $\alpha\beta$ matrix. Why could an $\alpha\beta$ matrix be useful even though the numerical values in it should be subject to uncertainty?
4. File entries within the same file, or within different files, can be linked together by name links or by address links. Suppose that you face a design situation in which you have to decide what kind of links to use. What factors would you take into consideration, and under what circumstances would you choose one solution or the other?
5. The missing data problem. Suppose a file represents the e concept $<O,A>$. Then we expect the file to contain for each object in O a value of the attribute A. However, for single objects in O the value of A may very well turn out to be missing at data base operation time.
   (a) What different causes of the missing data situation can you imagine?
   (b) If an $\alpha\beta\gamma$ query is being processed, missing data conditions may occur for the α attributes, β attributes, and the γ attributes. Discuss the problems in each of the situations.
   (c) The missing data situation is always irritating, whenever it occurs, in whatever kind of information system, be it conventional or data base oriented. However, the problem is particularly difficult to solve in a data base system. Why?
   (d) How would you design a data base system to solve its own missing data problems? Discuss both automatic and semiau-tomatic (conversational) methods.
6. Split yourselves into two groups and discuss the ISO versus the PDO method. For each argument in favor of the ISO method, supplied by

the ISO student group, the PDO student group should try to find a convincing counterargument. Summarize the discussion by stating as precisely as possible under what conditions the ISO method could possibly be a better solution to the file organization problem than the PDO method. Are there any "typical ISO applications"? Which file organization method would you suggest to be "default option" in a data base management system (DBMS)?

7. Suppose that you want to use a particular random number generator as your file addressing algorithm, and suppose that the generator requires the starting value to be k characters (bytes) long. What would you do if your file entry identifiers are n characters long, and
   (a) $n < k$?
   (b) $n > k$?

8. How would you interpret Table 6.11 if the bucket size were, say, three instead of one? How would a larger bucket size than one affect each of the four synonym-handling methods discussed in this chapter? What are the advantages and disadvantages of large bucket sizes in PDO files?

9. If you are about to design your own DBMS, or if you are about to buy standard software, you should be interested in how the DBMS is modularized. Try to develop an alternative to the modularization shown in Fig. 6.3.

10. When a data base system is in operation, what interactions will there be between the scheduling and the accounting subsystems? Hint: Combine the discussion around Fig. 6.3 with the analysis of the process design task later in the chapter.

11. Enumerate as many IMUR subfunctions as you can think of.

LITERATURE

Bachman, C. W. 1969. *Data Structure Diagrams in File Organization. Selected Papers from File 68—An IAG Conference.* Swets & Zeitlinger N.V., Amsterdam.

Bell, J. A. 1970. The quadratic quotient method: A hash code eliminating secondary clustering. *Communications of the ACM,* 2(Feb.).

Bell, J. R., and Kaman, C. H. 1970. The linear quotient hash code. *Communications of the ACM,* 11(Nov.).

Bubenko, J. 1973. Contributions to Formal Description, Analysis and Design of Data Processing Systems. Doctoral Dissertation, Royal Institute of Technology, Dept. of Information Processing and Computer Science, Stockholm, Sweden.

Buchholz, W. 1963. File organization and addressing. *IBM Systems Journal* (June).

Carzo-Yanozas. 1967. *Formal Organization, A Systems Approach.* Homewood, Ill.: Irwin-Dorsey.

Churchman, C. W. 1968. *The Systems Approach.* Dell Books, New York.

Churchman, C. W. 1971. *The Design of Inquiring Systems.* Basic Books, New York.

Codd, E. F. 1970. A relational model of data for large shared data banks. *Communications of the ACM.* 13(6), p. 377.

Colin, A. J. T. 1971. *Introduction to Operating Systems.* American Elsevier, New York.

Denning, P. 1968. The working set model for program behavior. *Communications of the ACM* (May).

Dijkstra, E. W. 1969. Complexity controlled by hierarchical ordering of function and variability in software engineering. In P. Naur and B. Randell (Eds.), NATO Science Committee, Brussels, 1969.

Ghosh, S. P., and Senko, M. E. 1969. On the selection of random access index points for sequential files. *Journal ACM*, 16(4).

Jäderlund, C. 1974. The process control matrix. Private communication, Stockholm.

Langefors, B. 1961. Information retrieval in file processing. *BIT* (Nordisk Tidskrift för Informationsbehandling). Bind 1, Hefte Nr 1, and Bind 1, Hefte Nr 2.

Langefors, B. 1963a. Some approaches to the theory of information systems. *BIT* 3:229–254.

Langefors, B. 1963b. Toward integration of engineering data processing and automatization of design. In P. W. Howerton (Ed), *Vistas in Information Handling*. Washington D.C.: Spartan Books.

Langefors, B. 1965. Information system design computations using generalized matrix algebra. *BIT*, 16.

Langefors, B. 1973. *Theoretical Analysis of Information Systems* (4th ed.). Lund, Sweden: Studentlitteratur; and Auerbach. Philadelphia, Pa.

Lefkowitz, D. 1969. *File Structures for On-Line Systems*. New York: Spartan Books.

Lundqvist, T. 1973. Private communication, Stockholm.

Martin, J. 1967. *Design of Real-Time Computer Systems*. New York: Prentice-Hall.

McKinsey Associates. 1968. Unlocking the computer's profit potential. *The McKinsey Quarterly*, 5 (2).

Morris, R. 1968. Scatter storage techniques. *Communications of the ACM*, 1 (Jan.), pp. 38–43.

Mullin, J. K. 1971. Retrieval-update speed trade-offs using combined indices. *Communications of the ACM*, 14(12).

Nijssen, G. M. 1971. Indexed sequential versus random. *IAG Journal*, 4(1).

Nordbotten, S. 1967. *Automatic Files in Statistical Systems*. UN Conference European States/WG 9/Geneva, Switzerland.

Nunamaker, J. F. Jr, Nylin, W. C. Jr., and Konsynski, B. Jr. 1972. *Processing Systems Optimization through Automatic Design and Reorganization of Program Modules*. Purdue University, Indiana.

Radke, C. E. 1970. The use of quadratic residue research. *Communications of the ACM*, 2:103–105.

Schay, G., and Spruth, W. G. 1962. Analysis of a file addressing method. *Communications of the ACM*, 5:159–462.

Senko, M. E., Altman, E. B., Astrahan, M. M., and Fehder, P. L. 1973. Data structures and accessing in data base systems. *IBM Systems Journal*, 1, pp. 12, 30–93.

Slagle, R. 1971. *Artificial Intelligence*. McGraw-Hill, New York.

Sølvberg, A. 1972. Formal systems description in information systems design. Cascade Working Paper, No. 16, Sintef, Technical University of Norway, Trondheim.

Sundgren, B. 1969. Adressering i direktminnen med hjälp av divisionsrestmetoden. *Statistisk Tidskrift*, 3.

Sundgren, B. 1973. An infological approach to data bases. Doctoral Dissertation, Stockholm University.

Tansworthe, R. C. 1965. Random numbers generated by linear recurrence modulo two. *Math. Comput.*, 19.

Thorburn, H. W. 1971. *Några metoder för synonymhantering vid direktadressering*. National Central Bureau of Statistics, Stockholm.

Watson, R. W. 1970. *Timesharing System Design Concepts*. McGraw-Hill, New York.

Whitlesey, J. R. B. 1968. A comparison of the correlation behavior of random number generators for the IBM 360. *Communications of the ACM*, 11(Sept.).

Zurcher, F. W., and Randell, B. 1969. Iterative multilevel modeling; a methodology for computer system design. IFIP Congress-68, Edinburgh.

INDEX